THE PRACTITIONER INQUIRY SERIES

Marilyn Cochran-Smith and Susan L. Lytle, SERIES EDITORS

ADVISORY BOARD: JoBeth Allen, Judy Buchanan, Curt Dudley-Marling, Robert Fecho, Sarah Freedman, Dixie Goswami, Joyce E. King, Sarah Michaels, Luis Moll, Susan Noffke, Sharon Ravitch, Marty Rutherford, Lynne Strieb, Diane Waff, Ken Zeichner

(continued)

The First Year of Teaching

Classroom Research to Increase Student Learning

Jabari Mahiri
Sarah Warshauer Freedman
EDITORS

Teachers College, Columbia University
New York and London

National Writing Project
Berkeley, CA

Published simultaneously by Teachers College Press, 1234 Amsterdam Avenue, New York, NY 10027 and the National Writing Project, 2105 Bancroft Way, Berkeley, CA 94720-1042

The National Writing Project (NWP) is a nationwide network of educators working together to improve the teaching of writing in the nation's schools and in other settings. NWP provides high-quality professional development programs to teachers in a variety of disciplines and at all levels, from early childhood through university. Through its network of nearly 200 university-based sites, NWP develops the leadership, programs and research needed for teachers to help students become successful writers and learners.

Library of Congress Cataloging-in-Publication Data

The first year of teaching : classroom research to increase student learning / edited by Jabari Mahiri.
        pages cm. — (The practitioner inquiry series)
    Includes bibliographical references and index.
    ISBN 978-0-8077-5547-1 (pbk. : alk. paper) —
    ISBN 978-0-8077-5564-8 (hardcover : alk. paper) —
    ISBN 978-0-8077-7317-8 (e-book)
        1. First year teachers—United States. I. Mahiri, Jabari.
    LB2844.1.N4F55 2014
    371.1—dc23   2014005251

ISBN 978-0-8077-5547-1 (paper)
ISBN 978-0-8077-5564-8 (hardcover)
ISBN 978-0-8077-7317-8 (ebook)

Printed on acid-free paper
Manufactured in the United States of America

21 20 19 18 17 16 15 14   8 7 6 5 4 3 2 1

To Kobie Santiago Mahiri Jr.
A Son Rising
To Emma, Eric, Adam, and Alex Berg
New Days Dawning

Contents

Acknowledgments

This book reflects contributions on many levels. Its core chapters were selected in connection with several foci that are central to teacher learning and professional development from a large corpus of teacher research projects of the Multicultural Urban Secondary English (MUSE) program. There are many exceptional research projects from MUSE teachers, and we want to acknowledge the collaborative roles that all these teachers played in strengthening one another's research and writing. So the featured chapters reflect important contributions from many educators. In addition to teaching peers, we want to acknowledge the significant work of numerous mentor teachers who helped guide MUSE teachers in critical phases of their professional development. We drew on the networks of the Bay Area Writing Project and the National Writing Project to place new teachers with exemplary practitioners in urban schools in Northern California.

We particularly acknowledge other "teachers of teachers" working with the MUSE program, beginning with Christine Cziko, the program's coordinator and a main instructor. Also, the administrative coordination of Billie Jo Conlee has been crucial to the program, while Ann Kim provided editorial support on this book project. Other key faculty for MUSE are Verda Delp, Richard Sterling, Glynda Hull, and Laura Sterponi, as well as other professors in the University of California, Berkeley Graduate School of Education who graciously and insightfully read and respond to MUSE research papers. Additionally, we acknowledge important contributors to aspects of the book's development, including editorial work on selected chapters. They are Jennifer DiZio, Katherine K. Frankel, Exequiel Ganding, José R. Lizárraga , and John M. Scott. We also thank Donald Lamm for his advice about publishing, the Center for Advanced Studies in the Behavioral Sciences at Stanford University for supporting Freedman's work, and the family of William and Mary Jane Brinton for their support of Mahiri's work.

CHAPTER 1

Learning to Teach in Urban Schools

Jabari Mahiri and Sarah Warshauer Freedman

"I was so focused, my mind wasn't anywhere else," Victor wrote in evaluating his participation in the fourth Socratic seminar in Julia Daniels's 11th-grade American literature class, the focus of the research reported in Chapter 2. He also gave a 9-out-of-10 rating for whole-class participation in this final Socratic seminar of the term. "Everyone seemed to really care and want it to work," he wrote on his evaluation sheet. "We wanted us to do well and wanted to be smart together." Janisha's ranking for the final seminar was a 10. "I think we should be hella proud cause we all were in it, and we all talked and tried, and we came up with smart things," she remarked. With regard to her own participation she wrote, "I think I made our conversation more deep."

Victor and Janisha were two of the focal students in Daniels's research project on her first year of teaching in an urban public school. Together they reflect the two major groups in this high school that has 45% Latino, 35% African American, 10% Asian, and 10% Middle Eastern students. Academically, it is one of the lowest-performing schools in a large school district that itself is one of the lowest-performing public school districts in California. More than 95% of the students qualify for free lunch and breakfast programs, many are undocumented immigrants, and the surrounding neighborhood is rife with a complex network of violent gangs.

Daniels, though in her first year, is truly a professional, able to make informed decisions and solve problems encountered in her daily practice in order to be successful in what many consider a very difficult teaching setting. Working in similar types of schools, all the teachers in this volume show how teacher education can lead to teacher professionalization. They show the benefits of reflective thinking in preparing beginning teachers to contribute to closing the achievement gap between young people who live in conditions of poverty and whose schools have all too often failed them and more privileged students. These teachers position themselves as learners.

They do not claim to know everything, but they do know how to work on solving the problems they face. If we are to reform low-performing public schools, we cannot rely on the policies that have failed time and time again. More testing mandates and punishments for poor performance do not work. Rather, we need to develop, support, and place our faith in thoughtful teachers supported by thoughtful administrators who foster caring communities and a thriving intellectual life in their schools.

Despite the demographic characteristics of their school, Janisha and Victor's comments indicate that they were highly stimulated intellectually and actively involved in analysis and discussion of a rhetorically sophisticated, book-length text. Through an array of data sources, Daniels documented how all her students were continually referencing the text itself and methodically using it to support their arguments and interpretations. In their preparation and execution of Socratic seminars, these students were developing and exercising the kind of social capital that is traditionally valued and legitimized by school culture, although as Conchas (2006) and Delgado-Bernal (2002) have argued, it is often missing in the schooling of racial minorities. One might suggest that these students were simply getting better with each successive seminar experience, but as Daniels demonstrated through her research, things were at times going the opposite way until she refined the structure and implementation of each seminar in line with the findings from her evolving data and analysis of them.

It is significant that all six standards of the California Standards for the Teaching Profession (1997) were directly addressed by the processes of teaching and learning reflected in this seminar: Engaging and Supporting All Students in Learning, Creating and Maintaining Effective Environments for Student Learning, Understanding and Organizing Subject Matter for Student Learning, Planning Instruction and Designing Learning Experiences for All Students, Assessing Student Learning, and Developing as a Professional Educator.

Key aspects of the Common Core State Standards (National Governors Association Center for Best Practices & Council of Chief State School Officers, 2010) were also effectively addressed, particularly with regard to how the Common Core focuses on instruction to develop a range of key thinking skills within and across the disciplines (Bellanca, Fogarty, & Pete, 2012). This is in line with notions that 21st-century schooling needs to focus more on the development of critical cognitive abilities, beyond the mastery of individual academic subjects.

Importantly, both the California and the Common Core standards were not set forth to regulate and control the day-to-day actions of teachers but rather to guide them in implementing and improving their teaching practices. As the most recent nationwide educational reform, however, the ultimate realization of the Common Core's perspective toward guiding (rather than specifying) the performance of teachers will be seen in how it is actually implemented state by state. Thus far, it is working best in schools where teachers feel they can take control of its implementation, while it is more problematic when implemented as a top-down mandate. And this gets to essential questions: Will teachers be seen and treated as highly skilled professionals capable of designing learning experiences that prepare young people intellectually and emotionally to meet the challenges of an increasingly complex world, or will policies and programs that work to deprofessionalize teaching prevail?

This book answers the former question with a resounding yes! Its aim is to give further, explicit guidance for continued professional development by providing a rationale and a set of compelling demonstrations for how classroom research can be a powerful process of *learning* how to implement and improve instruction, beginning in the first year of teaching and extending throughout a teaching career.

The First Year of Teaching dramatically reveals how new teachers can be immediately positioned as learners within a systematic process to improve their effectiveness and meet new teaching challenges in complex, diverse urban school settings. Clearly, many considerations for learning are similarly relevant for teachers as learners as they are for students as learners. But there are also important differences in the learning demands on teachers. They are constantly (and often quickly) making complex decisions while both designing and implementing instruction to increase student learning. As Bransford, Darling-Hammond, and LePage (2005) noted,

> Teachers must be aware of the many ways in which student learning can unfold in the context of development, learning differences, language and cultural influences, and individual temperaments, interests, and approaches to learning . . . [and] teachers need to know how to take the steps necessary to gather additional information that will allow them to make more grounded judgments. (pp. 1–2)

Reviews of research summarizing hundreds of studies over several decades conclude that fully prepared and certified teachers are significantly more successful in increasing student achievement than those without such preparation (Darling-Hammond, 1997, 2000). Our argument is that positioning new teachers as researchers, having them step back and take an inquiry and reflective stance on immediate challenges or questions they are encountering, is one of the best ways to continue their development as teaching professionals beyond preservice preparation.

This book is supported by significant theoretical and empirical work that identifies teacher research as a unique genre and acknowledges teachers as generators rather than just recipients of knowledge (Cochran-Smith

& Lytle, 1993, 2009; Freedman, Simons, Kalnin, & Casareno, 1999). Our work is directly informed by Cochran-Smith and Lytle's (2009) notion of "inquiry as stance," which calls attention to the critical role of practitioners in the process of making small- and large-scale changes in education. It is also informed by scholarship that explicates key roles for participatory inquiry in bringing about social justice in and through education (Duncan-Andrade, 2007; He & Phillion, 2008; Hopkins, 2004; Noffke, 2009).

In line with other scholarship, we are not suggesting that improving learning and professional development of teachers through research in their classrooms alone is a panacea for ailing urban public schools (Anyon, 1997; Payne, 2008). Anyon (2005), for example, illustrated how "the failure of city school systems . . . was a function of 100 years of urban political and economic history [and policies] . . . . that delimited the capacity of cities to support their schools" (p. 2). Wacquant (2008) further delineated the conditions characteristic of intentionally marginalized people and places within the structures and hierarchies of the larger urban metropolis in terms of historical, social, and economic forces that position marginalized zones in cities in relation to the functions they perform (or are made to perform) for the broader metropolitan system. He analyzed how urban structures and their resultant cultures that penalize some and privilege others are not accidental. They are human-made, they permeate the structures and cultures of schools, and they present the greatest challenges for educators at all levels.

Despite these complex, historically evolved structures and cultures of schooling, our book demonstrates how teaching and learning can be improved by positioning new teachers as researchers within a systematic process for increasing their effectiveness in their immediate school contexts. Beyond the belief that all children can learn and be successful understanding and communicating comprehensive ideas within and across school subjects is the problem of actually achieving this in diverse school contexts.

The research of all the teachers in this book took place in urban schools that reflect diverse and often intractable conditions. Weiner (2006) critiqued the distinguishing characteristics of these contexts to clarify what makes preparation to teach in them so critical. Most often, she noted, these schools have high concentrations of African American, Hispanic, immigrant, and poor students, as well as high levels of cultural and religious diversity; usually, they are in extremely large, centrally administered school districts; generally, they are severely underresourced, understaffed, and overcrowded; and they tend toward standardized, textbook-driven curricula with highly prescriptive approaches to teaching and learning (Weiner, 2006, pp. 16–17).

Comprehensive structural and policy changes (Anyon, 2005) along with culturally responsive teaching approaches (Gay, 2010; Ladson-Billings, 2009; Milner, 2010; Moll, 2000) are needed to address the severe inequities that foster underachievement in urban schools. Importantly, the needed changes and approaches must overtly address the dynamics and tensions of race/ethnicity, gender, religion, social class, privilege, and poverty (Delpit, 2012; Duncan-Andrade, 2007; Freedman, Simons, Kalnin, & Casareno, 1999; Jensen, 2010; Howard, 2010; Pratt, 1991). Clearly, teacher research cannot address all these complexities, but the chapters in this book reveal how taking an inquiry stance on these issues in conjunction with an inquiry stance toward understanding and improving the impact of instruction with urban students provided not only keen insights but also pedagogical strategies that contributed to educational success. We feel their learning and their contributions are persuasively demonstrated in our concluding chapter, where the various strands of our teachers' work are dramatically brought together in a final dialogue among them.

TEACHER RESEARCHERS

The chapters in this book describe and explicate how new teachers intentionally used research to gather, analyze, and act on data to inform more grounded judgments on how to ameliorate student learning in urban school contexts. Over the years, we have seen a few instances in which new teachers were overwhelmed by exigencies in these contexts, and having to do research simultaneously became problematic. But overall, as reflected in the concluding chapter, teachers found this process to be valuable for their professional and personal development. Their research chronicles an array of opportunities and challenges new teachers face as they design and implement instruction in their first placements in urban schools. Daniels, for example, encountered many challenges in crafting and implementing a curriculum that eventually engaged Victor and Janisha, as well as all her students, in rigorous, multilayered learning activities.

Through systematic, recursive analysis of her data on four implementations of the seminars, Daniels generated findings that clarified what was working and what needed changing in her approach. Her research allowed her to learn more about her students, but also to learn from them. Her analysis of a wide range of data revealed that her desire to help her students did not necessitate a dominating teacher presence. Instead, she wrote, "my students have taught me that after providing necessary scaffolding, I have to step back and offer independence, responsibility, and leadership."

Daniels is joined by eight other first-year teachers who report on research they conducted in their first year of teaching in urban public schools. These nine teacher research chapters were selected from over 300 research projects undertaken by teachers in their first professional placement after receiving their secondary English single-subject teaching credentials through the Multicultural Urban Secondary English (MUSE) credential and MA program in the Graduate School of Education at the University of California, Berkeley. In this university system, people wanting to be teachers must possess a bachelor's degree prior to enrolling in their formal teacher-credentialing program.

These chapters were written by students when they were in the MA portion of the program. Concurrent with teaching in their first, postcredential position, MUSE students complete the master's degree portion of the program by taking a two-semester teacher research class. Over the academic year, they are guided and supported in the development and implementation of qualitative research skills and perspectives in their individual sites of practices. This process culminates in the students' writing their master's project teacher research reports, which are reviewed and approved by two professors at UC Berkeley. At the end of this process, each student must also formally present her or his research to an audience of researchers, practicing teachers, prospective teachers, and community members.

Sarah Freedman implemented this program in 1998. Christine Cziko became the program's first academic coordinator. She and Freedman designed and taught the methods course, which Cziko took over after a few years. Freedman also designed the yearlong teacher research seminar and taught another core program requirement, Language Study for Educators. Early in the development of MUSE, Jabari Mahiri began teaching another core course in the program, Urban Education. Later, he joined Freedman as one of the main instructors for the teacher research course.

Although a number of publications are available on many aspects of teacher professional development, the voices and work of new teachers immersed in the complex dynamics of designing instruction, building relationships, and developing an array of crucial professional skills all while attempting to master time, stress, and management issues are rare. Freedman's book *Inside City Schools* (Freedman et al., 1999) offered a productive starting point for this current book. It illuminated the significance of urban teachers' researching their own practices for the field of education. It also piloted a novel approach to university–school collaborative research through the M-Class Project model, the Multicultural Collaborative for Literacy and Secondary Schools. Mahiri's book *Digital Tools in Urban Schools* (2011), chronicled another approach to university/school collaborations. It focused on the professional development of urban teachers to gain the confidence and competence to use appropriate digital tools in mediating learning. Freedman and Appleman (2008, 2009) also wrote about the MUSE program, focusing on what helps teachers remain in urban teaching. Although we build on these earlier works, the importance and uniqueness of this current book is its dedicated focus on the use of research by new teachers specifically to understand and improve their practices during their first year of teaching— presented in the voices of the teachers themselves.

Other recent books address important considerations for understanding and improving teaching in urban schools, but they don't reflect the voices and perspectives of new teachers as they are revealed through their own research. For example, Richert (2012) explored the conundrums of learning to teach by collecting and reading more than 300 narratives of the ethical dilemmas that her graduate students encountered while learning to teach. To understand what it means and what it takes to learn to teach in urban schools, Richert provided a discussion and analysis of 22 of these dilemma narratives clustered around four themes (or commonplaces) that directly connected to the realities of teaching in urban schools.

Ballenger (2009) focused on the practice of teacher research as a way for teachers to better understand what she called "puzzling moments" they encounter with students who do not excel in school. She discussed how teacher research could turn puzzling moments into teachable moments. Frank (2009) showed how teachers can use ethnographic interviewing specifically to improve their teaching practices and to communicate better with students and parents, while Cochran-Smith and Lytle (2009) provided a more radical view of the possibilities of practitioners' creating significant transformations of education through an inquiry stance for teacher research. Achinstein and Ogawa (2011) also explored the possibilities of teachers as powerful change agents, with a particular focus on the conflicted roles and responsibilities of new teachers of color working in urban schools that are often difficult to staff. Amid these and other recent works, we feel that *The First Year of Teaching: Classroom Research to Increase Student Learning* offers a unique set of penetrating perspectives on and insights into the demanding process of becoming an effective teacher in some of the nation's most challenging schools.

There were many exceptional research projects in the corpus from which these chapters were drawn. After reading hundreds of these research papers, we found that three areas continued to come up as major challenges for new teachers to master: Crafting Curriculum, Complicating Culture, and Conceptualizing Control. The nine texts that became the core chapters of this book illustrate something of the substance of these three themes and reveal a range of ways that the beginning teachers used research to illuminate and help them grapple with the issues that underlie each theme.

Because a first-year teacher's job is so challenging, the research requirements for the teachers' reports did not include extensive literature reviews. Our book addresses this, however, by providing prologues that frame and conceptually ground the discussions in the specific chapters within each part. Guided by the editors, these prologues were written by five contributors—Jennifer DiZio, Katherine K. Frankel, Exequiel Ganding, José R. Lizárraga, and John M. Scott—who were doctoral students in a seminar taught by Sarah Freedman on teacher research. As part of this class, they formed collaborative teams to review drafts of chapters being developed for each of the book's thematic parts and wrote the framing discussions for each part. They also helped guide the MA students with their MA projects and read a great deal of academic literature on teacher research, deepening their knowledge about both the theory and practice behind teacher research. Finally, three of them helped with the editing of selected chapters: Frankel on Chapter 3, DiZio on Chapter 5, and Scott on Chapter 9.

CRAFTING CURRICULUM

The chapters in the book's first part reveal how three teachers learned to implement curricular content in ways that fostered student and teacher independence, responsibility, and leadership in the classroom and beyond. Fundamental requirements for new teachers include engaging students in learning curricular content, developing students' abilities to meet state and Common Core standards, and preparing them for college or careers. While institutional approaches to curricular designs differ, all three authors in Part I came to see through their research the value of extended projects that ultimately transfer control and responsibility for learning to their students.

Following Daniels's discussion of Socratic seminars in Chapter 2 is Nicola Martinez's Chapter 3, "Assessing the Impact of Project-Based Learning on Students' Academic Achievement in English Language Arts." Martinez studied what students learn from creating exhibitions of projects designed to demonstrate mastery of aspects of the curriculum. Martinez faced a significantly different challenge from Daniels's as she worked within the confines of her school's existing curriculum. She focused on how the exhibitions worked to meet (or not meet) the specific learning objectives required for her high school English class. She found that the exhibitions were important for differentiating learning and enabled a range of access points for students to purposefully engage the curriculum. She provides insights into two important challenges for first-year teachers as they craft curriculum: The first is finding continuity between one's own teaching and learning objectives and the established objectives of the larger school context. The second is paying close attention to students' understandings of the curriculum and how these understandings may or may not align with one's own intentions and interpretations.

In Chapter 4, "Building Bridges of Hope Inside the Urban Classroom," Paula Argentieri describes her work to implement a social justice–focused curriculum in an urban continuation high school for students who had not made it at other schools. This school represented their last chance to get a high school degree. This chapter takes readers on Argentieri's semester-long "reflective journey" as she recounts how she and her students worked toward student empowerment through piercing critiques of the past combined with earnest imagining and planning for the future. The curriculum she crafted offered genuine opportunities for students to see how their lives were interwoven with many critical societal issues. As a consequence of their work together, Argentieri found that her students were able to move from resistance to hope—not by being pushed, but by learning how to push themselves.

For each teacher in Part I, a key goal of the curriculum was to provide students with the tools to be independent thinkers and learners. Daniels, Martinez, and Argentieri offer incisive, yet differing, views of the challenges facing first-year teachers as they crafted curriculum in their different school contexts. All assert their own agency and identities as teachers while simultaneously navigating the existing curricular goals of their larger school, district, and state contexts.

COMPLICATING CULTURE

The chapters in Part II express how three first-year teachers navigated and complicated the cultures of learning in their respective schools. Each took a different approach: the first chapter looked at complexities in cultural dynamics between home and school; the second examined these dynamics within the institution itself; and the third addressed these dynamics inside the classroom. Yet the authors all sought to understand how aspects of their students' cultural practices in and out of school affected their performances and behaviors in the school.

In Chapter 5, "Academic Self-Sabotage: Understanding Motives and Behaviors of Underperforming Students," Sophia Sobko examines a particularly problematic aspect of academic culture in her classes—why some of her underperforming students engaged in behaviors that clearly contradicted their stated academic goals. Her research revealed definite but elusive conflicts between in-school and out-of-school cultures that negatively affected some of her students' academic performances and practices.

Sobko's focal students were performing at a D level, and although each one expressed a strong desire to attend college after completing high school, they continually failed to turn in homework, essays, and other assignments that would raise their grades. In other words, their academic behaviors directly undermined or "sabotaged" their academic goals. Through her research, she began to see how these students' judgments and behaviors regarding completing and handing in required work was tied to personal/cultural perspectives that differed from the traditional stance of schooling. In becoming more aware of influences her students faced, she was eventually able to develop ways to better support and scaffold these students toward academic habits and perspectives needed to increase their success in school.

Perhaps the complications of culture are nowhere more pronounced than in some California urban schools that serve a wide range of immigrant students. In Chapter 6, "Approaches to Teaching Language Minority Students," Paul Lai looks at teaching and learning in a high school setting with a mosaic of different and often disparate languages and cultures. Lai was drawn to examine how English language learners (ELLs) crossed the terrain to becoming proficient speakers and writers of English, in part because he underwent the same journey after immigrating to the United States during secondary school. His research probed and illuminated the complexities of how different ELL groups were perceived and engaged in specific English language development programs at his school.

Danny Martinez's research in Chapter 7, "*Chumpas, los Bilis,* and *Peros?* The Intersection and Collision of Language Communities in a Middle School Newcomer Classroom," focused on similar issues, but at the middle school level. He looked at complex and creative ways that culture was manifested in a learning environment where conflicting linguistic scripts often collided. His study challenges narrow views of Spanish-speaking ELLs as a homogeneous group. He showed that although Spanish was shared by many students in the classroom, that environment was also rife with substantively differing language and cultural practices.

Interestingly, Martinez revealed how this context served as a time and space for "productive tension" in which cross-cultural learning and the creation of new hybrid ways of meaning-making occurred. He further found that the hierarchical role of the teacher as arbiter of classroom culture was challenged by shifting roles and levels of expertise that often came into play. He used his research to guide his work to build a viable classroom community that honored and enabled the learning of students with diverse languages and cultures. This chapter in conjunction with the other two in Part II help us see both possibilities and problems in how different languages and cultures intersect, interact, and even clash in contemporary schools.

CONCEPTUALIZING CONTROL

In the book's third and final part, two dramatically divergent approaches to student discipline are reflected in the research of Eva Marie Oliver and Nischala Hendricks. Oliver's research on a dramatic, restorative discipline process for two students in her class provided a stark contrast to the consequences that Hendricks found for implementing her school's "progressive discipline policy" in her classes, where "progressive" meant that sanctions for misbehavior became increasingly severe. Rafael Velázquez Cardenas's research in the final chapter of Part III offers yet another conceptualization of the cause of class disruptions and how they can be mitigated. Through the lenses of their research, these first-year teachers worked to better conceptualize ways of establishing productive control in school environments in order to enhance student learning.

In Chapter 8, "Restorative Discipline: Healing Students and Mending School Culture," Oliver assessed the successes and shortcomings of her school's first "restorative discipline process." This process included a structured conflict management protocol that her school's administrators and teachers adopted in an effort to resolve peer conflicts. Its first use was in an attempt to "mend and reify the overall school culture" as a result of an intense, volatile conflict that had been going on between two 12th-grade females students. Oliver examined this extended disciplining process from its beginning to its conclusion, including the central feature of its "restorative circles." She also probed the broader ideologies behind this approach to school discipline. Ultimately, she found that this comprehensive, months-long process did both facilitate students' ability to restore their place in the school's culture and help heal that culture. Through her experiences participating in and studying the entire process, she also gained important insights into the conflict resolution strategies for her own classroom.

Although Hendricks's teacher preparation courses had taught that engaging, relevant curriculum would diminish negative student behavior, she immediately saw that this was not the case in her first teaching placement. In Chapter 9, "Examining the Effectiveness of 'Progressive' Discipline Policies," Hendricks investigates the actual and perceived successes of a new schoolwide disciplinary policy from the perspectives of students in her classes as well as those of her school's administrators. Through a nuanced analysis, she identifies aspects of the discipline policy that worked well and those that required rethinking. Both Hendricks's and Oliver's chapters uncover the intended and unintended consequences of very different approaches to student discipline and control of the learning environment and show how each teacher gained crucial insights into better serving the academic and personal development of their students.

In Chapter 10, "'Why You Gotta Keep Muggin' Me?' Understanding Students' Disruptive 'Yell-Outs' in Class," Rafael Velázquez Cardenas provides a micro-examination of what he terms student "yell-outs in class," student behaviors in his classes that disrupted the flow of learning. Early on, he began to create a list of the types and times of student yell-outs based on observations in other teachers' classes as well as his own. He developed this initial list into a comprehensive taxonomy that identified the frequency, kind, context, and contributing factors to yell-outs. Through this taxonomy and other qualitative data, he was able to demonstrate, contrary to his initial beliefs, that the majority of yell-outs were actually directed toward seeking attention from either the teacher or peers. Rather than his seeing them as simply being acts of defiance, the other motives he found helped him understand the real needs his students' disruptions were attempting to call attention to. This discovery significantly changed his strategies for managing and mitigating these kinds of behaviors.

For the chapters in this part, notions of control and discipline are not framed as a teacher's desire to garner unflinching respect and exercise hierarchical power over students. Rather, each framed behavioral control as crucial to fostering a sense of school and class community, where respectfulness, compassion, and a sense of obligation to the well-being of the broader school culture were essential to student learning and personal development. *All the chapters by these teachers use pseudonyms for the schools, students, and adults discussed in the research.*

REFLECTING ON URBAN TEACHING

Taken together, the nine chapters by first-year teachers provide powerful accounts of the complexities of building rigorous, engaging curriculum; of honoring and enabling the play of diverse cultures in the classroom; and of understanding and facilitating the development of classroom communities that are safe and conducive to the kind of learning that must take place in schools and beyond. As the book was being prepared, the chapter authors were asked to write their reflections on the focus of the part in which their chapters appear. Mahiri synthesized these reflections and wrote the Authors' Dialogue sections at the end of each part. These discussions provide insights into the chapter authors' views on the issues addressed in their research.

The book ends with an additional, more extensive dialogue among our nine authors on key considerations for teacher research and for teaching and learning that were raised and engaged across their individual chapters in the book's three thematic parts. In writing the book's final chapter, "Reflecting on Urban Teaching Then and Now: Synthesizing the Power of Research by First-Year Teachers," Frankel and Mahiri created an extended dialogue. They built on a set of themes that emerged from the teachers' written responses to questions about their ongoing teaching, learning, and research in urban schools. The teachers updated their thinking about the challenges and affordances of teacher research. Since six of the chapter authors are White women and the other three are men of color, we also asked them to reflect on and respond to our inquiry about their experiences teaching urban students of color from their specific positionalities. Consequently, our final chapter pulls together what became a lively, passionate discussion in which they considered their positions as well as what they felt teachers needed to know and be able to do in order to be successful in urban schools and what teacher preparation and professional development programs needed to do to ensure teacher effectiveness.

Through the research in *The First Year of Teaching*, we all learned about the complexities of building rigorous, engaging curriculum; honoring and enabling diverse cultures; and understanding and encouraging classroom communities that are safe and conducive for the kind of learning that must take place in schools and beyond.

Part I

CRAFTING CURRICULUM

Prologue: Designing Learning for Student Independence, Responsibility, and Leadership in Classrooms and Beyond

Katherine K. Frankel and Exequiel Ganding

Beginning teachers are responsible for the critical task of defining and facilitating the work that their students will participate in over the course of the school year. More important, they must also rationalize how such work contributes to meeting larger learning objectives, whether those objectives are self-, student-, school-, district-, or state-defined. Depending on the institution, teachers are responsible for designing, preparing, and revising curriculum to varying degrees. Some are responsible for executing a detailed curriculum, predesigned with course learning objectives. Other teachers have full autonomy to determine learning objectives and the types of work their students will do. Regardless of where they fall between these polarities—most teachers find themselves somewhere in between—new teachers engage in an ongoing process of exploration, reflection, and negotiation as they become effective facilitators of their curricula.

Although institutional requirements and approaches to curricular design differ, all three of the authors in Part I demonstrate, through their research, a shared understanding that learning is co-constructed between teachers and students with the ultimate goal of fostering student independence and agency. These teachers recognize the importance of student dialogue and conversation to the curriculum (e.g., Applebee, 1996; Nystrand, 1997). They ground their thinking in common classroom activity systems (Engeström, 2005; Leontiev, 1977) that include the tools of the Socratic seminar, the exhibition, and the critical classroom. These systems change across time and are sensitive to local conditions.

Each teacher conceptualized curriculum, then, as building an entire course, not as planning a series of separate units. Their search was for the underlying structures that would guide their work. Following Freedman,

Delp, and Crawford (2005), they built curriculum with a whole-course vision that would support their students' learning across time. As Freedman and her colleagues found, it is important to have an extended view of student development and to plan across this longer time period. They write: "A year-long curriculum rather than the common division of separate units provided opportunities for the recycling of many ideas across time in Delp's class and a growing complexity of thinking and depth of understanding on the part of her students" (p. 116). Not coincidentally, Delp had taught most of the authors in this book a course about teaching reading and literature, and others had taken courses from Freedman.

Together, the three chapters reveal a variety of dimensions to consider in curricular design, including Julia R. Daniels's iterative refinement of a common type of classroom activity, the Socratic seminar; Nicola C. Martinez's evaluation of a schoolwide exhibition project; and Paula L. Argentieri's design and implementation of a yearlong course saturated with personal meaning-making that raised the possibility of making a new future. Each one aimed to craft curriculum in ways that supported students as they took responsibility for their own learning.

Daniels builds on foundational theories and applications of the Socratic method (Benson, 2000; Guthrie, 1968; Vlastos, 1983) and its contemporary use in schools (Chorzempa & Lapidus, 2009; Copeland, 2010; Gose, 2009) in order to understand her students' engagement. Besides documenting her students' progress, Daniels details her own process of development and how she sought ways to improve the seminars' effectiveness and tailor the curriculum to her students' needs.

Martinez investigates how her school's learning model—grounded in theory and research related to authentic, project-based learning (Bell, 2010; Blumenfeld et al., 1991; Dewey, 1938; Newmann & Wehlage, 1993) and its potential to transform teaching and learning in schools (Barron et al., 1998; Ravitz, 2010)—supplemented the learning objectives of her high school English class. In her study, she looks specifically at her school's required exhibition projects (Cushman, 1990; Davidson, 2009; Sizer, 1986), which asked students to make connections across their subject-area classes, and how these projects contributed to her students' academic achievement in her English class.

Citing and inspired by Freire (1998, 1993), Giroux (1988), and hooks (1994, 2003), Argentieri draws on critical perspectives on education that view the classroom as a potentially transformative and emancipatory space for students and teachers. Argentieri shows what's involved in providing meaningful educational experiences to students who come with a history of school resistance and with many life problems. She helps them experience a kind of schooling that taps into their concerns and that respects rather than oppresses their spirits and dreams (Lantieri, 2001; Miller, 1997).

All three first-year teachers in Part I chronicle their experiences crafting curriculum in ways that foster independence, responsibility, and leadership for their students. For each of them, a fundamental goal of the curriculum was to provide students with the tools to be independent thinkers and learners. At the same time, their experiences speak to the challenges facing first-year teachers as they craft curriculum that asserts their own agency and identities as teachers while simultaneously navigating the existing curricular expectations of their students and of the larger school community.

CHAPTER 2

Implementing Successful Socratic Seminars in a Challenging Urban School

Julia R. Daniels

MY FIRST SOCRATIC SEMINAR DID NOT TAKE FLIGHT

When I began my first year of teaching at Lafayette Union High School, I was excited to replicate the Socratic seminars I witnessed in my master teacher's classes while student teaching the year before. She used these seminars on a regular basis as part of the way she taught literature. Socratic seminars (also known as Socratic circles) use a dialogic approach to enhance understanding of a text. As a pedagogical approach, they offer systematic ways to examine texts by posing questions and answers. They are based on Socratic beliefs that all thinking comes from asking questions, that all new knowledge is connected to prior knowledge, and that participants can work together to construct meaning. My master teacher was adept at guiding student preparation, providing support structures to help define and inspire participation, and helping students to reflect and deepen the meanings they explored. Her seminars moved smoothly and almost effortlessly, with many opportunities for students to speak freely and critically about rhetorically sophisticated, academic texts.

Even though she had taught seniors and my students were juniors, I assumed I could provide similar structures and supports and expect relatively similar—if slightly less sophisticated—results. I was wrong! In my first Socratic seminar, only a few students actively participated and maintained focus. Often, they engaged in sidebar conversations and other distractions. Some of them actually seemed daunted by the expectations for their participation, and almost all were visibly frustrated by the time we concluded. Afterward, sitting alone in my classroom, surprised, confused, and slightly defeated, I was frustrated too.

The first seminar came 4 weeks into the school year and centered on the novel *Flight* by Sherman Alexie, the same text my master teacher had used approximately 4 weeks into her school year. The day of the seminar, I organized the chairs in a circle (just as my master teacher had done), made sure I had a place to sit outside the circle to observe, and placed a stack of clean white paper on my desk for taking notes on my students' discussion. Despite my excitement and expectations, the seminar was clearly unsuccessful—according to both my students' and my own follow-up assessments. My students were smart, thoughtful readers whom I had led through 2 days of careful seminar preparation. Yet their first seminar had been chaotic, vague, and unfocused, and the students had seemed lost and confused.

Given the stark contrast between my students' Socratic seminars and those I had witnessed in my master teacher's classroom, I decided to explore the following questions:

> What structures can I design to make Socratic seminars most useful, effective, meaningful, and safe in my classes, and what will be the effects of creating those structures?
> When structures are successful for the students, what are the most viable teacher roles in designing, implementing, and supporting those structures?

To pursue these questions aimed at helping me learn how to better design and support student learning, I focused my research on one of my 11th-grade English classes. Over a 7-month period, I documented and analyzed how my students experienced each of the four seminars in this class. Additionally, I centered my analysis on the learning experiences of three focal students who reflected something of the range of the class's diversity.

I found that my students experienced the seminars as most effective, useful, meaningful, and safe when I provided them with adequate support structures and then restricted my involvement in their actual execution and took minimal responsibility for their success. In other words, they worked best when I fostered and then relied on the students' collective responsibility for the seminars' execution and success. I learned that seminars were more effective when students had the tools and then were left to take responsibility for their own and their peers' learning—rather than when I was significantly involved in the seminar's execution. A key implication is that teachers need to create structures that support students in developing the skills and motivation to take responsibility for their own learning and then trust them to follow through.

TEACHING IN CHALLENGING CONTEXTS

Trusting students to take responsibility was not always easy for me in my school, Lafayette Union, where a challenging context of inconsistency and chaos characterized most students' experiences. It is a large public high school that, because of consistently low test scores, was reorganized into five independent small schools in 2003. I taught in the Mathematics and Design Academy (MADA), the largest of the three schools, with approximately 380 students enrolled; however, the next year the school district decided to turn it back into one large school, making the students the victims of the consequences of quickly shifting whole-school organizations.

Nearly 100% of Lafayette students qualify for free lunch/breakfast programs. It is also the case that a significant percentage of Lafayette Union's school population (an exact number is nearly impossible to gauge) are undocumented immigrants and therefore receive few economic, social, and health support services. The student population is approximately 35% African American, 45% Latino, 10% Asian, and 10% of Middle Eastern extraction (almost entirely Yemeni American) and Tongan. Also, inextricably connected to this demographic/economic context is the school's relationship to a complex network of gangs. It is one of the lowest-performing schools in the entire district, which itself is one of the lowest-performing school districts in California, although test scores at Lafayette have been consistently improving, albeit modestly. This is the larger school and community context for the research in my classroom.

The class where I did my research had 26 students: eight Latinas, eight Latinos, three African American males, three African American females, three Asian males, and one Tongan male. Three of these students were English language learners, and two were special education students. There was a range of academic skills among these students, and although an AP English course was offered for juniors, my students had either chosen not to take it or had been encouraged not to take it by their 10th-grade English teacher. Nevertheless, when I informed my class that I would be doing a research project that focused on their Socratic seminars, they were excited and immediately asked me how they could help.

The mood was almost always upbeat, and the class had its own rituals and idiosyncrasies. Students usually walked into class with smiles; one student always sat at my desk and pretended to be the teacher; another sometimes brought his ukulele and played music softly during Author's Chair (when students read their writing aloud to the class); another regularly showed off his fancy, highly coordinated outfits by strutting up and down the classroom, garnering great attention and often applause. Yet they were also a group of serious and engaged students who were learning to share their personal perspectives, critical analyses, and individual experiences with the class. Consequently, the general learning context in the class seemed conducive to my research.

THE SOCRATIC SEMINARS

Over the course of this study, a Socratic seminar was an integral part of the unit on each of four readings: *Flight* by Sherman Alexie; *Sula* by Toni Morrison; *The Tortilla Curtain* by T. C. Boyle; and a packet of short stories that included works by David Sedaris, Alice Walker, Gary Soto, Langston Hughes, Ernest Hemingway, Amina Susan Ali, and Sandra Cisneros.

I provided the students with different, albeit plentiful support structures and formats for each seminar. While the format and structure of both the preparation for the Socratic seminars and the seminars themselves varied dramatically, there were some constants and predictable patterns. Desks were arranged in a circle, and students were allowed to sit wherever they wanted. All focused thematically on the "Essential Questions" that framed each unit. For each seminar students were required to develop questions that were divided into three categories (Literal, or Level 1, questions; Interpretive, or Level 2, questions; and Applied, or Level 3, questions). Students brought their questions, as well as specific quotations they had identified, to the seminar to share. Each seminar had a student facilitator, and each had a student timekeeper to help the facilitator. Additionally, students sat in a circle of desks facing one another during each seminar. Each Socratic seminar counted heavily in the students' grades. The students received credit for preseminar preparation work, participation in the seminar itself, and written and oral analyses and reflections after the seminars.

COLLECTING AND ANALYZING MY DATA

To learn about the seminars, I collected each student's preseminar work, their notes from the seminars themselves, and their postseminar reflections and analyses. I collected and transcribed audio recordings of each of the four seminars and wrote descriptive field notes during my observations as well as reflective and analytic memos after each one. In addition, as I worked on structuring the seminars, I observed two other teachers conducting seminars in their classes and wrote descriptive and analytic notes about each of those observations. Last, I emailed several other English teachers and asked them to send me their Socratic seminar materials as well as any theoretical or analytical writing that they had regarding the goals, structures, and implementation of Socratic seminars in high school classes.

An important question for this research project was how I would determine the level of success of the seminars in my class. Consequently, an early step in my research process was to create an operational definition for a successful Socratic seminar. More specifically, I needed to determine what I would use as central components of success. That way I could ascertain if the seminar was successful in some ways, but not in other ways, and thereby know what to work on specifically in order to increase their overall effectiveness. Beyond the model from my master teacher's classes, I wanted to create my own definitions of success for myself and for my students in our implementation of Socratic seminars.

I reviewed my initial field notes, memos, and student writing prompts to establish categories that both the students and I used in setting individual and whole-class goals for the seminars. In this process I noticed the following words coming up most frequently: *effective, useful,* and *meaningful.* Although these words may not seem to index separate concepts, my students thought about them as being separate. While the first three criteria were developed as categories from my students' own writing, I developed the final criteria around the word *safe,* although it was not often used by the students. I included this word to denote a category for all the ways that students wanted themselves and their peers to feel (comfortable, relaxed, etc.) during the seminars. In addition, seminars in which students felt safe enough to take risks and make personal connections seemed to be a prerequisite to the other three criteria for success. So, drawing on categories that represented both my own and my students' goals, I established four criteria for success—that the Socratic seminars were meaningful, useful, effective, and safe as defined below:

- *Meaningful:* The seminar helps students to deepen and broaden their personal connections to the characters and themes in the text. The seminar helps students to understand and articulate the ways in which the text affects them personally and academically.
- *Useful:* The seminar helps students to engage in critical and analytic writing about the text. The seminar provides students with opportunities to explore both new and diverse arguments, vocabularies, and perspectives (in relation to the text) that they will later use in formal writing.
- *Effective:* The seminar is focused and centered on the text itself as well as the Essential Questions framing the unit and the specific perspectives, lenses, questions, and arguments in which students have expressed particular interest.
- *Safe:* All students contribute to the seminar and feel valued and respected throughout the seminar process. The seminar itself deepens the class's sense of community and connection by fostering

honesty, sharing, and curiosity in and between all students. Students feel free to take academic and personal risks and to support their peers in doing so.

First, I examined all of my students' experiences with and responses to each of the four Socratic seminars as reflected in the entire corpus of data I had collected. Then, I divided their reactions and experiences into three main categories: students for whom all the Socratic seminars had been relatively successful, students whose experiences in the seminars had varied dramatically, and students for whom none of the seminars were particularly successful. Within each of these three categories, I selected one focal student. In selecting each one I took into account the range of identities represented in the classroom such that the focal students somewhat reflected the various identities represented the class's heterogeneity (particularly in relation to race, gender, and language).

The first focal student, Victor, is a Latino male whose skill and confidence in his analytic thinking and writing is impressive. While Victor does not always complete all his work for my class—he had a C+ during the time of this study—he is consistently one of the leaders of our Socratic seminars. Janisha, the second student I focused on, is an African American female whose experiences in each seminar varied dramatically. She was one of the most thorough workers in the class and had an A during the time of this research. However, her participation in the seminars was uneven, but representative of a large number of students in the class.

Anayeli is a Latina female who was particularly quiet and soft-spoken in my class. While Anayeli completed enough of the classwork to pass—she had a D+ during the time of this project—she rarely participated orally. Originally, Anayeli was an English language learner, but she was redesignated while in 9th grade. Nonetheless, English literacy and oral fluency remain a challenge for her. Anayeli did not successfully participate in any of the Socratic seminars in my class. In other words, she never fully experienced them as safe, meaningful, useful, and effective.

FINDING MY PLACE IN THE PROCESS

A central finding from this study had to do with my role in designing specific formats and structures (which included my place in the process) for implementing Socratic seminars in my class. In this section I discuss my findings on the students' varying levels of success with regard to meaningfulness, usefulness, effectiveness, and safety as they progressed through the four seminars. I reveal the findings with respect to these four attributes of success largely through the experiences of my three focal students. I also show how my own process in researching and developing the different formats and structures for the seminars contributed to the students' varying degrees of success in terms of the four attributes.

For each seminar, I first provide background on how I developed and structured it. Then I discuss how the students experienced it, including my analysis of its success or lack of success according to my criteria of its being meaningful, useful, effective, and safe for each focal student. I provide detailed descriptions of the first and last seminars and shorter descriptions of the two in between.

Flight Seminar

Four weeks into fall semester, we had our first Socratic seminar on the book *Flight* by Sherman Alexie. For this seminar, I relied almost entirely on materials developed in collaboration with my master teacher for her classes. I provided word banks, suggested themes, and detailed explanations of the various types of seminar questions. I provided only basic information regarding the Goals, Process, and various student Roles in a Socratic seminar. I chose and met with the first student Facilitator ahead of time to discuss strategies for maintaining, supporting, and guiding the discussion. I also assigned a Timekeeper. Finally, and important for my research on the structuring of the seminar, I included a detailed seminar reflection handout that would allow me to learn about the ways in which the supports and structures were adequate and inadequate for my students.

At the beginning of the seminar, I reviewed the procedures that were outlined in the packet on their desks and explained that the Facilitator would call on students to ask the questions they had prepared and then call on other students to comment and respond.

I sat just outside the seminar circle in a large and prominent chair so that most of the students could see me throughout. While I did not make any overt contributions, I wanted the class to know that I was there supporting and encouraging them and listening intently to their discussion. When students made jokes, I laughed; when a student spoke to his or her neighbor out of turn, I stared and cleared my throat to get their attention; when students asked questions or brought up new ideas, I smiled or made encouraging noises. A few times, the Facilitator got stuck and turned to me. Each time, I counseled the Facilitator and made encouraging comments to the class as a whole. Throughout the seminar, I tried to make eye contact with students who were not talking and smiled encouragingly. In other words, while I sat outside the circle and did not make overt oral contributions to the discussion, my presence was prominent.

Flight **Student Experiences.** Victor was one of the few students who actively participated in this seminar. Although he was daunted by the highly detailed seminar questions that the preseminar materials demanded he develop—"This is too much, Ms. Daniels!" he told me as I passed them out—he nonetheless completed the majority of the preseminar preparation work. The questions he developed were sophisticated and insightful, showing deep understanding and multiple perspectives on the themes in the text.

During the seminar, Victor spoke six times (more than anyone else in the class). Each time he spoke, he turned and seemed to speak directly to me, ignoring his peers. But his answers were thorough, and he twice referred directly to the text, using quotes to make a point. However, he made no personal connections to the text and did not speak or pose questions with real interest or passion. Nevertheless, he gave himself a 9 out of 10 for participation. "I talked a lot and I asked two questions. I came up with answers to questions, and I used quotes from the book," he wrote in explanation of his score. He graded the class's participation as a 7 and wrote, "We came up with some answers. More people should have talked. There was too much silence, but people were prepared and had their questions written. We did good for the first time."

Janisha spoke only twice during the seminar. She had completed all her preseminar materials and had developed questions that showed a burgeoning understanding of the distinctions between Level 1, 2, and 3 questions. Her questions drew more overtly on the supports and scaffolding that the preseminar materials had provided. She used the words from the question word bank and relied heavily on the list of themes that the class had generated and that had been included in the handout. She also picked thoughtful quotes to write down that clearly connected to the questions she developed and showed a thorough understanding of themes in the text.

However, Janisha barely participated. Like many students, she spent most of the seminar doodling on her seminar preparation worksheet, staring at her hands, looking nervously at me, or trying to avoid the facilitator's eye so as not to be chosen to speak. Her self-evaluation (4 out of 10) was quite critical, as was her class evaluation (5 out of 10). She wrote that she "should have talked more" and "should [have been] less shy and [said] more stuff." For the class she wrote that "people should have talked more. People should have participated more and been sharing their questions more. We didn't really come up with any good answers to any questions, so I don't think we did that well."

Anayeli did not speak at all during the seminar. She came to the seminar with most of her preparation materials completed, but her questions were formulaic and did not indicate a sophisticated analysis or understanding of the text. During the seminar itself, she frequently shifted in her seat, appeared quite uncomfortable, and made little eye contact with anyone. At one point she leaned over to whisper to her friend, but immediately stopped and looked down at her desk when she saw me looking. Even when the conversation became humorous, she did not laugh or smile and rarely even looked up from her lap. Her 5-out-of-10 evaluation of her participation was not completely genuine. She wrote, "I was prepared and had my questions, but I didn't have anything to say, so I didn't say nothing." She gave the class a 9 out of 10, saying, "They talked a lot about the book and had lots of questions. They did good." Interestingly, Anayeli seemed to distance herself from the process and perhaps from the classroom community by her use of the word "they."

***Flight* Findings.** After the first seminar, it was clear that the majority of my students were not adequately able to engage in a high level of dialogue and text-based analysis. My findings in the framework of the four criteria I had established for successful seminars further illuminated the problems encountered in this seminar on Alexie's book *Flight*.

Had the seminar been meaningful? Students did not use the seminar to draw connections between their own lives and the text, themes, or perspectives addressed in the seminar. The seminar did not—according to both my own and my students' writing—help students to articulate the ways in which the text and its themes related to their own lives. In this way, it was not very "meaningful."

Had the seminar been useful? According to both my own and my students' evaluations, the seminar had not offered students new insights into the book or allowed them to experiment with new ideas or perspectives. For the most part, they had been too quiet and too uncomfortable to participate in and learn from a seminar in that way. Although orally reviewing the text's main themes might have been somewhat helpful in preparing a piece of writing, there didn't seem to have been any part of the discussion that provided important insights for subsequent writing.

Additionally, had the seminar been effective? Both my focal students and I noted that the students had remained on task throughout the seminar. There were few major distractions, and students took turns posing questions (albeit with prolonged silences in between). While there had been little discussion, the questions and few comments that students made were all directly connected to the text, major themes, and essential questions. In this way, the seminar was "effective."

Finally, had the seminar been safe? While there had been no overt rudeness or hostility, there was a general feeling of tension and anxiety during the seminar. It did not seem to deepen the students' sense of connection or community. Rather than speak to one another, the students had almost all spoken directly to me, ignoring and de-emphasizing their connection with their peers. So, the seminar did not seem particularly "safe."

Sula **Seminar**

The second Socratic seminar focused on the novel *Sula* by Toni Morrison. While the students (particularly the male students) were not as engaged in the text as they had been during our reading of *Flight*, they nonetheless completed the reading and engaged in several in-depth teacher-led informal discussions around the novel's themes of sexual liberation, promiscuity, feminism, and hedonism.

After the first seminar, I decided to return to my master teacher's classroom and observe one of her seminars; I thought perhaps I had missed or forgotten an important component of the process. I did notice a few structures she provided for her students during the seminar itself that I had not provided, but I also noted that I used the same preseminar supports that she did. In light of the difficulties my students were having and the structures I observed her using, I added three active roles for students: Process Checker, Recorder, and Participation Monitor. The Process Checker was responsible for taking notes on the dynamics and logistics of the discussion. The Recorder was responsible for writing down important and interesting questions raised during the discussion. The Participation Monitor was responsible for keeping track of how often students participated and for giving credit when students posed or answered questions thoughtfully and thoroughly.

I made no other significant changes in the seminar structure, the preseminar materials, or the postseminar evaluation and reflection. The goal of these new roles was to encourage the students to be more aware of the process of the seminar itself: to consider who was speaking, what he or she was talking about, to whom the student was speaking, how the student was speaking, and how frequently he or she was speaking. I hoped that by giving students the responsibility of monitoring the discussion, they would take more responsibility for the success of the seminar and become more invested in making the experience meaningful, useful, effective, and safe.

The experiences of my focal students in the second seminar varied. Victor arrived with all his preparation materials completed and spoke 10 times during the seminar. However, the presence of a Participation Monitor, Recorder, and Process Checker changed how he participated. He seemed markedly aware that I was no longer the only person taking notes, recording and considering his every word. Instead of directing his questions and responses to me (I again sat in a prominent chair just on the outside the circle), he directed his questions to the Participation Monitor and the Recorder, and occasionally made eye contact with other classmates. His postseminar reflection and evaluation also indicated significant changes. Although he assigned himself a slightly lower grade, his written insights about his participation indicated a deeper understanding of the seminar process and a new perspective on his own role in relation to his class members. "I talked a lot this time,"

Victor wrote. "But . . . I think I should listen more next time and try more to encourage other people to talk." He gave the class as a whole a higher grade than on the first seminar. "I think we worked together more this time," he wrote. "More people were trying to make the seminar work. . . . I could have helped the class more, and the Facilitator could have encouraged more people to try to speak. But the people who talked had good stuff to say and they asked good questions."

Janisha also completed all of her preseminar materials but spoke only once. However, she clearly had a newfound understanding of the complexity and nuances of the various types of seminar questions as a result of work we had done since the last seminar. Although her verbal participation was minimal, her participation overall had shifted. Instead of spending the entire seminar staring at her paper or looking nervously at me, she made eye contact with her peers as they spoke and even nodded or smiled when someone made a particularly interesting or poignant comment.

The one comment Janisha did make seemed to indicate a new level of comfort with and ease in the seminar. When a peer referred to the two main female characters in the novel as "friends," Janisha commented, "I think they're not just friends. They not havin' sex, but they both be wantin' to have sex. They kinda girlfriends or lovers or whatever 'cause look at that chapter we were just reading." With a comment that took both courage and confidence, she attempted to broaden her peers' understanding of the characters, and did so by referring to evidence in the text. Janisha gave herself a slightly higher grade than she did for the first seminar and wrote, "I didn't talk a lot, but I really listened. I also wasn't that nervous. . . . The one time I talked, I think I said good stuff, and I used the book." She also significantly raised her grade for the class as a whole and wrote, "We did a lot better because more people talked and people cared more this time. . . . They wanted the Participation Monitor and the Recorder to be sure they knew they talked."

Anayeli did not complete her preseminar materials, but she did speak for the first time, which indicated a key change from the first seminar. Instead of looking down at her desk and shifting nervously in her seat, she spent the hour making eye contact with students, smiling supportively at their comments, and not engaging in side conversations. When a fellow student drew a connection between the characters in *Sula* and the characters in *Flight*, she slowly raised her hand and said, "Um, isn't that kinda wrong, I'm not bad, but, 'cause in *Flight* the character didn't really have no home at all . . ." Although she gave herself and the class the same rating as that of the first seminar, her reflection no longer referred to the class as "they." Thus, she was no longer excluding herself from the class community and the seminar process.

My major conclusion was that student participation in the second seminar had improved (though not as much as I had hoped). I felt it was more "meaningful" for my students in that it provided more opportunities for them to articulate connections between the text and their own lives. Across the group, they spoke more and seemed more engaged in their peers' comments and questions. It still was not as useful as I wanted it to be in that the students did not significantly explore, expand on, or experiment with issues in ways that might later be useful in their analytic writing. I felt, however, that the seminar had been "effective" to the extent that my students remained focused on the text itself. Yet they were almost too narrowly examining the text in efforts to draw direct, but less complex, answers to their questions. Finally, the second seminar seemed safer to participate in than the first. Students took personal risks, exposed themselves, and strengthened their sense of community. They directed their comments and questions to one another (instead of me) and seemed to feel supported by peers who had taken on the roles of Process Checker, Recorder, and Participation Monitor. Therefore, this seminar was more welcoming than the first as partially evidenced by 16 out of 26 students actively participating.

"Beauty . . . " Seminar

Our third seminar centered on a short story by Alice Walker titled "Beauty: When the Other Dancer Is the Self." I deliberately choose a shorter text, thinking that its brevity might allow students to delve more deeply into its nuances and complexities. After the second seminar, I wanted to find additional ways to facilitate students extending their intellectual and emotional insights, analyses, and perspectives in the seminar. So I emailed several English teachers and asked them to send me the Socratic seminar materials that they used with their classes. In putting together the materials and structures for the third seminar, I hoped to provide students with more information about the process of discussion and analysis and the goals of the Socratic seminar.

As usual, students worked in groups to develop their seminar questions. However, when I handed out the seminar materials this time, I included information about the theory and goals behind the Socratic seminar as well as the qualities that characterized sophisticated intellectual dialogue in contrast to debate. For homework the night before the seminar, I asked students to use the theoretical information I provided to set goals for themselves for the next day's seminar and to make predictions about any difficulties they foresaw in integrating the theoretical perspectives into the actual seminar preparation. Other than this, the preparation and structure for the third seminar was exactly the same as for the second. Despite (or perhaps because of) these additions, student experiences plummeted in the third seminar.

Victor completed his preseminar materials, but spoke only four times during the seminar itself. Although the homework questions he had developed showed deep insight and analytic skills, he brought none of that sophistication to the seminar discussion itself. Instead, he limited himself to surface-level comments and to answering literal questions about the events in the text, and he often looked toward me as if gauging my responses. Victor gave himself an exceptionally low grade (3 out of 10). In reflection he wrote, "I didn't say complicated things cause I said mostly stupid things. I didn't do all the stuff Ms. Daniels said about dialogue and questions and analyzing." He seemed embarrassed that he had not participated in a more "complicated" way that reflected the theoretical reading he had done before the seminar.

Janisha also completed all the preseminar prompts and spoke twice during the seminar. She seemed highly inhibited, even though she participated orally one more time than earlier. But neither her preseminar materials nor her actual participation reflected the complexity or sophistication I expected of her. She seemed anxious and made little eye contact with her peers, although she regularly glanced in my direction throughout the seminar. She evaluated her participation and that of her peers as lower than for both previous seminars, writing that her comments were not "smart or connecting to the stuff Daniels wanted us to do."

Anayeli did not participate positively at all and seemed frustrated by the very process of this seminar. She started off-topic side conversations four times and muttered under her breath when peers asked her to stop. Unlike in past seminars, when she either marginally participated or simply withdrew from the process, this time she seemed committed to refusing to participate and separating herself from the rest of the class. Although she did not give the class an exceptionally low rating, she gave herself a 1 out of 10.

My findings were that this was the least successful seminar. Instead of inspiring the students to deepen their discussion, the theoretical materials I provided seemed to overwhelm and intimidate them. Attempting to integrate these concepts into their seminar participation was either too challenging or simply explained too poorly by me. The theoretical information also seemed to underscore my role in the seminar—and my own agenda and goals. As a result, the students attempted to prove to me that they were working hard—rather than attempting to learn, discuss, or explore ideas in ways that were "meaningful" to them. Essentially they had not drawn any new or meaningful connections between the text and their own lives and experiences.

This seminar also had not been very "useful" for my students in terms of providing them with new insights that they might later use in their writing. The majority of the class had been too intimidated or nervous to experiment with new arguments or to take risks exploring new perspectives. It was marginally "effective," however, in that it did remain focused on the text of the short story throughout the period, with just a few side conversations and distractions from individual students. But it was the least "safe" of the three seminars thus far in the class. The students were trying hard to do something that was difficult for them, and they were somewhat embarrassed that they seemed to be failing. They were consequently very anxious and visibly frustrated. Like my students after the first and third seminars, I was also frustrated.

The *Tortilla Curtain* Seminar

Before undertaking *The Tortilla Curtain* by T. C. Boyle, a satirical novel that addressed issues of immigration and social responsibility, I decided to visit another English teacher who regularly used Socratic seminars. I observed her using many of the strategies I had tried; however, she structured her seminars slightly differently. She divided the class in two and assigned each student in one group to observe and document the several aspects of participation of a specific student in the other group while engaged in the seminar. Then the two groups switched roles.

For *The Tortilla Curtain* seminar, however, I decided to randomly pair students to observe, take notes on, and grade each other's participation, but to have them all work together in a whole-class seminar instead of breaking them into two separate ones. I told them I would not be grading their participation: Students would be grading each other, using notes on a detailed handout that I developed. Their new roles eliminated the need for a Participation Monitor, since all students had the responsibility of monitoring participation. I also did not have them use the theoretical information that I had included for the previous seminar. Otherwise, their preparation for the seminar was similar to that of the previous seminars, but during the actual execution, I decided to seat myself in the far corner of the room so that only a few students could see me, and I did not take any notes, although I listened intently. I did this to underscore that the students themselves were responsible for conducting the seminar, grading participation, and engaging in the kind of dialogue to make it a success.

The *Tortilla Curtain* Student Experiences. Victor completed all his preparation materials and was actively involved throughout the seminar, making eye contact and constantly writing down detailed observations about his partner. He spoke six times—twice to pose challenging questions that drew rich connections between themes in the novel and four times to offer thoughtful responses to questions or comments of fellow students. He was verbose in his evaluation of himself, his partner, and the class. He rated his participation a 9 out of 10. "I was so focused, my mind wasn't anywhere else," he wrote. He also wrote that his partner "seemed to be trying really hard and listening," and he gave the class as a whole a 9 out of 10 too.

"Everyone seemed to really care and want it to work," he noted on his evaluation sheet. "We wanted us to do well and wanted to be smart together." It did not bother him that all his classmates were taking notes on each other.

Janisha also completed all the preparation materials. She spoke three times during the seminar itself. At first she had expressed trepidation about taking notes while participating in the seminar. Once it began, however, she became completely engrossed in the process. Two of Janisha's comments were in response to her peers' questions, and they each pushed the conversation to new levels of complexity by drawing in vocabulary, literary techniques, and themes that we had explored as a class outside of the seminar. The last comment that Janisha offered drew a surprisingly personal connection to the text. She shared an experience with racial profiling that was similar to the experience of a character in the novel. I felt that this kind of participation indicated a new level of comfort on her part.

Janisha gave herself an 8 out of 10 and wrote, "I talked and said stuff that I think helped us. I think I made our conversation more deep." When evaluating her partner, she thoughtfully wrote, "My partner really focused; and even though he got confused once, he seemed like he tried; and then he understood again." She gave the class as a whole a 10 out of 10, writing, "I think we should be hella proud cause we all were in it; and we all talked and tried; and we came up with smart things."

Anayeli did not speak at all during the fourth seminar; however, her presence was in no way disruptive to the process (as it had been in the previous seminar). In fact, while she did not complete any of her seminar materials, she was very active in taking notes on and evaluating her partner. Throughout the seminar she continually observed her partner, took detailed notes, and seemed very engaged in her partner's contributions to the discussion. Her partner spoke over 10 times. And at no point did she engage in side conversations. She gave herself only a 3 out of 10, writing, "I didn't talk, but I listen." But her evaluation of her partner was quite detailed and complimentary. "My partner basically led the seminar. He said smart things and was ready and helped everyone." Anayeli gave the class as a whole an 8 out of 10, and wrote, "We tried, and a lot of people talked and helped each other. We were nice."

The Tortilla Curtain Findings. The fourth seminar clearly was the most successful. In part, this might have been tied to the fact that it was the last seminar, and the students had finally gained confidence in their seminar skills. It could also have been tied to this particular novel's themes surrounding immigration and social justice. But the other texts had also addressed provocative personal and political themes, and it was definitely not a simple evolution, as indicated by the near disaster of the third seminar. Essentially, I found that the structure of the fourth seminar itself contributed greatly to the students' experiences of success. The four criteria I established for a successful seminar illuminated the importance of the fourth seminar's structure.

This seminar was "meaningful" for the students in that they took more risks and drew more extensively on personal connections between themselves and the text. Students' comments and questions built on their real-life experiences to interrogate themes and events in the text, sometimes creating moments of profound, shared understanding. While perhaps this seminar did not prepare students to write a formal essay on *The Tortilla Curtain*, it was certainly "useful" because it offered them rich opportunities to share their ideas and perspectives and to explore one another's arguments. Students often referenced the text itself and used the text to support their arguments more in this seminar than they had in any of the previous ones. The seminar had also been effective in that (like the other seminars) the students remained focused on the text throughout the seminar. Even those students who did not orally contribute to the seminar seemed focused and highly engaged in the process, as revealed by the copious written notes on their observations of their partners and other aspects of the seminar. Importantly, this seminar seemed not only uniquely productive but also "safe." In their own evaluations the students commented on how well they had worked together and supported one another in developing and exploring ideas. The students also commented on how "kind" they had been to one another.

Through my analysis of all the data sources, I found that the final seminar was by far the most successful. This was not simply because it was the last seminar in the series. Instead, I found that it had more to do with ways my students were relied on to take leadership and responsibility for its execution. There were definite structures that facilitated them in being able to do this. They were able to establish a genuine sense of community within their circle of desks. They actually felt their independence, responsibility, and the need for their leadership in concretely structured ways. This was aided by the fact that I sat in a place in the room that was physically distanced from the seminar process, but I also placed myself outside the role of directing the seminar process. Importantly, key structures had been established building from earlier seminars (such as the roles of a Facilitator, Timekeeper, and Process Checker and having students develop thoughtful questions ahead of time) to provide the scaffolding needed for my students to succeed.

WHAT I LEARNED RESEARCHING MY TEACHING

As a teacher, I constantly question my roles in the classroom. Every day I wonder how I can better support my students by offering them more information, different skills, and more complex perspectives. In the midst of trying to learn how to be more effective, however, I sometimes forget that students should be their own best teachers—regardless of how varied or valuable the perspectives that I supply might be. Further, I needed to provide lots of support for that independence, of a nonthreatening kind, and I needed to carefully adjust the support, depending on my students' responses.

I believe in the importance of Socratic seminars partially because they can be organized to explicitly validate and encourage student voice and leadership and offer students the opportunity to collaboratively guide and complicate their own learning. The structures that most supported my students in having a successful Socratic seminar were ones that furthered their sense of independence, collective responsibility, and leadership, as well as ones that demanded appropriate levels of thinking and probing of the texts themselves.

While engaging in this research and exploring ways to best support my students, my findings revealed that my desire to help did not necessitate a stronger teacher presence in the moment of the seminars. Instead, my students taught me that once I have provided adequate structures and supports, I have to step back and offer them opportunities for independence, responsibility, and leadership. As teachers, we often become so involved in attempting to design and direct learning experiences that we sometimes forget that being individually and collectively responsible for learning is empowering and inspiring for students. Through this process, I have been reminded that experimentation in the classroom does not always mean inserting my own presence more pervasively—sometimes it means stepping back after providing the necessary support, and letting students take the lead in learning for themselves and with one another.

CHAPTER 3

Assessing the Impact of Project-Based Learning on Students' Academic Achievement in English Language Arts

Nicola C. Martinez

Project-based learning at the Academy of Arts and Technology High School (AATHS) is an opportunity for students to synthesize the material that they are learning in their courses and beyond into one project that showcases their critical thinking and leadership capabilities. As a preservice teacher at AATHS, I was captivated by the project-based approach to learning that the school had designed and implemented for students in every grade level. In their English language arts (ELA) class, students were learning about the complexities of equality in society by analyzing the text *Animal Farm* by George Orwell. In their history class, they were investigating the historical components of the Russian Revolution by analyzing the notions of power and inequality in a communist government. Students were asked to work in small groups to create their own utopian society using digital software and then present this creative design to parents, teachers, staff, and other members of the community. As I observed the preparation and implementation of this project, I was intrigued by the level of critical thinking it required and wondered whether a high-stakes project like this one had an impact on students' academic achievement in their core courses.

When I began my own teaching at AATHS the next year, I collaborated with the other 10th-grade teachers across content areas to weave the concept of transformation into our separate semester projects. I was excited and inspired by the fact that my students were going to learn about social, biological, digital, geometric, and literary transformations and then have the opportunity to synthesize these elements into a larger project. Since my students were going to be engaged in deep learning of and critical thinking about the concept of transformation in each of their classes, and because I had witnessed this same kind of learning the prior year as a student teacher,

I decided to investigate how my students' academic achievement in our English class was affected by their participation in the project. I define *academic achievement* as a student's ability to earn satisfactory or above-satisfactory grades based on AATHS's holistic grading system, which was designed for all instructors to use to assess students' academic performance in their course(s). Therefore, in this chapter, I address the following research question: How does project-based learning affect students' academic achievement in their high school English class?

TEACHING AND LEARNING AT MY SCHOOL

AATHS is a small charter high school located in the San Francisco Bay Area. It has been in operation since 2004. At the time of this study, there were 170 9th- through 12th-grade students enrolled at the school. Fifty-seven percent of these students were students of color, 43% were first-generation college bound, 38% qualified for free or reduced-price lunch, and 13% were English language learners. Many of the students commuted to the school from other cities in the Bay Area, some with commutes of an hour or more each way.

Project-Based Learning and Exhibitions

AATHS takes a project-based learning approach to academics, in which students explore core academic content within a system that requires their active participation and input. Students create projects that demonstrate their mastery of complex questions and problems in a variety of academic subjects: literature, art, math, science, and digital media. To encourage this type of active learning, students are expected to participate in Exhibitions, which are public projects and presentations that showcase students' knowledge and mastery of core concepts. Exhibitions require students to work individually or collaboratively to create high-quality and in-depth demonstrations of their learning. A vital part of the Exhibition process is the student reflection component, which encourages students to reflect on their work leading up to, during, and after the Exhibition event.

Each year, students in the 9th through 12th grades participate in an Exhibition at their grade level. The focal point for each grade's Exhibition depends on the subject matter that students are learning in each of their core academic courses. The fall Exhibition for 10th-graders, which is the focus of this study, asked students to explore the notion of transformation by answering the question, How does transformation occur? The 40 students in the sophomore class learned about the concept of transformation in each of their academic disciplines—geometry, global studies, English, digital media, and biology—and then created projects (e.g., revolutionary voices blogs, literary analysis essays, digital animations, and evolution reports on a wild animal) for each course that demonstrated their understanding of transformation in the context of each discipline. In order to synthesize the information learned in each of these courses, students designed a thesis statement that articulated the connections between each of their course projects. On the night of the Exhibition, students displayed their thesis statements and semester projects on trifold poster boards at individual tables. Parents, teachers, staff, and other community members walked through the seven rows of tables asking students critical thinking questions and commenting on their work. Teachers graded each student's responses using a rubric that assessed that student's ability to analyze and synthesize the meaning of transformation within and across the five academic disciplines.

The English Curriculum

During the fall semester, students read the Greek tragedy *Antigone* in our ELA class and analyzed the ways in which the main character, Antigone, transformed the world around her. Many students chose to write about how Antigone transformed the beliefs and actions of minor and major characters through her prideful determination to bury her brother, Polynices, an act that defied Theban law. Students articulated their understanding of transformation in this text through five-paragraph essays (introduction, three body paragraphs, conclusion) and used these essays as one of the four required artifacts in their Exhibition projects.

MY FOCAL STUDENTS

I chose four focal students—Taylor, Brasil, Jocelyn, and Jessica—for this study based on three main factors: their academic performance during the fall semester of my 10th-grade ELA class, their prior participation in the 9th-grade Exhibition project, and their willingness to speak openly about their personal assessments of the effects of the Exhibition on their academic achievement in English class.

Brasil. Brasil is African American and lives with her mother in San Francisco. She participated in the 9th-grade Exhibition at AATHS and stated that the experience contributed to her improved academic performance. During her sophomore year, Brasil demonstrated a willingness to strive for academic success in ELA. As an active participant in our ELA class, she enjoyed working with her classmates on skits, reading texts aloud, and presenting material to her peers. Even though she participated in the daily classroom activities, however, she inconsistently turned in homework assignments and earned low grades on tests and her *Antigone* essay. She therefore earned an NC (No Credit) in ELA prior to the Exhibition.

Jocelyn. Jocelyn is African American and lives with her mother in Oakland. She is a highly engaged student and demonstrated creativity in most of her academic work. As a freshman, Jocelyn participated in the 9th-grade Exhibition and expressed frustration in being asked to work on the project in a small group of her peers. She preferred the individualization of the 10th-grade Exhibition. Jocelyn was earning a B in ELA prior to the Exhibition.

Taylor. Taylor is African American and lives with her mother and younger brother in Oakland. She believed that her 9th-grade Exhibition project had a positive impact on her confidence as a student, and she was eager to discuss her observations about the positive academic impact the 10th-grade Exhibition had on her peers' performance. Taylor was earning a B+ in ELA class prior to the Exhibition.

Jessica. Jessica is Latina and lives with her parents and younger sister in Richmond. She has an Individualized Education Plan and was at a 3rd-grade reading and writing level during the study year. During her freshman year at AATHS, Jessica refused to participate in the 9th-grade Exhibition and earned NCs in most of her classes. In her sophomore year, however, Jessica chose to participate in the 10th-grade Exhibition even though two of her projects were only partially completed. Prior to the Exhibition, Jessica was earning an NC in ELA.

MY DATA AND ANALYSIS

I collected five types of data during the fall semester of the 2010–2011 school year: teacher logs, field notes, exhibition data, ELA grades, and interviews.

Teacher Logs. Teacher logs were journal-style reflections on classroom dynamics, student behaviors, and academic performances that I observed each day over the course of the fall semester. I used these logs to capture any trends and to narrow my research topic. Some of these logs included information on student academic performance before and after the Exhibition.

Field Notes. Field notes consisted of my ongoing observations of the focal students' behavior, perspectives, and academic progress. During the first 4 months of the school year, I wrote weekly field notes pertaining to my four focal students' attitudes toward and comments about their Exhibition projects. I recorded these quotes and highlighted any recurring themes.

Exhibition Data. On the night of the Exhibition, I asked the four focal students questions related to the theme of transformation and how this concept connected across the coursework they had completed in biology, English, global studies, digital media, and geometry. I wrote down their individual responses to my questions and also observed and recorded how they interacted with other teachers, staff members, and parents. Later, I read my notes and other teachers' notes regarding each student's responses to the questions and overall performance during the Exhibition.

ELA Grades. Using the holistic grading system and corresponding grade-tracker sheet supplied to teachers, I kept track of my students' grades before and after the Exhibition in order to monitor their academic progress and identify any changes in performance over time. This grading system enabled me to observe and compare academic achievement in English class in relation to the Exhibition for the four focal students and reflect on each student's academic strengths and areas for growth 1 month before and 1 month after the Exhibition.

Interviews. Four weeks after the Exhibition, I individually interviewed my four focal students and took handwritten notes of their responses. Each interview lasted 15 minutes. During these conversations, I asked each student the following questions:

- Describe your past Exhibition experience(s).
- Did the (prior) spring 2010 Exhibition impact your academic achievement in any way?
- Why does AATHS have Exhibitions?
- Describe your experience at this year's Exhibition.
- Did you notice if your English grade was impacted in any way?
- Were other students impacted academically by this year's Exhibition? If so, how?

After conducting these interviews, I read through the students' responses and highlighted any similar experiences and opinions they had discussed. I compared and contrasted these responses with my other data sources (teacher logs, field notes, Exhibition data, and ELA grades) and looked at each student's academic performance across time (before, during, and after the Exhibition).

MY FINDINGS

I found that the 10th-grade fall Exhibition project had a positive impact on the academic achievement in English of all four of the focal students. However, not all the students recognized that their performance had improved as a result of the Exhibition project. In the sections that follow, I first trace the academic trajectories of the two students—Brasil and Jocelyn—who believed that the Exhibition affected their academic performance in my class in positive ways. Then I trace the trajectories of the two students—Taylor and Jessica—who did not attribute their improved performance in English class to the Exhibition project.

Brasil

Brasil demonstrated a remarkable will and strove for academic success throughout the fall semester. Even though she exhibited these characteristics relentlessly, she was not passing English approximately 1 month before the Exhibition because many assignments were turned in late and were not at a proficient level. During the revision process for the *Antigone* essay, for example, Brasil submitted three drafts and earned a C on her final draft. She understood the concept of transformation as it manifested in the play but did not adhere to the analytical writing structure, and this greatly affected her grade. Two weeks prior to the Exhibition, Brasil inquired if she could continue revising her draft to earn a higher grade. She submitted a fourth draft, which earned her a C+.

Before the Exhibition. Brasil's attitude toward the Exhibition was a combination of excitement and anxiety. One day after English class about 1 month before the Exhibition, she commented, "I don't know the science stuff but I know the *Antigone* stuff. So when people ask me questions about *Antigone* I will know the answers. I hope I don't fail." As the Exhibition date approached, Brasil continued to exclaim to me and to her peers how nervous she was because she did not think she was going to know the answers to the questions. However, 3 days before the Exhibition, I held a review session in English class to assess students' readiness, and Brasil answered the questions with grace and fluidity. Even though she demonstrated that she was prepared for the Exhibition, she continued to make remarks such as "I'm going to fail" and "This Exhibition is going to be so hard."

During the Exhibition. Brasil displayed all four of her projects from English, global studies, geometry, and science on her trifold board and titled the board with the essential question, How does transformation occur? She waited patiently for teachers, parents, and other staff members to stop by her table to ask her questions about how the theme of transformation connected each of her projects. As I approached her table she smiled and said, "Okay, Niki, I'm ready." I asked her how Creon (the antagonist in *Antigone*) represents rotation and how that same concept can be applied to the Haitian Revolution, which she researched in her global studies course. First, Brasil defined *rotation* (a complete change; a flip). Next, she proceeded to explain Creon's transformation: "He was so selfish [at the beginning of the play] . . . only thought about himself and the laws he created . . . He wanted everyone to follow his demands. But then when Antigone buried her brother even though Creon didn't want her to, he felt sorry for what he had done." Then Brasil discussed how the slaves of Haiti completely changed their social status by at first complying with the demands of their owners but then rebelling against them.

As she was describing this connection, Brasil's high level of critical thinking impressed me. She was applying rotation, a geometric term, to a dynamic character in *Antigone* and then showing how this same concept applied to an historical revolution. Her freshman English teacher observed, "I have never heard Brasil speak so eloquently about English or history. She understood each term so deeply through her ability to make rich connections between the disciplines." During the Exhibition, Brasil showed great enthusiasm for the subject matter by elaborating on the specific ways each of her projects aligned with the concept of transformation. She used her display board to point to evidence, listened carefully to the questions asked, and made thorough analyses.

After the Exhibition. During our interview, Brasil stated that she "was so nervous" during the Exhibition but added that it enabled her to "put deeper meaning into the answers [because] I learned the projects deeply." Since Brasil spent an entire semester learning about and analyzing transformation, she felt competent to answer rigorous, critical thinking questions.

Academically, Brasil's grade in English class improved after the Exhibition, increasing from failing to a C. When I asked her about her past Exhibition experiences at the school, Brasil stated, "Exhibitions have helped with my grades. I had to revise my projects. I was actually failing English before [last year's] Exhibition, but then got a C afterward." Likewise, for this year's Exhibition, Brasil stated that the Exhibition contributed to her improved academic performance. She explained, "I was failing English [before the Exhibition] but passed after because I put a lot of work into it." According to Brasil, the Exhibition was the reason for her academic improvements.

Through my observations of Brasil's performance in English class, I also attribute her academic growth to the Exhibition process. During the first academic quarter, she lacked confidence in her writing skills and did not turn in classwork and homework assignments consistently. When she did turn in assignments, they were not at a proficient level. As a result, she was failing English. However, Brasil's academic performance in English improved dramatically after the Exhibition took place. She began to put more thought and effort into her assignments (especially the final project and the final exam for the course) and turned in classwork and homework more consistently, enabling her to earn a passing grade in my class. One of the other focal students, Taylor, saw a similar trend in Brasil's academic performance and observed, "Brasil's confidence went up. . . . Like she is doing better in her classes now." Showcasing her work during the Exhibition gave Brasil the opportunity to demonstrate her deep understanding of the concepts she had learned in her classes while also drawing on her performative nature. This, in turn, increased Brasil's engagement and confidence in her ability to succeed in her English class.

Jocelyn

Academically, Jocelyn showed consistent success throughout the fall semester. She submitted the majority of her classwork and homework on time and earned a proficient grade on the *Antigone* essay. During the essay-writing process, Jocelyn wrote four drafts, earning a B on the final draft, an achievement about which she showed enthusiasm and pride. In a written reflection, Jocelyn explained, "It took a few tries to get my essay grade to proficiency and I am so proud of myself because I worked really hard on it." Jocelyn was able to express her ideas effectively and convincingly by using the analytical writing structure that I provided and began to demonstrate rhetorical capabilities as well, a skill many students do not begin to illustrate until 11th grade. One month before the Exhibition, Jocelyn was earning a B in English class.

Before the Exhibition. As the Exhibition neared, Jocelyn showed confidence in her ability to achieve success. Approximately 1 month prior to the event, the students in my English class discussed questions that would be asked at the Exhibition and the types of answers that would be considered "advanced." Jocelyn contributed to this discussion by saying, "This Exhibition is going to be so easy. You don't have to work in groups. It's just you. I know the answers to these questions, so it shouldn't be a problem." As the Exhibition approached, Jocelyn came to my room one day after school to review the answers to the questions and asked for my assessment of her answers. The high level of critical thinking she demonstrated through her in-depth analysis of each subject area revealed her soaring confidence and readiness for this high-stakes event.

During the Exhibition. Jocelyn showcased all four projects on her display board and showed that she was ready to be questioned by standing upright with her hands folded behind her back, with a gentle smile across her face. Many teachers and parents stopped by her table to ask her questions and make positive comments about her work. I overheard one conversation between Jocelyn and another student's parent. Jocelyn was explaining to this parent how biological transformation (e.g., evolution) is similar to the transformational journey of Ismene (the sister of Antigone):

> Like evolution where there are changes over time, Ismene changed
> her opinion about Antigone's actions over time. She didn't agree
> with Antigone's decision to bury Polynices. . . . She even said to just
> follow Creon. But then Ismene began to transform her beliefs and then
> wanted to help Antigone actually bury her brother.

As she described this process, she pointed to her cladogram (a diagram that shows the ancestral relations of a particular animal) and her *Antigone* essay to provide visual evidence to the parent. The parent nodded her head as Jocelyn explained the connections between the two processes, and then the parent asked Jocelyn clarifying questions. The parent ended the conversation by saying, "Well, I have never thought about transformation in that way. So interesting." While witnessing this conversation taking place, I was impressed by Jocelyn's ability to effectively communicate such complex and highly analytical ideas. During an Exhibition grading meeting, her global studies teacher stated, "Jocelyn showed her capability to make deep and unique connections across each project. She really knew her stuff."

After the Exhibition. When Jocelyn and I sat down for our interview, she reflected on how this year's Exhibition differed from last year's in terms of her academic improvement. She described last year's Exhibition as "terrible" because her "group members didn't do any of the work . . . and [we] only got a B." She further indicated that her grades improved that year, but she did not attribute those improvements to the Exhibition. However, she did credit this year's academic growth to her Exhibition experience. This year's Exhibition enabled her to think critically and deeply about each class project. Practicing those academic skills during the Exhibition enabled her to implement them in English, thus improving her semester grade. Jocelyn's grade increased from a low B one month before the Exhibition to a high B after the Exhibition.

Jocelyn showed significant improvements in her English work once the Exhibition concluded. Her level of analysis in her formal and informal writing assignments deepened, demonstrating more critical thought and insights into the concepts she was investigating. On her final project, for example, she used scientific terms to symbolize the significance of a character's traits and actions and aligned those symbols and traits to the events of the French Revolution that she had studied in global studies. Her level of critical thought was evident because she used elements of a particular ecosystem to metaphorically represent and encapsulate historical and literary events. Because she practiced aligning the thematic notions of each class project for the Exhibition, she was capable of using this same kind of thinking for the final English project, which earned her an A and improved her overall grade for the course.

Taylor

During the fall semester, Taylor fulfilled the English requirements by completing all homework and classwork assignments and earning a proficient or advanced grade on this work. One month before the Exhibition, Taylor was receiving a B+ in English class, one of the highest grades among the sophomore class at that point in the semester. Taylor demonstrated the desire to succeed through her work ethic and passion for understanding the deeper meaning of content. While writing the *Antigone* essay, Taylor made appointments with me to discuss the strategies that she needed to use in order to convey her analysis more profoundly in her writing. She applied these strategies in each draft she wrote, which eventually enabled her to earn a high B on the final draft (one of the highest grades a sophomore received on this essay).

Before the Exhibition. Taylor demonstrated an optimistic and confident approach toward the Exhibition. While discussing the Exhibition procedures and questions that would be asked by parents and teachers, Taylor stated, "This is going to be so much easier than last year's Exhibition because you don't have to work with anyone else. I do so much better on my own." During a large-group activity on the question and answer component, Taylor answered each question using evidence and then connected the meaning of transformation across each subject area by analyzing how transformation in each of the disciplines is related to transformation in the others. This activity indicated that she was highly prepared for the questions that she would be asked on Exhibition night. One morning a few days prior to the Exhibition, Taylor came to my room to review her responses to each question and asked me to clarify questions she was having trouble answering. After meeting with me, she said, "I'm going to ace this Exhibition."

During the Exhibition. Taylor posted all four projects on her display board and waited eagerly for the Exhibition to begin. As participants approached her table and asked questions, she used her four projects to guide her responses. For example, she used the cladogram to explain the process of evolution and the evidence in her *Antigone* essay to support the ways in which certain characters in the play changed over time. Parents and other staff members seemed to have a clear understanding of the connections she was making across the subject areas through responses such as "I see what you mean!" and "That is a really interesting way to think about transformation." When I asked her the question, "Taylor, dilation occurs in *Antigone*. Describe this process in the play and then connect it to the revolution you studied in global studies," she answered with clarity and deep, critical thinking. She responded by first defining the meaning of *dilation* (when an idea spreads), discussed how this happened in the play, and then showed, using evidence, the ways ideas about revolt and rebellion spread before the French Revolution transpired. Her argument was very convincing because she spoke with such confidence and poise while using evidence to support her ideas. After the Exhibition, the principal of the high school expressed how impressed he was with Taylor's work and her ability to present and analyze the process of transformation within and across each subject area.

After the Exhibition. As Taylor and I conversed during our interview, she explained that Exhibitions "add to people's confidence levels because you show off what you have done." She went on to say that Exhibitions "might be the magic potion. . . . A lot of people change afterward." Although Taylor noticed academic changes among her peers, she did not believe that the Exhibition influenced her grades in English, because "everything is really easy to understand." However, as she reflected on the prior year's Exhibition, she stressed that her academic performance was affected by that experience because completing a rigorous and group-based project led to an increase in her confidence level. Even though she believed that her academic performance was not affected by this year's Exhibition, she highlighted a few students who were significantly affected by the event. These students were "not taking school seriously" but, afterward, approached school with a more focused and engaged attitude.

Although Taylor did not believe the Exhibition affected her grade in English, her academic performance did improve after the Exhibition. She was earning a B+ in English class at the time of the Exhibition but concluded the semester with an A-. Her analytical writing and final-semester project demonstrated more advanced critical thinking through her thoughtful and deep connections across characters and historical figures. For example, Taylor highlighted similarities across fictional characters and historical figures through metaphorical puzzle pieces as well as ancient animals she learned about in Biology. These elements enabled her to communicate her ideas about the fictional characters from the class novel and her chosen historical figure she researched in Global Studies in an effectively thought-provoking and convincing manner. Taylor did not demonstrate this level of deep thinking earlier in the semester. The Exhibition gave her the opportunity to take risks, and this mentality translated to her later work in our English class. For Taylor, the Exhibition engaged her in deeper, more critical thinking. Even though she did not have that perspective, her work later in the semester demonstrated this higher level of thinking.

Jessica

Jessica consistently struggled to complete classwork and homework assignments in the fall semester, which negatively affected her grade in English class. She did not earn above a D during the 4 months leading up to the Exhibition and completed only a second draft of the *Antigone* essay, for which she received a low C. After I indicated to her that a third draft was needed to fulfill the requirements of the assignment, Jessica promised that she would revise her essay, but she never completed this crucial step. Therefore, 1 month before the Exhibition, Jessica was not passing English class and it was unclear whether or not she would be able to participate in the Exhibition as a result of this series of incomplete assignments.

Before the Exhibition. While reviewing Exhibition questions and answers during a large group activity, Jessica resisted contributing her ideas. When one of her peers or I asked her a question, she would respond by saying, "I don't know." She continued to respond in this way to any follow-up questions. During a class discussion about the Exhibition process (room setup, question and answer session, etc.), Jessica said, "I don't care about this. Whatever." I approached Jessica numerous times before and after English class to assess her feelings about the Exhibition process as well as her knowledge about the information on which she would be tested. In regard to her feelings, she told me, "I feel fine about it," yet when I asked her about the content she stated unclear answers and showed confusion. Despite her lack of preparation, Jessica agreed to participate in the Exhibition. This choice was a major step forward in Jessica's academic career, as she had refused to participate in the 9th-grade Exhibition the previous year.

During the Exhibition. Although Jessica had only three of the four projects displayed on her trifold board—two of which were only partially completed—she seemed excited, if nervous, for the Exhibition to start. Prior to the official start time, I walked over to Jessica's table to ask about her readiness. She told me, "Niki, I don't know if I can do this. I'm scared. What if they ask me questions that I don't know?" I responded by telling her, "You can do it. You know a lot about transformation. . . . Make sure to refer to your artifacts on your board." She seemed to calm down. When the Exhibition officially began, parents and teachers walked by and stopped to observe Jessica's artifacts. As the participants asked Jessica questions, she would respond with short, curt answers and did not necessarily explain or analyze how transformation occurred across the disciplines. For example, Jessica's freshman English teacher asked her how Antigone transformed one character in the play and how this connected to transformation in global studies. Jessica responded, "Antigone? Well, I don't really know. People changed because of her, but I really don't know why." Later, I asked Jessica about the process of evolution and the ways this process connected to the Mexican Revolution, which she had researched in global studies. In her response, Jessica only explained evolution; no connection was made to the revolution. Although many participants were impressed with Jessica's clado-gram, with its hand-drawn images, she did not consistently demonstrate the ability to deeply analyze how transformation occurred within and across the four projects. However, she continued to answer questions throughout the evening, in stark contrast to her refusal to participate at all in the prior year's Exhibition.

After the Exhibition. Jessica described her Exhibition experience as "just okay" and said it was "just something to get over with." Even though Jessica used these words to describe her Exhibition experience, she showed a level of excitement while showcasing her projects and responding to questions that she had not exhibited during our preparation periods in English class. During our interview, she stated firmly that the Exhibition had no effect on her academic performance in English class and that it was "something to just do." Because Jessica had chosen not to participate in either of the 9th-grade Exhibitions the previous year, this was her very first time displaying and describing her work, and the very fact of her participation in the Exhibition demonstrated a distinct shift in her approach to school. Yet Jessica strongly believed that the Exhibition did not have any impact on her academics. When I asked her if any of her peers were affected by this event, however, she said, "Yeah, some people were because they were made to talk about their projects."

Prior to the Exhibition, Jessica was failing English class. Her work performance was very low and she did not participate actively in class activities. Yet after the Exhibition, she began to make positive progress in her academic performance. For instance, for the final project in English, Jessica aligned character traits of the main character from the class novel, *Like Water for Chocolate*, to Pancho Villa's traits, the revolutionary figure of the Mexican Revolution she was learning about in global studies using a colorfully hand-drawn map of Mexico with each color representing the common traits each character demonstrated. Jessica did not show this level of deep thinking earlier in the semester. She earned a proficient grade on the final project in English, raising her overall semester grade from a NC to a C-. Although

Jessica did not attribute her improved performance in English to the Exhibition, the experience was a turning point for her and her approach to school.

WHAT I LEARNED BY RESEARCHING MY TEACHING

As a first-year teacher, I learned about the positive impact of project-based learning on the academic achievement of four students in my 10th-grade English class. At the same time, I learned that my perspective on what happens in the classroom does not always align with the perspectives of my students. Two of the four students, Taylor and Jessica, did not believe that the Exhibition had any impact on their academic achievement in English class. However, I observed a completely different trend. My data indicate that all four students demonstrated deeper and more analytical thinking and writing skills on major class assignments after the Exhibition. The Exhibition provided students with an opportunity to develop and hone these skills, which meant that students were able to apply them more readily and willingly to our work in the classroom. Therefore, while some students did not recognize or attribute project-based learning to their improved academic performance in English class, my data indicate that this approach to learning did contribute to their academic success.

The Exhibition was a turning point for all four focal students. Each student demonstrated academic growth in ELA after they experienced this approach to project-based learning, but they did so in different ways. Jocelyn began writing more analytically, which allowed her to demonstrate her own thinking about the texts more clearly and compellingly. Taylor advanced her learning by thinking more deeply and critically about the ideas and concepts being taught in her classes and by synthesizing the information analytically. In contrast, Brasil's Exhibition experience was a means of improving her confidence in her academic capabilities. Because she participated in the Exhibition and noticed an improvement in her overall grade, she began to cultivate a more positive academic identity. Likewise, Jessica grew as a student by participating in her first Exhibition. Her perspective on her academic identity changed because of her improved grade in ELA as well as her increased depth of critical thinking in formal and informal writing assignments.

Project-based learning is a valuable way to foster critical thinking and alignment across disciplines. Through the Exhibition, students engaged in an enriching and relevant academic experience by learning how to obtain information in their academic courses and then apply that information to other disciplines. Students subsequently used this experience and the knowledge and skills they acquired in their work in my English class. At the same time, the experience was empowering for students like Jessica who were disengaged or not confident in their academic abilities.

Although the Exhibition provided students with the opportunity to think critically and creatively about subject material and enabled them to grow as learners, in order to foster applicable, "real-life" learning, the Exhibition process needs to extend beyond the school structure. For youth to gain knowledge about the applicability and relevancy of subject material, we need to provide them with leadership opportunities within the local community. In order to prepare them for their futures as college students and professionals, the project-based learning model needs to demonstrate the connections between school, community, family, and self. For example, Taylor's critical thinking was profound, yet it remained within the confines of school. Perhaps if the Exhibition challenged her to "transform" an aspect of her community that she felt passionately about, she could have developed a deeper, more global understanding of the real-life relevancy of transformation and the dynamic power that she has to create change. Furthermore, this approach to project-based learning could have enabled her to attribute her academic improvement in ELA to the Exhibition because of the personal connections she was making between these areas.

The mission statements of most high schools emphasize the importance of developing and fostering lifelong learning within each student. In order to address this mission effectively, we must provide our students with projects that take them beyond the classroom and into the community, rather than limiting the scope of their thinking to standardized tests and five-paragraph essays. We need to show our students that they have the skills, knowledge, and power to apply the information they are learning in their courses to current issues and events taking place within their local and global communities. This approach to education will foster the development of confident, capable, and dynamic learners, who take responsibility for their learning by actively contributing to the success of their communities, their families, and themselves.

CHAPTER 4

Building Bridges of Hope Inside the Urban Classroom

Paula L. Argentieri

> The ultimate objective of education should be to help create not only a balanced and harmonious individual but also a balanced and harmonious society where true justice prevails, where there is no unnatural division between the "haves" and the "have-nots" and where everybody is assured of a living wage and the right to live and the right to freedom
>
> —Arun Gandhi, "Gandhian Education: The Difference Between Knowledge and Wisdom"

At Belvedere Alternative High School, where I was a new teacher, the average student enrolled had a history of at least 1 to 2 years of successive academic failure and truancy. Students were categorized as "at risk" and faced common street life issues, including drugs, violence, teenage pregnancy, depression, extreme poverty, homelessness, poor mental and physical health, and suicide. I felt that teaching these students to eke out a living in our society didn't seem to be enough. Teaching them to survive wasn't enough. If I provided them with only such basics, it seemed that the legacy of their struggles would repeat indefinitely.

I was interested in enacting the philosophies and pedagogical theory that had inspired me to become an educator. Henry Giroux (1988) wrote, "In short, educators must explore the meaning and purpose of public schooling as part of a discourse of democracy grounded in a utopian project of possibility" (p. 208). And, according to the Annenberg Senior Fellows at Brown University, urban schools are an integral part of the richness and promise of a vital world. The public provision of spaces for personal and collective agency in schools is the core of a vision to revitalize democracy (Annenberg Senior Fellows, 2000). bell hooks (1994) noted that school was the place where she could invent herself over and over again. Her vision is that the classroom is the most radical space of possibility and that educating as the practice of freedom is access to hope and empowerment for our students (pp. 3–15).

I agree with these ideas and therefore believe that educators need to take on the roles of transformative intellectuals who work to actualize an emancipatory social vision. Teachers can aspire to be radical intellectuals who, according to our job descriptions, sign up to create society. We can choose to mirror dominant ideologies, or we can choose to challenge the limiting dimensions of school life for our students and thus challenge the inequities of political and social life.

Giroux suggested many approaches for critical educators to take, such as guiding students to become critical citizens by using historical and social analyses to understand how knowledge is constructed. In this regard bell hooks's notion of reinvention is also key. In essence, students begin to rethink their lived experiences in relationship to the wider society and, as a result, hopefully, become capable of reinventing themselves. Consequently, critical citizenship aims to increase empowerment and hope.

Guided by these ideas and my personal commitment to develop as a critical educator working to transform constraining structures in public schooling, I embarked on a semester-long journey with a group of dynamic students to critically examine and seek answers the following question:

> What is the nature of learning and development when students in an urban alternative high school, who have previously not had success in school, are exposed to a curriculum designed to create self-empowerment opportunities in an intentionally constructed environment where they think and write about past and present experiences in their lives and then identify and take action around new possibilities for the future?

MY SCHOOL, MY STUDENTS, MY CURRICULUM

Belvedere has only 150 students. Of those students, about 75% are African American, 12% Hispanic, 6% White, 5.5% multiethnic, and .6% Asian. Students come with a range of challenges and are typically behind in grade-level credit requirements. The students would be classified by other schools as a homogeneous group of low-tracked students. In fact, they bring a multitude of complex life issues to school, but their intelligences are multiple and robust.

The class that is the focus of this research is one I was hired to design. It is an English class elective with a social science emphasis and is called Life and Society Explorations. In this class, I sought to create opportunities for students to see their lives interwoven with many societal issues and to help the students begin to tell the story of their lives from multiple perspectives. The curriculum included three units: Building Community (4–6 weeks of activities that included thinking about what a community is and how to build one in the classroom); The Story of My Life: Part I (8 weeks centered on the text *Our America* and a four-chapter autobiography that explored their pasts from their point of view and the points of views of others); and The Story of My Life: Part II (4 weeks of activities in which they wrote varied versions of their imagined futures).

Through this curriculum I hoped my students would have an opportunity to consciously learn about themselves as individuals, to learn about their connections to their families and family history, and finally to learn about their connections to the society that they've grown up in. I ultimately hoped they would learn that their identities are mutable. Telling their life stories, interviewing family and friends, and declaring multiple versions of the future, I reasoned, might help them transform a societally constructed story of failure into a self-constructed story of success. Beyond learning about their individual identities, this study of place, I hoped, would allow them to see the structures of the society that affect them negatively and to see possibilities for working toward changing those structures.

To support this personal work the students would be doing, I also consciously worked to create a particular type of community that would be a safe zone. In addition to agreeing on what constitutes a safe classroom with students, I defined three core values as integral to the safety in the room: communication, respect, and integrity. The sign on my door said, "Welcome to Ms. Argentieri's Room. Practice listening, being present, receiving others, and being authentic."

I encouraged failure and admission of failure as being tied to growth, self-empowerment, and hopefully, transformation, by which I meant students seeing new possibilities and then seeing themselves as agents in creating those possibilities. I wanted my students to have a space where they could search carefully and intently for meaning and purpose.

I also knew that as a teacher I had to be fully "present" with the students. Besides working on being present, I consistently reflected on my own positionality as a White woman and worked to respond rather than react to the different behaviors, comments, and interactions that occurred, often unpredictably.

DATA COLLECTION AND ANALYSIS

My research question focused directly on my curriculum and teaching, including the specific classroom environment I was developing to support that process, to see if I was actually helping students acquire a new set of life skills. I kept a record of my daily/weekly/monthly plans and my rationale for their design. Throughout the semester, I took daily field notes to capture the essence of what was happening in the room and to record teacher-student interaction and student-student interaction. I gathered background data about students' lives, their past achievement at school, and their future aspirations by referring to student introduction letters, journal entries, and daily exit cards, which included comments written at the end of class. I also collected student work, which provided a sense of student engagement and progress. Finally, I ended the class with extensive course evaluations, and I interviewed 10 students to expand on the information they provided in writing.

After gathering all the artifacts, I transcribed my handwritten notes into a complete teacher log and matched student debrief comments to corresponding days. This allowed me to examine my observations adjacent to student comments about the class. I then compared student work from the beginning of the semester with that at the end to get a sense of what happened in the course and more specifically to track how student attitudes and behaviors shifted over the semester.

I began by narrowing my focus to one student in particular who demonstrated a transformational shift. I chose Michelle because I thought her case would help me get close to what actually happened in my class and what worked from the students' perspective. Her participation in the class was the most complete, and she had nearly perfect attendance and completed every assignment, so I had a lot of data on her. I then looked for themes that she evidenced that were more general for the group, comparing her self-identified transformation with other students' growth.

THE BEGINNING

At the beginning of the semester I wrote in my teaching log:

> Every day I'm confronted by a room full of students who identify
> as "failures" or as the "black sheep" of society. My students see no
> purpose in striving for success in school. On the first day of school, I
> asked them what their goal for the semester was and the majority of
> the answers were "to pass." They shoot for the minimum to get by,
> and they respond to high expectations with backlash and complaints.
> They don't see a purpose for themselves in school and a purpose
> in life is even foggier or nonexistent. One student recalled a middle
> school teacher telling him that his life would be "shit," or maybe this
> is a notion he started to believe in middle school. When I asked him
> to think about what excites him about his life, he said, "Nothing,

I'll probably get shot in the head when I'm eighteen." The not unreasonable despair present in my students' lives is evident in their behavior and attitudes in the classroom.

FROM RESISTANCE TO HOPE

At the beginning of the school year, most of the students expressed discomfort about being part of the kind of community I was trying to create: personal, intimate, quiet, and reflective. Many revolted and three students dropped the class. However, those who stuck it out found that the curriculum provided them with important tools they needed to deal with their current lives, and it was helping them imagine a different future as well. By the end of the semester almost everyone experienced personal, communal, and academic growth, and some experienced what I would call true transformations.

But there was significant resistance at the beginning. I wrote in my observation notes at the start of the year that students reported angrily that this class was different from the other classes on campus. "It's too quiet!" and "too slow!" I also wrote how "another student put it less eloquently: 'I hate this f***ing class!'"

The students wrote exit cards an average of three times a week as a closing exercise to lessons. Below are typical samples of students' comments during the first month:

The class was boring as usual, hella dull.

I hated today.

Today I really didn't understand this class.

Why did we have to write so much?

I learned some things, but I don't know what.

Class was the same but I still came I learned about poetic devices.

It was ok just a little boring.

This class was almost interesting.

At the end of the first week and a half, those students who couldn't hack it either acted in complete defiance or dropped the class. One student arrived late to class (I'm assuming in part to avoid the quiet time at the beginning) and after a few minutes she exclaimed, *"Nuh uh!* I need a pass to the office. This class is too slow!!" She got up angrily and stormed out of the room. Later, I heard from the counselor that two other students had requested to drop the class. In response to these complaints, I was asked to justify my curriculum and approach to the administration, which I did.

In the midst of these responses, I considered whether I should change my plans and my style, or stick to my intention to create classroom learning experiences that were reflective, authentic, and predictable enough for students to begin to transform their perspectives and goals. With each negative comment and each disruption, I felt an increasing pressure to change my plan, to give in, to accommodate to what I saw as requests for chaos. However, I decided to keep on the path that I believed in because in my heart I knew it could work despite how my students were squirming. My continuing reflections, like the following, helped me keep my focus.

> There is sparkle and light in my students' eyes that has been clouded over by years of conditioning in school and on the streets. It is my intention to provide a classroom experience that allows them to identify that light and then learn how to grow and nurture it.

My students are lucky to be at an alternative high school that is attempting to fill in the gaps where past educational experiences failed. Many of their counterparts at mainstream high schools in the area have dropped out or are in the process of failing out. My students chose Belvedere Alternative as a new beginning. This tells me that beneath my students' stories of failure, there are persistent, resilient human beings who aren't willing to just take what they've been given (in school and society) and settle for it. They want something more and they just don't know how or where to find it, but they are looking. My students are the transformative hope for the future. If they get access to transforming their own lives, I believe they will transform the greater society.

Freire wrote that "the more completely they [students] accept the passive role imposed on them, the less they develop the critical consciousness which would result from their intervention in the world as transformers of that world. . . . The solution is not to integrate them into the structure of oppression, but to transform that structure" (1993, p. 54). I believed I could turn Freire's theory into informed action.

SHIFTING ATTITUDES ACCOMPANIED READING, WRITING, AND DIALOGUES AROUND LIFE'S CHALLENGES

A slight shift in student attitude and performance began approximately 1 month into the semester when I introduced the second unit, The Story of My

Life: Part I, and the book, *Our America*. As we got into the unit, students began to respond eagerly to opportunities to engage in dialogue around life issues, including school, poverty, street life, drugs and dealing, and short- and long-term life satisfaction and goals. I noticed the occurrence of the shift most directly in the daily class debrief comments the students wrote on their exit cards. The following comments written were typical:

> I learned more about their lives, and what other people put up with. Also, about how hard it is for some people to make it in life because of the struggles they face daily, but some never give up and make it.

> I learned about how this book is about what goes on in "Our America" and "Their America." It is really terrible to me in both worlds because people don't care about each other at all. I also enjoyed talking and having open talks with the whole class. I think that we should do this more often, talking as a group.

> Its good that we have dialogue about real life issues because that way we all communicate with each other and work as a class.

The issues raised in *Our America* seemed to give students opportunities to talk about life, and more specifically ghetto life, without necessarily revealing anything personal. Students also saw that their personal life challenges were not unique and that some people face more struggles than they do. Michelle explained in her journal, "I thought my life was crap, but after reading this book I realized it's not as bad as I thought." Jaime revealed, "I learned that no matter how bad your hood is, you can still make it." Jody wrote, "Well, I've learned that no matter where you come from you can make a difference in your life."

SHIFTING ATTITUDES AND RE-VISIONING THE FUTURE WITH SUPPORT FROM UNDERGRADUATE MENTORS

These shifting attitudes were directly related to and possibly accelerated by the curricular choices I made and the environment I had been constructing from the start. One of those choices was to involve undergraduates from a nearby university in leading the class on Fridays. These students were members of a class I taught there titled "Current Issues in Education." I approached four students of color who had formed a cooperative group in the class to work on a community-based project. Each of them had worked through socioeconomic struggles to achieve success in high school in order to enter college. The high school and university students identified and related to one another almost immediately.

The college students offered hope and accountability to my students as they shared their personal stories of challenge and what it took for them to overcome them and make it to the university. Veronica, a college sophomore from South Central Los Angeles, told my high school students, "We are a source for what you want in your life. We can help each other out. I can't make it alone out here. You need connections. We know what's up. It's attainable. I mean, shoot, what is your fantasy?"

I wrote in my observation notes that it was becoming apparent that the antisocial tendencies of some students in my class were survival strategies that kept them "safe" in unpredictable places. I further noted that these learned survival strategies could be dismantled as we all continued to build this intentional, hopeful community. The college students' weekly visit became an integral part of that intentionality. Each week the visits became more and more meaningful as students eased into opening up and sharing their personal dreams and the challenges that stood in their way. For example, after the second visit the students wrote things such as the following:

I learned about . . . applying for college. We also learned the difference between high school and college.

Today the class was fun. The [college] students should come more often. This visit was better than the last.

I want to go to college.

It was nice having choices of where I want to go.

Today I stepped it up a lot. I felt like a leader.

I learned a lot and I really like the way that people opened up and expressed themselves.

I learned that I have many goals to reach. Make sure I come to school.

It'll help me because I'll be informed. Just don't give up on us/me.

Besides demystifing the college experience, these older students allowed students in my class to see themselves in a place of success in this society. This realization shifted some of their perceptions of success and achievement in school. They realized that they needed to come to school and do well now, but they also acknowledged that they had had challenges in the past because they had seen no hope or path to success. Through their interaction with the college students, I learned that the students' views of themselves and their future could be transformed, and that they could be fully engaged in high-level intellectual work. It was inspiring to watch my students make connections between their own personal struggles, society as a whole, and the notion of choice as it relates to empowerment through their interactions with the college students. Since I wasn't leading and directing these interactions, I was able to participate in small groups or work individually with my students in the process of unraveling the past and re-visioning the future.

SHIFTING ATTITUDES ACCOMPANIED MAKING SENSE OF THEIR PASTS

The students conducted family interviews as a step in the effort to write the story of their lives, past, present, and future, using *Our America* as a model for style and tone. Many students demonstrated signs of resistance in composing the story of their lives, not wanting to relive the memories of their childhood. Yet at this point in the semester, they were more able to overcome their discomfort than at the beginning of the year. I wrote in my log about their quick turn to enthusiasm for the project:

> Today was a personal day. I shared about my family and the students were silent and engaged. The students are really interested in interviewing family and friends about themselves. This is huge!! First of all, they never volunteer to do work outside the classroom, homework is nonexistent at BAHS [Belvedere Alternative High School]. Students planned out who they are going to interview and some included relatives that they have not spoken to in a long time and some that they don't even get along with. The excitement level is high. One student asks for 10 interview forms, the minimum is 2 and most students are planning to do 4 or 5.

The most significant breakthroughs came before, during, or after student-conducted interviews. Students reported being hesitant or nervous to interview family members. They didn't know what to expect. After the first interviews were complete, the students brought tape recordings back to the class to share. They were proud of the work they did outside of class and were eager to share the recordings. They also jumped right into transcribing the interviews, a task that seemed engaging to them. They moved quickly into typing their stories for publication and liked seeing them in a published form.

The interviews allowed students to get closer to family members. They called relatives from the computer lab to ask clarifying questions: "How old were you when my daddy came and got me?" and "How old was I when you went to jail?" It was obvious that students took the opportunity of the project to ask family members questions that they might not have asked previously.

I could see students shifting the dynamic in some family relationships, and some students' self-perceptions shifted, too. Students and immediate family members sat down to talk to each other about the students' lives. One student recorded an interview with her older sister. During the interview the siblings realized that they never hung out any more like they used to when they were little. They decided to make a point to hang out with each other more. Another student and his sister reconnected after being angry at each other for several years. An additional student, who no longer lived with his mother, was able to find out some important information about why he lives with his grandmother.

The following excerpt from my daily log shows some of the students' behavior as they were while writing in class: "They are quiet and engaged as they write and one student puts her head down and cries. Students stop periodically to share with their neighbors about their lives and then are drawn right back into writing more about it." Ninety-five percent of the students completed this project and most written pieces were between 10 and 20 pages long. The only obstacle to completion was student attendance.

SHIFTING ATTITUDES ACCOMPANIED COMPOSING A FUTURE

Writing their future stories in the final unit, titled The Story of My Life: Part II, clearly solidified the growth students experienced in my class. Writing about their future lives allowed them to construct hopeful, productive present lives. I encouraged them to write more than one version of their future story to emphasize the important notion that the future is fluid and that ultimately they have the power to say how it goes. Discussion of the future was a consistent theme from the start of the course, and students wrote and thought about it weekly, but it was during this final unit that I first asked them to declare their future lives in a published piece of work. As a result, the students began to define their future plans publicly and in detail. I wrote in my log at the start of this project:

> The students are openly talking about their future plans without prompting. Today Tanya exclaimed, "Ms. A, I'm not going to be a lowlife. I'm going to Alabama State!" She spoke enthusiastically about how she had decided on this school versus staying in the Bay Area, and all the details that she had planned out. The other students listened intently and were soaking in everything she said.

Students wrote on their exit cards toward the end of the project:

> Today's project for Part II was good because it kind of got my mind-set on the future. I like the story, it sounded like real life.

> I think that I'm getting better in your class and I'm trying to stay on track I think that you are a good teacher and I'm learning a lot. Today I learned that we only have one life and I have to do my best to reach my goals so I'm in school and I will try to be a fire fighter.

> I like how in this class in order to get your work done, you have to focus on yourself and learn about yourself. When people just say be yourself sometimes it scares me because I still really don't know who I am I hope by the end of this class I will know a little better Thank you for being a great teacher

We had crossed the barriers of resistance together. The results seemed spontaneous, but I knew they were the result of much hard work. The students chose engagement and empowerment, and the group dynamic and momentum brought all the students along this path. Importantly, they witnessed their own success daily, and there was no turning back.

At the end of the semester, the students acknowledged that intimate connections and conversations with one another, the college mentors, and me as their teacher were their favorite parts of the class. I learned quickly that quiet reflection and sociopolitical analysis are skills that needed to be taught. At the beginning, the students preferred chaos because it was entertaining, and it was what they were used to. Over time students became comfortable with stillness in the classroom, and it allowed them to sink into a deeper understanding of themselves than they had experienced before.

MICHELLE'S STORY

I took a look at one student's growth and subsequent transformation over the course of the semester to get closer to what actually happened in my class and what worked from a student perspective. Michelle's story offers detail about what is involved in shifting attitudes and changing views about the future, in ultimately moving from resistance to hope.

At the beginning of the year, Michelle was shut down and hard edged and complained about the "peaceful" atmosphere in my classroom. Before school one day early in the semester she told me that the class was different from her other classes and insinuated that I didn't know about the hidden code of alternative high school classes, "don't expect a lot." I realized that the class was asking her to be personally reflective in a way that felt challenging and foreign. Early on, however, when many of my students reported that they didn't want to learn anything, that they just wanted to pass and needed the credit, Michelle wrote that she wanted to learn about making good choices for the future.

Similarly, when I asked the students to reflect on a piece of poetry that they had written about their current lives to say how they thought their lives might be different or the same in 10 years, Michelle made a proud declaration about her future: "I am from music, and harmony feeding my soul. I am from performing on stage with over a thousand people watching." Later on in a free-write she declared that she wanted to be a hip-hop and R&B singer, but she felt frustrated by the fact that it seemed almost impossible to accomplish her dream. This far-fetched dream left Michelle feeling powerless and uninspired in the present.

Additionally, when the college students were helping my class think about their futures, Michelle wrote, "Well, lately I've been hearing many different things about college and it's so much. . . . I get lost. I want to get my hopes up about going to college but at the same time what if I don't for any reason. It's a scary thought to think that maybe I don't make it in life, and become a no one."

All of Michelle's comments at this time revealed her internal struggle over deeply wanting to be successful in her future and not really knowing how to do it or even what she was good at in the "real world." This left her in a place of despair and frustration that she expressed with defiance, boredom, or apathy in the classroom.

Michelle's attitude started to shift after we began delving deeper into the real-life issues raised in *Our America*. After a heated conversation about being poor in the United States, the students wrote responses to the question, Do you agree with the statement "In this country, only the rich get richer and the poor get poorer"? Michelle wrote:

> I don't fully agree, but half of me does. The rich or wealthy people most of the time keep getting wealthier, even when the poor person tries. It's best to be wealthy. There are always going to be more struggles for them [the poor people] than for those who have been involved with money all their lives. In life there are more opportunities for those with money because to some people it means that they come from a good background not knowing that people who are poor or have low income, come from good backgrounds too, and have been through more experiences that's made them gain knowledge compared to others.

Michelle was beginning to practice some higher-level analytical skills in her writing, and simultaneously her class participation shifted. She started to formulate her strong feelings into clear arguments. Michelle was frustrated and fearful about her future until she started expressing her concerns.

Michelle's confidence continued to build and escalated to an even higher level after a field trip to the nearby university. In her journal entry following the trip, Michelle wrote, "What stood out for me was that they [the college students] talked about all the options they get and the classes they take. This impacted my life because it makes me feel motivated and it brings my hopes up."

This trip proved to be a turning point for Michelle as she began to feel some hope about her future. Shortly after, Michelle wrote, "I will go to college. I will be dedicated to my work. I will study Civil Rights. I will graduate from college." This was the first time Michelle mentioned anything about college in her written plans for the future, and simultaneously Michelle's engagement in the class shifted, too.

In the weeks following the field trip Michelle wrote a journal entry about not doing the family interviews. She also shared that she wasn't getting along with her sister and her father. "Man. I haven't done my interviews yet cuz I keep forgetting. Lately, I've been good, except that I've been arguing with my dad and sister." Meanwhile, Michelle began to write more freely about personal issues of identity and culture. She wrote a beautiful political poem about being Latina in which she referenced many times that she wasn't stupid and that she wasn't limited to having children or being a caretaker and that she was actually going to "make it."

> Just because I'm a Latina . . . doesn't mean I have kids and even if I did who says I'm not going to make it? . . . Yeah I'm a Latina and I'm proud. . . . Before you open your mouth you should think before you speak. I am like everyone else in a unique way. . . . Just because of my race I have no rights. . . . Why don't you come talk to me and see what I'm all about.

She finally interviewed her mom and learned that her mother still had some negative perceptions of Michelle's past behavior. During a journal entry written about forgiveness, Michelle spoke about forgiving her parents despite the exchanges that they had in the past. "I want to forgive my parents. I will say all the things I've been meaning to say, but never had the courage to. My parents have a horrible concept about me, and it bothers me because I'm not that type of person. Even though I'm going to forgive them for all the things they've said to me. I will tell them how much I appreciate them and some of the ways they've raised me to be."

At the end of the semester, Michelle began to imagine who she would be six years into the future. She talked about developing her confidence and courage in the class. She said, "Little by little I've grown stronger, and I've noticed because I've done things I never thought I'd do and I've said things I never thought I'd say." She wrote her futures chapter with enthusiasm:

> Life is good, I can't complain. I am 22 years old and I have everything I need and want. I still have a long way to go but I'm getting there. . . . I haven't left school. I'm still in college and studying for law school. . . . I've realized a lot of things. Life is really precious. We only get the chance to live once. I mean, "Why live without life?" and "Why have a life without living?" To all you out there feeling like there's no hope, yes there is! I thought life was worthless to the point I wanted to commit suicide, but then I realized . . . what for? I can't give up so soon, I'm not even half way through with life. They say that "the sun shines after the rain." . . . If I would have done something stupid like taking my own life away, I would have only given up on myself and that would have proven to people that I was a failure, and I'm not!

Michelle's transformation over the course of the semester was profound. She blossomed from a cynical student who held onto her stories about failure in the past to a student who was excited about future opportunities, confident that she could achieve whatever she wanted. She also related to her family as a whole new person. Michelle taught me that once students enter a space of hope, the possibilities that are available to them in their lives are endless because they begin taking responsibility for generating possibilities. Michelle no longer appeared as cynical, resigned, or confused. She smiled and was genuinely happy. She was not the same student I had met 6 months earlier.

One of the first of many inspirations I shared with the students that semester was a quotation from bell hooks (2004): "Home was the place where I was forced to conform to someone else's image of who and what I should be. School was the place where I could forget that self and, through ideas, reinvent myself" (p. 3). It is clear that the seeds of hope I had intentionally planted, even though initially met by much resistance, had grown and were blossoming. In my teaching log at the end of the semester I wrote:

> On the second to the last day of class my students beamed with accomplishment. It seemed as if a distinct peace and calmness emanated from the walls in our classroom. We did it, we have built a highly functioning, enjoyable environment and my students are speaking of their successes, some of them for the first time ever. No it isn't a model class, students still speak out at inappropriate times and they still have trouble giving their undivided attention to each other, but there is a noticeable shift in the room after 5 months of

hard work. The students were proud of themselves, clearer about their futures, connected to each other and me, and most importantly present to success and hope.

CO-CREATING SPACES OF HOPE AND HEALING

Whether or not my class was solely responsible for the students' transformations, in reflection, it is clear that my students and I co-created a healing space in our classroom that reached out into my students' lives beyond school and into the future. I practiced accepting the students where they were and the status of the class as a starting point. This acceptance allowed my students to be okay with where they were and from there to move forward. I consistently gave up making them wrong for being resigned and making myself wrong for not doing it right. Acceptance gave us access to a space of hope that provided the context and possibility for transformation.

Teaching students to articulate, declare, and actualize hope is essential. This work begins with and is centered on students, and on critical educators who choose to open their hearts to their students with love, care, commitment, and hope on a daily basis. Within this context students are able to become advocates for themselves so that they might begin to understand and transform the systems that oppress them (Freire, 1993) while also developing the motivation to achieve in school.

On the last day of class, we sat together in a circle for the last time. A few students read pieces of their stories out loud to the group, revealing their transformed visions for their futures. Michelle's words provided a fitting conclusion:

> Whatever it is, I'm going to be. . . I'm going to do my best at it. Never giving up, always with my head up high, never looking down, but even if I fail, I will get up.

Authors' Dialogue on Crafting Curriculum

Jabari Mahiri

The central consideration that emerged across the responses of Julia Daniels, Nicola Martinez, and Paula Argentieri was that crafting curriculum was much more than designing a series of discreet units or lessons to enable students to achieve highly specified learning goals or standards. Instead, they see curriculum building as a yearlong (or even longer) process of developing themes and activities that cross larger spans of time than the thematic units that are staples of most curriculum guides.

For example, Daniels noted, "I have always struggled with the concept of 'learning targets,' not because I don't have something very specific I want my students to get out of each class, but because I think learning is amorphous, vague, recursive, and chaotic. Learning to think critically or to use language to explore ideas or to feel deeply and express emotion can't be captured by filling in the simple sentence: By the end of today's class, students will be able to do 'X.'"

Martinez explained how her use of project-based learning helped her think more broadly about crafting curriculum. Rather than just mastering a specific content, it allowed students to "apply information they were learning in each of their classes to a broader, more encompassing context" and to "understand the concepts, themes, and facts more deeply and fluidly . . . through application." She argued that these active, embodied ways of learning through creating and presenting exhibitions helped break the limiting effects of traditional classroom teaching and learning. "It provided students with the opportunities to apply their thinking to their local communities and to incorporate current-day social, political, and environmental issues" such that they could see "the interconnectedness of what they learned to major social structures impacting their world, while also seeing ways to impact those structures themselves."

Argentieri believes the challenge is more than just crafting relevant curriculum and teaching as well. For her, it was co-creating a transformative environment in an urban classroom setting and pushing boundaries every day about ways of being, thinking, and engaging each other as a community in such a space. Even though she feels that even the best teacher, curriculum, pedagogy, and classroom context matter, she also understands that many marginalized urban students are still underserved because "one class or even a few aren't enough to turn the tides of institutionalized oppression."

Daniels captured key sentiments of all three authors. She talked about teachers being guides, mentors, and mirrors for students to ultimately create authentic learning experiences for themselves. "I have come to believe that everything that happens in the classroom is a part of the curriculum," she noted. "The informal moments of intimate intellectual connection between students when working on a project and the collaboration between a teacher and a student when they talk after school about an assignment—all these experiences and relationships are just as important and require just as much planning and thought as any specific assignment. They all add to the arc of learning and to the chaotic and emotional process that is education."

Part II

COMPLICATING CULTURE

Prologue: Mediating "Superdiversity"
in Urban Schools

Jennifer DiZio and José R. Lizárraga

> Working with students at the English Language Center plunged me deeply
> into questions that I have consciously and unconsciously faced throughout
> my life, the questions of identity, communication, and meaning when the
> surrounding world's language is not yours.
>
> —Paul Lai

Certainly over the past 2 decades, educators, researchers, and students
have found themselves at the forefront of discussions of culture—the
myriad intersecting and conjoining identities, including those expressed
through language, ethnicity, race and gender—in the classroom (Clauss-
Ehlers 2006; Loreman, Deppeler, & Harvey, 2005). Indeed these
intersections are even more striking in California public schools, which are
home to one of the most diverse student populations in the United States
(census.gov 2011). Such considerations are becoming increasingly relevant
in the complex, globalized world we inhabit, with its manifestations
of "superdiversity" (Vertovec, 2007). Although there may be intuitive
understandings of these nuances of culture experienced by new teachers,
addressing them is often in conflict with their schools' own responsibilities
to adhere to rigid state standards (Delpit, 2006; Valdés,1996; Valdés &
Figueroa, 1994). The majority of California public schools, for example,
beholden to strict accountability measures, are often forced to delineate
their student populations along strict binary categorical boundaries:
"White/non-White," "English proficient/limited English proficient,"
"high-performing/low-performing," and so on. Such categorizations are
problematic for both teachers and students in that they obscure the fluidity
of these many aspects of identity and lead to missed opportunities for
innovative, transformative, and liberatory learning experiences.

The chapters in Part II reveal how three first-year teachers learned to navigate cultural and linguistic complexities in their classrooms and in their schools. Each new teacher took a different approach and theoretical frame: Sophia Sobko looking at differences in cultural dynamics between the home and school, Paul F. Lai examining these dynamics within the institution, and Danny C. Martinez addressing them from inside the classroom. All sought to understand how gradations of their students' cultural practices in and out of the institution affected their performance and behavior in the schools.

Sobko examined conflicts in student performance and practice connected to differences between in-school and out-of-school cultures. Her work extends understanding of the connections between home and school first identified in the foundational ethnographic work of Shirley Brice Heath's *Way with Words* (1983). Although Sobko does not observe her students in their respective communities, she, like Heath, wanted to understand the linkages between school performance and home identities.

This work is framed within the context of Bourdieu's (1973) notions of "cultural capital" and the "habitus" in noting how the effects of "capital" from home (in the form of values, culture, and language) are or are not transposed to the school space. Indeed over the course of this study, Sobko "opened [her] eyes to the reality that for many of [her] students, 'school' and 'home' (or whatever exists after school) are two separate worlds that seldom meet." Bourdieu's theorization helps us see that deeply embedded expectations linked with spaces outside of school can provide obstacles to student success, even when their desire to succeed is strong. To conclude, Sobko offers suggestions for interventions that may provide students with the necessary scaffolds to achieve their academic goals.

In Chapter 6, Lai examines approaches to language and culture adopted by an institution within his school, the English Language Center (ELC), which is dedicated to helping recent immigrant students develop their English skills. His school reflected a diverse body of students; however, the majority (80%) were Spanish speaking, and most of these students were of Mexican descent. The school's articulated approach was in an additive framework (Valenzuela, 1999) of "emerging bilingualism" (Bartlett & Garcia, 2012; Garcia, 2009; Garcia & Kleifgen, 2010) that placed emphasis on building on rather than losing the first language (Genesee, 1987).

Lai grounded his methods for teaching English language learners (ELLs) in a specific theoretical approach because each one incorporated particular views on the nature of language, the language-learning process, and the learner (Lindholm-Leary, 2001; Richards & Rodgers, 2001). By probing how different-language student populations were perceived in the ELC, Lai reveals how members of the Spanish-speaking population traversed from "minority" to "majority" and negotiated their own identity formations. Further, through examining the phenomenon from within a frame that contextualizes the students' experiences in practicing both language and social identity skills, Lai reveals the complexities behind the school's approach to, and assessment of, the language-minority students.

In Chapter 7, Martinez looks at the complex and creative ways that student cultures were manifested in a learning environment where different linguistic scripts collided. His qualitative study with recent Latino immigrant middle school students challenges views of Spanish-speaking ELLs as a homogeneous group and centers on three conceptual lenses. In this milieu, the first lens focuses on understanding that language is a primary tool that mediates learning and also the key tool for social interaction and socialization (Schieffelin & Ochs, 1986).

Second, Pratt's (1991) concept of "contact zones" and the concept of a "third space" (Gutierrez, Baquedano-López, & Turner, 1997) are used to frame the negotiations and collisions of diverse cultures, but with an understanding that these tensions are often productive for language development. Third is Moll's (2000) notion that there are always multiple, dynamic cultures that each individual is part of—*la cultura vivida*.

Martinez reveals a classroom environment where even the shared culture of language was complicated by differing culturally and nationally situated dialectical practices. He describes how this classroom context served as a time and space for productive tension, whereby cross-cultural learning and the creation of new hybrid ways of meaning-making occurred (Gutierrez, Baquedano-López, & Tejeda, 1999).

As these three studies show, cultural and linguistic practices in diverse urban schools are inherently complicated. They reveal aspects of the intense challenges for teachers to accommodate and integrate multiple identities linked to cultural diversity and language differences. They also contribute to better understandings of how urban schools are being transformed by complex, fluid, and hybrid ways of being and making meaning. They help us see how meeting the academic and social needs of contemporary students transcends the mere sanctioning of *diverse cultures* in schools and requires sustained attention to how new expressions of culture (particularly through language) are co-constructed in these spaces.

CHAPTER 5

Academic Self-Sabotage

Understanding Motives and Behaviors of Underperforming Students

Sophia Sobko

The warning bell rang, signifying the impending start of 3rd period, and 25 rowdy juniors and seniors piled into my tiny third-floor classroom. One student's voice cut through the cacophony of students shuffling to their desks: "Why did you give me a D on SchoolLoop [the online gradebook]?" Jasmine demanded. Some students kept going about their business; others turned to look at her. "Hmmm," I answered, setting up the projector, "I think it might be because you didn't turn in that *Death of a Salesman* essay." She paused for a second, before announcing, "Well, if I fail as a student—*you* fail as a teacher."

The students who were looking at Jasmine turned their heads in anticipation of my reaction. I stood there, paralyzed, staring back at her and wondering if she was right. After all, Jasmine was a student who never missed a day of my class. Without fail, when the bell rang for 3rd period, she was there, engaged and ready to learn. And yet Jasmine's single line in my grade book was a disaster of zeros, half-credit scores, and incompletes. Her grade for the first semester was a D—passing but not University of California/California State University eligible.

Jasmine's performance concerned me greatly, and thus I sought advice from a veteran teacher. "If that girl were in my class every day," the teacher said curtly, "there is no way she would have a D." Jasmine's reproachful outburst, and my follow-up conversation with the veteran teacher, haunted me. After all, I was convinced that I was doing everything possible to ensure the success of my students—*all* my students. I sincerely believed in their potential; I worked tirelessly to create relevant, engaging curriculum; I stayed hours and hours after school offering extra tutoring and support; I reflected constantly on my practice. And yet, like Jasmine, too many of my students were not "successful" in the way I had hoped they would be in my class. The years I had spent philosophizing about "equity" now seemed useless; they did not tell me what to do when a student did not turn in an essay that the class had been working on for weeks.

It might have been easy to stop at the answer offered by colleagues in other disciplines: "The students just don't care." Yet this response seemed at odds with the expressed desire of most Franciscano High School students to do well in school. On the first day of class, the students shared their motivation for doing well in high school and going on to college. In response, I set high expectations for them, exemplified by rigorous lesson plans, nightly homework assignments, and ongoing project work. As the quarter progressed, however, a surprising and disturbing number of zeros began to fill my grade book. It became increasingly clear that some of the students were not turning in classwork I knew they had completed, while others were simply not completing their homework, and still others, like Jasmine, had completely missed important project deadlines. Although I made relentless attempts to intervene and support these students, their failure to complete or turn in assignments resulted in their earning Ds in my class.

The implications of these low grades were grave: a D does not count toward fulfilling admission requirements and therefore makes a student ineligible to apply to California public universities. This aside, I also was deeply concerned with my students' learning—if Jasmine wasn't submitting her essays, did that mean she did not know how to write them? Was she lacking in the composing skills that I had assumed she had? Or was there another reason behind her failure to produce them? Without the product, I was not able to fully evaluate her abilities, nor was I able to assess whether I was teaching writing effectively.

The concern I felt for my struggling students was intensified by the school's commitment to serve *every* student, exemplified by the administration's decision to implement an "antiracist" framework to its professional development and practices. In compliance with this framework, all teachers are required to disaggregate grades by race, charting the number of Ds and Fs given to Latino and African American students. We discuss our grades in both department-wide and one-on-one meetings. This disaggregating process, though painful and exasperating at times, forced me to look more closely at some of my struggling students. I began to ask myself more strategic, pointed questions: What assignments had my students missed, and which had they completed? How had I set up those assignments? What patterns could I see in their behavior? By conceptualizing these questions, I began to realize that I had the power to try and change these dynamics. I could conduct a directed inquiry with select students wherein I probed questions related to patterns of behavior and motivation.

Hence, I arrived at the following research question: Why do some students who clearly value academic success fail to complete or turn in important essays and homework assignments?

MY SCHOOL

Founded in 1890, Franciscano High School is an inner-city public high school located in Northern California. Like its surrounding neighborhood, Franciscano's student body is both racially and linguistically diverse. As indicated on the school's website, among the total 850 students 45% are Latino, 22% are Asian, 17% are African American, 8% are White, 4% Filipino, and 4% are students who identify as mixed race or "other." Roughly 14% are classified as having learning disabilities and have been assigned Individual Education Plans (IEPs). Nearly half (45%) fall under the category of "English language learners" (ELLs); many of these students have only recently immigrated to the United States from countries like Mexico, Honduras, China, the Philippines, Yemen, and Ethiopia. While the majority of ELLs are initially placed in English language development classes, there is a big push at Franciscano High to mainstream the students. As a result, many recent immigrants are enrolled in mainstreamed classes, creating a dynamic in which U.S.-born students work together with students who have been in the country for only a year or two. The school also has many cultural clubs for students to participate in and learn about each other's cultures; in this way we seek to build a diverse yet integrated community.

Over 60% of the student body is considered to be socioeconomically disadvantaged, and a large number of these young people have responsibilities that extend beyond their schoolwork: They hold jobs to help support their families, take care of younger siblings, and perform housework duties. While the school's official academic mission is to "prepare *all* students for college and careers with rigorous courses," the reality is that many students are not being prepared for life beyond high school. Despite recent gains in test scores and graduation rates, the school continues to be on the federal government's "persistently low achieving schools" list. Moreover, of all Franciscano High students who go on to attend 4-year universities, very few actually graduate within 6 years. In fact, only 10% of students test as "college ready" for the California State University system. Consequently, despite the school's best intentions, students are *not* being prepared to attend college.

Ironically, these grim statistics are at odds with the motivations of Franciscano High School's faculty, who are passionate, professional, and committed to social justice. Time and again, I witnessed teachers staying late into the evening to tutor their students or helping them apply to universities and gain access to scholarships. The teachers are committed and infinitely patient and will stop at nothing to facilitate their students' academic achievement. Again, I was led to wonder if their passion and sincere caring might actually be working *against* us. For example, because most teachers accept late work, the students have come to understand that deadlines are very flexible. Within this context, teacher and student engage in an accountability tug-of-war. Thus, I couldn't help but wonder whether we've kept students from developing work habits they need for high school and beyond.

Currently, I teach 4 periods of English 11/12 (classes that combine both juniors and seniors), one period of English 9, and an Advisory class that meets 2 times a week (made up of some of my 11th-graders). For my research, I decided to focus on juniors in my 11th-/12th-grade classes, since they'd already spent several years in high school and are expected to have developed high school "work habits." Ultimately, I was interested in exploring why some of my juniors, even after 2 years of high school, continued to struggle with turning in assignments and essays in my class.

HOW I COLLECTED AND ANALYZED DATA

To address my questions within this context, I selected three focal students who had earned Ds in the first semester and collected a variety of data on them, including attendance records, grades, questionnaires, and one-on-one interviews. Unlike the students earning Fs, who were constantly truant, my students earning Ds were usually present but failed to turn in homework assignments or essays and projects. In addition to the behavioral criteria, I selected a group that ranged in race and gender. Although I do not claim that the experiences of three students can represent those of the entire student body, I did want to gain insight by selecting students who I felt represented something of the diversity of the school. Of the three juniors, two are female and one is male. One female student is Latina and the other mixed-race African American and Filipino; the male focal student is Latino. The female Latina student was born outside the United States, while the other two were born in this country.

To deconstruct exactly why I had given these students D grades, I accessed their Semester 1 grades using the online gradebook SchoolLoop. This program allowed me to see the students' overall grades, as well as a breakdown by category (Classwork, 35%; Formal Assessments, 25%; Informal Assessments, 25%; Homework, 15%). This subdivision was important because it allowed me to see in which areas students were strong and in which they struggled.

I conducted two initial surveys with my focal students to gain insight into their beliefs related to academic success and responsibilities to complete assignments. Then, I conducted one-on-one interviews that allowed me to probe student motivation more deeply. I requested that the students elaborate on why they did not do their homework by asking, "What do you do when you get home from school?" and "Do you have a place where you write down your homework?" When asking about specific assignments, I posed questions such as "Why did you not turn in the literary analysis essay? Did you start it? If you started it, why didn't you complete it?" and "Do you feel you could write an essay at home by yourself? What happens when you get stuck?" In conducting the interviews, I used these questions as guides only. While I hoped to have all questions answered, I allowed the interviews to progress organically—using the student's responses to tailor the order and wording of subsequent questions. This approach allowed for a more "conversational" style interview. All the interviews were recorded, and I also took handwritten notes while conducting them.

I organized my data by making a chart of the information I gathered and used it to look for patterns. In reviewing the data from both the pre-interview surveys and the interviews, I noticed that there were clear categories in the data that reflected "homework" and "essays," on the one hand, and student "behavior" and "motivation," on the other. As a result, I coded and organized the data within these four categories. Through this process of data analysis, I began to understand each focal student individually and holistically.

WHAT I FOUND REGARDING THE FOCAL STUDENTS

After documenting the findings that resulted from my analysis of the focal students, I offer possible explanations for patterns of behavior and motivation regarding their academic performance.

Jasmine

Jasmine, who identifies as mixed-race African American and Filipino, epitomizes the brilliant-but-struggling student; she is perceptive, insightful, and quick thinking but does not turn in the assignments she needs to, to earn a high grade. Jasmine expressed a great desire to succeed academically, stating that her ultimate goal is to attend a California university as an engineering student. She explained, "Without an education you can't really do anything. Most jobs won't even hire you without a high school diploma." Yet her stellar attendance record (she only missed one class in the first semester) and consistent in-class participation were not enough. Jasmine's D (63.5%) for the semester broke down as follows:

Category	Weight	Score
Classwork (including participation)	35%	92%
Formal Assessments (essays, tests)	25%	27%
Homework	15%	42%
Informal Assessments (quizzes, projects)	25%	73%

As indicated by the chart, Jasmine's strongest areas of performance were "Classwork and Participation." Unsurprisingly, she also rated participation, classwork, and attendance as the most important categories of academic tasks. Although she is younger than many of the other students in my mixed 11th-/12th-grade class, Jasmine often offered her opinion confidently during class discussions. For example, in a recent classwide discussion of the "American Dream," Jasmine disagreed with many of her classmates that hard work guarantees success in the United States. She boldly stood her ground, critiquing Horatio Alger's argument by discussing the many inequalities that impede certain groups of people from achieving their goals. She voiced her opinion readily on provocative topics and avidly participated in debates and Socratic seminars. Jasmine also completed the majority of her classwork. These assignments are usually short and manageable; they include quick writes, text annotations, vocabulary sentences, and reading-response questions.

Jasmine's performance in school was at odds with her lack of completion of out-of-class tasks—indeed, with her perception of the latter. In her questionnaire, Jasmine reported that she "often" does homework, but, as evidenced by her homework performance (42%), she rarely completes homework assignments, and when she does, she turned them in late for partial credit. When asked to clarify the obstacles impeding her from completing her homework, Jasmine reported, "I get lazy and I sometimes forget." In an effort to understand *why* Jasmine "forgets," I asked her a series of more specific questions about her life after school. "I don't write down my homework anywhere," she revealed. "I don't even think of it when I get home."

Jasmine recounted that when she gets home, she either watches TV or chats on the computer. She continued, "If I don't do it at school, it won't get done." Jasmine's explanation revealed that she does not "forget" to do homework; rather, she does not even think about it outside of school. Homework is not a part of her routine.

It is important to note that Jasmine *did* make an effort to complete some homework during the *school day*, specifically during class. This effort signified that she indeed cared about her education, as discussed earlier. However, she reported that on the occasions she did do English homework, she usually "will start but not finish it." She explained, "Most likely I'll get stuck and not know an answer." As a result of "getting stuck," Jasmine often stopped working on the assignment entirely.

The problem of "getting stuck" was exacerbated when Jasmine attempted longer written assignments, usually essays. As evidenced by her grades, she did not turn in the major writing assignments of the semester and, as a result, earned a 27% in the Formal Assessment category. While we worked on these major essays in class through both writing workshops and computer lab time, I required all students to finish their work outside of class. Hence, although Jasmine began and worked on these large assignments in class, she did not finish and submit her work. When probed, Jasmine reported that when working on an essay, she will usually "finish it but not turn it in."

My assumptions around Jasmine's early failure to turn in work were that she was either defiant or lazy. I knew, from the examples of in-class writing I had received from her, that she was an eloquent writer. In addition, her paragraphs were well organized and she was facile with syntax, using a variety of complex sentences. And yet when I devoted an entire class period to outlining an essay, she would write only a few lines. Every time I asked her if she needed any help she shook her head no. It always seemed to me that she just needed *time*, but even when 50 minutes were allocated she would produce less than a paragraph of writing. I admit that I grew frustrated, and thus I would spend the period helping my other 24 students. I would thus send Jasmine home to finish her essay, but it would never come back.

I remembered Jasmine's struggle with academic writing during a timed in-class essay-writing assignment. Following our dynamic class discussion of the "American Dream," during which Jasmine was a key speaker, I asked students to write an argumentative essay in which they sided with either Horatio Alger or Harlan L. Dalton. Jasmine began writing immediately and after several minutes paused and called me over. "When was the 14th Amendment ratified?" she asked. "Don't worry about that," I said. "Just leave a blank and you can come back to it and fill it in." A few minutes later I circled back to her and noticed she hadn't written anything new. "I'll look it up," I told her. As soon I shared the information with her, she filled it in and continued writing furiously for the rest of the class period, but ran out of time before getting to the conclusion. It was shocking to me that this small piece of information had impeded her from moving on with her writing. This made me think back to a literary analysis piece we had written a few months earlier: Had a similar roadblock prevented her from getting past the introduction of her essay?

Rather than grading the "American Dream" essay as incomplete, I decided to give Jasmine a chance to complete it for a better grade. Like the other essays, this one went home and disappeared. Yet surprisingly, several weeks later, the essay reappeared along with a conclusion. I asked Jasmine what had motivated her to finish the essay. "I was at home flipping through papers," she said, "and I seen my grade had gone from an A to an F. So I found the paper and finished it." Intrigued, I asked her why she hadn't finished it earlier. "I forgot or got lazy," she replied. "What do you mean you 'got lazy?'" I probed. "I like it to sound good," she explained, just as in her questionnaire; "I need to find the right words so it takes me a long time." Again the same issue caused Jasmine's struggle: She could not express herself in a way that seemed adequate. Yet this time, she persevered. She explained that the grade motivated her and that the topic was easier than others because she knew a lot about it.

Rather than forgetfulness or laziness, it seemed that a peculiar *perfectionism* might be behind Jasmine's struggle with writing. Jasmine admitted to me, "I feel like I *could* write an essay by myself, but I just *choose* not to . . . because I can't concentrate. I get stuck because I don't know what to write." Her struggle therefore seemed to be mostly with concentration, figuring out what she wants to write, and finding ways to express herself that she considers appropriate: "I think of a sentence before I write it, but I don't know what to say. I get stuck. I like to sound educated so I get stuck." As elucidated, Jasmine was troubled by a desire to get the words just right, or sound "educated." Given Jasmine's high level of oral expression and critical thinking, it must be frustrating for her to not be able to express herself on paper with the same ease.

Hence, Jasmine's propensity to "get stuck" when completing assignments indicated a perceived perfectionism around academic writing. When she "got stuck," Jasmine stopped and waited to "get back to it, at school." The reality was that if the assignment was required to be typed, as most of my longer assigned essays are, Jasmine did *not* get back to writing. As a result, she did not complete the assignments and did not receive credit.

Mateo

Mateo, a sixteen-year old Latino male born and raised right near the high school, contributed great energy to my 4th-period English 11/12 class. Much like Jasmine, he was insightful, confident, and engaged and offered a strong voice in our class. Although he faced significant adversity every day, including personal family problems and health issues, he consistently came to class with a positive attitude and desire to learn. Mateo did not think about life beyond high school, and he had no idea what he might want to pursue as a career. Still, he understood the importance of academic success. Echoing Jasmine, he explained, "Getting good grades and passing school is important to me because a high school diploma means nothing in this world." Over several months Mateo came to my classroom at lunch every day to make up the homework that he did not do at home. He was determined to pass, but given that he didn't do schoolwork outside of class, achieving this goal was proving to be difficult. Like Jasmine, Mateo earned a D (67.45%) in his first semester of English 11:

Category	Weight	Score
Classwork (including participation)	35%	82%
Formal Assessments (essays, tests)	25%	68%
Homework	15%	20%
Informal Assessments (quizzes, projects)	25%	75%

Similar to Jasmine, Mateo almost always completed his in-class work. He was also an avid participator—often volunteering to read aloud and voluntarily answering questions when called on. In my informal observations of Mateo, I noticed that although he was quick to respond, he worked slowly, especially when the task involved writing. Further still, his written responses were usually brief and lacking in depth. I found myself having to push him to explain his argument or develop a complex analysis.

In the many months that Mateo was my student, he never turned in a piece of work that was to be completed outside of class. Cognizant of and truthful about his own performance, Mateo noted that he never did his homework. This is in part explained by Mateo's perception of the weight of homework on his overall performance. While he said that homework was "important" for his academic success, he stated that it was less important than attendance, participation, classwork, and essays: "Small homework assignments are not so important, so I don't really pay attention. I just don't do it."

While Mateo reported that he "forgets" about his homework, his later comments also indicated a lack of overlap between his school and home life. He explained, "My activities after school consist of me doing my workout at the gym or going out late with friends. Doing these activities caused me to forget about my homework." Clearly, the activities that Mateo enjoyed did not *cause* him to "forget" about his homework; rather, homework was simply not part of his after-school routine—neither his family nor his friends encouraged him to bring academics into the home sphere. "Some days homework crosses my mind, some days it doesn't," Mateo explained, adding with a smile, "I'm distracted by other activities." He spoke about homework with a lightness that suggested a casual approach to academics; he cared about his education, he wanted to succeed, and yet he didn't understand the importance of continuing to practice reading and writing outside of the classroom. Even though I explained that class time is *not enough*, Mateo did not change his habits. His reality once he stepped out of Franciscano High School was disconnected from school, and my nagging voice was drowned out by other priorities and other realities.

One of Mateo's great strengths was his ability to recognize when he needed help and to request it. As such, Mateo managed to complete several major writing assignments last semester. While I was helping him with these essays, I came to understand that he lacked confidence in his own writing abilities. He explained, "When I start an essay I have help from my teacher. The reason I don't finish the essay is because without help I get lost and I just give up." Unlike Jasmine, Mateo did *not* feel that he could write an essay on his own. "I don't trust my own writing," he explained, "I don't think it's up to the standards so I don't even do it." Indeed, in the beginning of the year, Mateo was behind his peers in terms of writing ability; he did not know how to construct a topic sentence or critically analyze a quotation. Yet he answered brilliantly when I asked him to justify his rationale orally, and he flourished when I helped guide his writing assignments. Once these scaffolds weren't present, though, I struggled to convince Mateo to trust in his own writing abilities. He still preferred to have "teachers sit down with us and work on the essay with us." Thus, because he couldn't "ask for help" when writing at home, Mateo did not even start.

Esperanza

Esperanza was a soft-spoken, sixteen-year-old Latina in my 2nd-period English 11/12 class. Given that she was very quiet and nondisruptive in class, it was easy to imagine that some teachers failed to notice her. When I talked to her individually, though, she was quite gregarious, eager to share her perspective. "I know I need to do well in school and go to college to be successful," she began. "One of my dreams is to become a teacher. That's what my parents want for me too." Yet this drive to succeed in school was highly inconsistent with her academic behaviors. Most of the time she completed all her classwork but failed to transport it from her binder to the turn-in tray, while for other work, she shrugged and mumbled that she didn't do it. Given her highly inconsistent performance throughout the semester, Esperanza earned a D (68%), with a breakdown as follows:

Category:	Weight:	Score:
Classwork	35%	83%
Formal Assessments	25%	62%
Homework	15%	48%
Informal Assessments	25%	65%

One of Esperanza's greatest strengths was her ability to offer deep text analysis. Although she was one of the quietest students in the class, when I called on Esperanza to share, she offered interesting inferences and analyses of both fictional and expository texts. She also worked well in groups, but if paired with friends, she would go off task. Or she would begin listening to someone else's conversation when she was supposed to be working.

Esperanza explained, "I get distracted easily. With anything in front of me I could get distracted." On other occasions she just would not finish classwork that she didn't like (usually writing). As with the other focal students, Esperanza's perception of the importance of certain academic tasks mirrored her own strengths. While she labeled homework and participation as "not important," she rated attendance, classwork, and essays as "fairly important." As with the others, Esperanza's failure to work at home hurt her grade in the class.

In the first semester of school, Esperanza completed less than half her homework. Many of these assignments were turned in late for partial credit, meaning she completed them late in class. Esperanza recognized this and stated that she only "sometimes" does her work. She explained, "I have some teachers that leave me a lot of homework and it is really hard so I forget on doing it sometimes." As with the other students, her initial response was that she "forgets." Given her brief comment about the workload, though, it seemed that there is something behind her reported forgetfulness.

Unlike my other focal students, Esperanza stated that when she comes home from school, she does her chemistry homework. She continued, "I do chemistry because that class is the hardest and that teacher gives the most homework." She then did homework for her other classes if she "remembered" to. Esperanza did not write down her homework in a planner or on a piece of paper; rather, she flipped through her binder to see if there were any assignments she needed to do for the following day. She explained that "it's hard—I forget what we learned when I get home." Esperanza did not seem to feel the urgency or importance of doing homework, nor was she used to completing all of it every night. As a result, she completed her homework on some days and not others. When I gave her an opportunity to complete homework in class, she almost always took advantage of the time and turned the assignment in for partial credit.

Unlike with daily homework assignments, Esperanza *did* keep essays in her mind beyond the school day. Her reasoning was that "an essay is harder so I focus on it in my mind." Similarly, she indicated on a class survey that essays were more important than homework to her academic success. After much pestering on my part, Esperanza did turn in the three major essays from the first semester. However, all these essays were submitted late, and in one case *so late* that I did not even have time to factor it into her final grade.

Esperanza offered several explanations for her behavior toward writing essays. She acknowledged that when she was assigned an essay, she would usually "start but not finish it," or complete it after the deadline. Like Jasmine, Esperanza did believe that she could go home and write an essay. Indeed, Esperanza was a fairly high-skilled writer and could produce a well-written essay. Rather, then, her struggle seems to relate to her difficulty with completing a longer written piece. When asked directly, she wrote, "Sometimes I don't have any more ideas. Other times I forget to finish it or I just don't want to keep doing it." When I probed her to reveal what happens after she "runs out of ideas" (usually after the third paragraph), she stated, "I first ask my brother for help. Then I think even harder. Finally, 10 minutes later, I just give up. I decide just to not do the essay." Despite this candid explanation, Esperanza *did* eventually turn in her essays, and the last was submitted on time. I therefore asked her about this last piece. She stated, "I wasn't going to do the essay, but then I remembered I needed to get my grades up. So I found some information, I got notes, and I finished it." In the end, the value she placed on academic success motivated her to finish the essay: she was able to connect her future goal of becoming a teacher with her current reality of being a high school student. Although she still "got stuck," in the end she pushed herself through the process of completing these essays.

FURTHER EXPLANATION OF MY FINDINGS

Getting Stuck

As the preceding case studies revealed, all three focal students reported that they started their essays for English class but often gave up before they finished them. The difficulties the students faced with writing were unique to each of them: Jasmine struggled to find the "right words" to use, Esperanza "ran out of ideas," and Mateo reported having trouble with everything from organization to analyzing quotations. Their shared struggle, however, was "getting stuck" while writing.

In my experience, it's natural for students to hit roadblocks during the writing process—especially for a substantial essay of five or more paragraphs. These difficulties are not uncommon, even for more experienced writers. However, unlike these writers, my focal students lacked strategies to help them overcome these roadblocks, or resilience that would enable them eventually to persevere. As Mateo asserted, "The reason I don't finish the essay is because without help I get lost and I just give up." Esperanza hit her wall while trying to write the topic sentence of the third body paragraph of a literary analysis essay, while Jasmine became blocked when she didn't "know what to say" or how to find the words to "sound educated." When these students hit a wall, they gave up.

With every essay completed, the writing process became a little easier, and students' endurance strengthened. For example, while Mateo admitted that he did not "trust" his own writing, he recognized that after completing a thematic analysis essay he had more confidence. He did not believe he could complete an essay on his own, but he felt as though he was getting closer to that goal. This evidence suggests that as students practice formal essay writing, they are likely to gain confidence and develop resilience strategies. The implication is that teachers, then, must provide numerous and varied opportunities for students to write essays and be confident that students can work on their own before asking them to. We can also explicitly teach strategies for overcoming writing roadblocks to help students gain the ability and confidence to write independently. Teachers can also emphasize the importance of revision with the hope that students will not feel their first drafts need to be "perfect." Students will benefit from understanding that writing is a process and a struggle that can be approached in multiple ways—but as with all struggles, students need support.

A Home–School Connection

As I walked around collecting homework from students, it was not uncommon or surprising to hear students mumble that they forgot to do their homework. However, I *was* surprised when all my case study students confirmed this in their written surveys. A closer look at their questionnaire responses elucidated the motives behind their "forgetting" behavior: Jasmine wrote, "I get lazy and I sometimes forget," while Mateo shared, "My activities after school consist of me doing my workout at the gym or going out late with friends. Doing these activities causes me to forget about my homework." Esperanza offered a third reason: "I have some teachers that leave me a lot of homework and it is really hard so I forget on doing it sometimes." Hence, behind "forgetfulness," the students suggest more probable reasons for not doing homework. Going to the gym does not *cause* one to forget about homework assignments, nor does the rigor of the expected work. Rather, for myriad reasons, these students have not formed a consistent habit of doing or thinking of schoolwork outside of school.

The excuse of "forgetting" is so common perhaps because it enables students to relieve themselves of responsibility. If students develop a habit of saying "I forgot," they do not have to think more seriously or deeply about their patterns of behavior or motivations behind their behavior. Indeed, we all tend to "forget" when faced with a task we don't feel comfortable with or find overwhelming. All my focal students became uncomfortable when I asked them to elaborate on their reported forgetfulness. Jasmine, for example, looked away from me or down at her paper, her voice quieting. Her body language suggested an internal struggle, which signified that I had forced her to recognize her explicit academic self-sabotage. Yet I feel bad because I played a role in what became self-sabotage by not offering sufficient support.

All three students reported that homework was "important" to academic success. They also all rated homework to be less important than attendance and in-class work. While it is possible that they did not realize the importance of these tasks, it is also not uncommon to justify to oneself a choice to avoid difficult tasks by downplaying their importance. Mateo offered some insight in his interview, explaining, "Small homework assignments are not so important to me, so I don't really pay attention. I just don't do it." Mateo decided these short assignments did not matter, and thus he put them out of his mind. Esperanza also shared that while she did not think much about homework, "essays are harder" so she "focuses on them in [her] mind." It therefore followed that students were not completing homework possibly because they found it insignificant, or they believed (or hoped) they could do well in the class without doing it, or because they felt unable to complete the task without support and so gave up.

Concurrently, I was shocked to discover that none of my focal students wrote down reminders of their homework assignments. In the first week of school the students are all given planners for keeping track of their homework assignments. The interviews revealed that none of my focal students used these planners (several months into the school year, they did not even know where their planners were). While this was initially surprising, it became clear that all the focal students decided, consciously or subconsciously, that they wouldn't do schoolwork beyond the school day. The problems with doing homework seemed to have a history for these students.

Indeed, students' failure to write reminders about homework signified that these students had over time come to see "school" and "home" as *two different worlds*. Jasmine divulged that her after-school routine involved watching TV and chatting on the computer, and did not think of homework when she got home. "If I don't do it at school," she said, "it won't get done." Mateo shared a similar pattern of behavior: after school he went out with friends or went to the gym. He often came to class with stories of being out until four in the morning with friends and sleeping in his car. "Homework doesn't cross my mind," he said, "I'm distracted by other activities."

These students are not to blame for their separation of their "school" and "home" lives. There are countless reasons to explain why, from 1st grade through 11th, they did not develop the habit or skill of working at home. We mustn't turn to "blame," but instead look to ways that we can support their success. When my students enter college, they will be expected to read and write independently for sustained periods of time; these skills must be taught so that students like these three can gradually learn to assume responsibility for working outside of class, both in the present and to prepare them to achieve their dreams of higher education in their future. The discussion then turns to *how* to help students learn to work independently.

IMPLICATIONS FROM WHAT I LEARNED

When I began this project I admit that I felt a certain amount of frustration toward my focal students. While I recognized their many strengths and appreciated them greatly as people, I was aggravated by their failure to turn in homework assignments and essays. I sincerely felt that I was doing all I could for them, and yet they were not succeeding. The chasm between their dreams of success and the obstinate Ds they were earning seemed to be a black hole, inexplicable and destructive. After doing this research, I developed a radically different perspective on this phenomenon of what appears to be student academic self-sabotage, and have renewed my empathy for struggling students.

First, I have reopened my eyes to the reality that for many of my students, "school" and "home" (or whatever exists after school) are two separate worlds that seldom meet. I knew this was true for many socioeconomically disadvantaged students, but somehow, in the flurry of first-year teaching, I had failed to think about my students as people with lives outside of school. Perhaps because there are other, more pressing priorities, there is no one at home forcing them to complete their homework. And then for any number of other reasons, just because something was assigned, they did not necessarily complete it, regardless of its importance to their school success.

These findings hold several important implications for my practice and for other high school teachers, especially those teaching in socioeconomically disadvantaged neighborhoods. We simply cannot take for granted that if a student is motivated to succeed, she or he will automatically do schoolwork outside of school.

With regard to writing, I think that I need to provide students with frequent opportunities to write a variety of academic essays and I need to give them more help throughout the process. At home, assignments will have to be something they can accomplish without the support of the classroom. Given my students' struggles with writing essays of five paragraphs or more, I will consider starting the year by assigning several shorter essays—about one page in length—to be completed during class. These one-page essays will require students to follow the structure of a formal academic essay and will ask of them the same critical thinking and analysis they use in any essay. Given the short length requirement, I hope the essays will be less intimidating than traditional essays. Once they master writing these, I will try to move them toward writing longer essays, also at first in class. This will give all students, regardless of their skill level or experience with independent writing, time to practice their writing skills, ways to get help throughout the process, and ways to demonstrate to the teacher their strengths and weaknesses. With this method, as students gradually gain both skills and confidence, the teacher can then assign some independent writing to be completed outside of class, carefully monitoring what students can and can't do without support.

In addition to offering ample and frequent opportunities for students to write and ample and frequent support for writing, teachers could think about how to help students develop strategies for overcoming roadblocks in their writing. Specifically, teachers might guide students to understand themselves as writers by asking them to reflect on instances when they "get stuck." Teachers could remind the students that *all* writers, regardless of skill level, run into roadblocks when writing, but that they use strategies to keep going. Together, then, the class could brainstorm the various strategies they use to persevere in writing. These strategies could include asking a friend, sibling, or parent for help; checking notes from class; asking the teacher for help (in class or through email); or perhaps even taking a risk and writing something they are not fully confident in. After each essay, students could write a reflection in which they think back on their writing process, identifying both the roadblocks they encountered and the strategies they employed to overcome the problems and finish the essay.

Beginning in the first weeks of school, teachers need to identify those students who do not complete homework assignments or miss deadlines, and intervene as soon as possible. Once students are fully supported academically, teachers may still need to monitor the pull of the daily movement from home to school. If students are still having difficulty, teachers might try contacting parents or caregivers of these students to inform them of homework assignments and to explain explicitly *why* it is important to work outside of class.

If the "forgetting" problem persists, teachers might try using cell phones and computers to help students track their homework and grades. Teachers at Franciscano High School have long been employing planners and graphic organizers for homework tracking to no avail. However, students are incredibly adept at using cell phones. Teachers could instruct students to record their homework in their cell phones and to set up reminder alarms. The alarm could serve as a temporary interruption of the "home" realm, carrying with it reminders of the "school" realm. Although many teachers may feel nervous about permitting cell phone use in class, we could set a designated period of time to set up these alarms and teachers could walk around the room to monitor the process. Students could even act as "experts," instructing the teacher and other classmates how to set up reminders and alarms. The task could therefore be empowering for students and encourage them to take ownership of their academic achievement.

In addition to facilitating the setup of homework reminders, teachers could try giving students who are still struggling weekly progress notices in which they track their grades and get feedback from teachers about their strengths, weakness, and missing assignments. These progress notices could provide students with constant feedback that may help them see a more direct, instantaneous connection between their assignments and their grade in the class, and they could give teachers additional information about where students continue to get stuck.

In the end, teachers will only learn about their students by *listening* to them and hearing about their strengths and struggles, about their perceptions of the work they are expected to do. Too often we wonder about what is going on with our students, why they are acting a certain way or *not* doing something we want them to do. Rather than speculate, we can get the answer directly from the source. We can ask students what they need and want from us as teachers. When I asked this of my focal students, Jasmine offered, "Constantly remind me. Explain and show me what I need to do or how to do something." Mateo echoed, "I personally don't like it when a teacher gives you a hard time about your work but it has helped me do my work." Esperanza concluded, "I don't know. Maybe every week give me a report of what I'm missing and make me stay on lunch or school to do it." In essence, the students intimated that they *wanted* to be pestered, reminded, and harassed to turn in work. Their suggestions remind us that we must not give up on these struggling students. Rather, we must recognize what they *are* doing and pushing them to do what they are not.

Finally, we must keep in mind the goal of helping all students achieve academic independence. While I believe I can help by reminding and pestering my students, I want my students to appropriate the work habits and strategies and learning they need to work on their own. If I can achieve this, perhaps Mateo will have the confidence and skill to produce an essay without my help, and Esperanza will have the resilience and ability to return to a difficult part of her essay and finish it before the deadline. And maybe Jasmine will no longer explain her grade—whether a D or an A—by what I, her teacher, did or did not do. Instead, she will be empowered with the confidence and skills to complete her work on her own and earn the grade she aspires to receive.

CHAPTER 6

Approaches to Teaching Language Minority Students

Paul F. Lai

When the Vietnamese, Korean, and Japanese students at the English Language Center (ELC) met me, a Taiwanese American teacher, they looked hopeful that there might be a member of the staff with whom they could communicate freely and fluently. In fact, *hopeful* aptly describes most students at the ELC. As this California district's secondary school for recent immigrants from Mexico, Pakistan, the Philippines, and literally a world of other places, the ELC is a mosaic; students and faculty speak various tongues, wear disparate fashions, and maintain diverse cultural outlooks and traditions, but they all bank in the same currency of hope. An atmosphere of optimism and anticipation permeates the classroom talk, the faculty discussions, and even the students' social exchanges. Although troubled with the same dilemmas as other urban schools, the ELC affords a small-school attention to students that humanizes and personalizes each of them.

As a new teacher, I was drawn to this unique environment and the opportunity to pay special attention to the English language development of secondary immigrant students. As an immigrant schooled as a member of a language minority when I was a child, my concerns were personal as well as professional. Working with the students at the ELC plunged me deeply into questions that I have consciously or unconsciously faced throughout my life, questions of identity, communication, and meaning when the surrounding world's language is not yours.

While I knew of the strengths and challenges of the ELC's context, I have become increasingly aware of a particular phenomenon. While all the students are language minorities in the broader American culture, and for the most part they are language minorities in the school setting, the ELC provides unique contexts where, for some students, they are the language majority. While there is a great diversity in the students' primary languages and national origins, the majority of them, in the 70–80% range, speak

Spanish. And while many of these Spanish speakers may come from El Salvador, Peru, and other Latin American countries, most come from Mexico. Although on a daily basis they experience being language minorities, in many situations in the ELC they are the school's language majority.

Despite their diversity, the predominance of Spanish speakers is exhibited in moments such as when a Punjabi student jokingly responds *"Presente!"* during roll call. The students chuckle, even those who do not speak Spanish, at the ironic preponderance of Spanish in the common culture of a center for English development. And despite moments of light-hearted repartee and mutual appreciation, at other times non–Spanish speakers appear frustrated by their exclusion from the social world of the Spanish speakers. The Arabic student is placed in an all-Latino group to provide heterogeneity but is shut out of the conversation. Announcements for activities are delivered in Spanish and the non–Spanish speakers are left guessing about whether and how they can participate.

While the staff urges the inclusion of all students, the understandable emphasis on the Spanish-speaking majority is institutional as well as social. Bilingual classes, progress reports, and parent announcements often have Spanish as their default language. Administrators work hard to have translators available for all languages and to cultivate appreciation for all cultures, and yet appealing to and empowering the Spanish-speaking majority merits special attention. The ELC provides a rare kind of midpoint between institutions and locations where Spanish speakers are shut out because of their primary language and those where Spanish gives them access.

Meanwhile, as language minorities among language minorities, students with other primary languages have different experiences of the ELC. They too struggle and succeed as immigrants in the United States. They too must clutch at language while going through turbulent adolescent years. Yet, for better or worse, they find fewer of those midpoints between the culture, experiences, and languages of home and the social and academic world of the school.

The differing experience of these two groups of students—those who find a context within the school to be language majorities and those who remain language minorities—led me to question the effects of being a language majority or language minority on English language development as well as social and identity development. As a teacher researcher, my work with these students involved teaching English; facilitating their reading, writing, speaking, and listening; and assessing their learning needs. Beyond the classroom, I got to know my students through building informal personal relationships, getting involved in extracurricular activities with them, and being in spaces designed for communicating with students. Amid these various encounters, I wondered, What are the official and unofficial spaces where students can use their primary language and, temporarily, constitute a "language majority"? How do these spaces function in the students' academic and social development? What is the difference in language acquisition and identity development between language minority students who have contexts within the school setting to be a language majority, and those who do not have such a context?

COLLECTING DATA FOR MY STUDY

I collected two different kinds of data to answer these questions: information about the entire school, through surveys, promotion rates, student work, and observations of various primary-language spaces; and information about individual students and spaces, through classroom observations, interviews, and observations of students through following them during the school day.

I compared 3 years of promotion rates for Spanish- versus non-Spanish-speaking students. I also observed various spaces—combinations of time, place, and social arrangements—where staff paid attention to students, where students provided one another academic support, and where personal relationships and social dynamics were at play. These included the student-led Club Wake Up, the primary-language Homerooms, and the cafeteria at lunchtime. Put together, these data helped me paint a general picture of the school and compare the experiences of the speakers of Spanish and non-Spanish language minorities at the school.

I interviewed 13 students, 8 Spanish speaking and 5 non–Spanish speaking, and followed them for at least some portion of a day to observe how and where they used their primary languages at the school. In the interviews, I asked them about their years at the ELC, experiences inside and outside of classes, views about school, educational background and history, and opinions about the effect of primary-language spaces and the Spanish-speaking majority. When I followed students, I observed them in and between classes. These observations proved the richest source of information, as I either caught a glimpse of their daily lives or caught them in the midst of incidents that invariably involved their position as language learners and speakers of other languages.

HOW I ANALYZED THE DATA

My analysis involved grouping my observations about various primary-language spaces to see how these spaces affected students' social and academic development. From observation notes, interviews, and surveys, I assembled a detailed picture of both the official spaces, sanctioned and set up by the school, and the unofficial spaces created by the students. I then examined how students interacted with one another in those spaces; what aspects of students' academic, interpersonal, or linguistic personalities were brought out in each space; how much students got to use their primary language; and how others, from classmates to faculty, responded to the primary-language use. I then had a sense of how the various primary-language spaces functioned and what impact they had. I also tried to learn about how primary-language spaces affected the ways students related to one another and formed their identities, how they developed language proficiency, and how they interacted with the school. The findings I present are the patterns that I noticed, theorized, and confirmed.

MORE OFFICIAL SUPPORT FOR SPANISH SPEAKERS

My first major finding was that the school's official, faculty-initiated primary-language spaces provided a unique, supportive environment for Spanish speakers, but such environments were unavailable to the non–Spanish speakers. From one perspective, the ELC offered a supportive environment sensitive to the strengths, needs, and limitations of newcomers. From another perspective, it seemed strange that Spanish-speaking students were bused away from an English-saturated school to learn English among peers who predominantly spoke Spanish. That situation may have seemed even more strange for the non-Spanish-speaking students. While the clear objective of the school was to teach English, separating the earliest newcomers in a different campus created, on occasion, what amounted to a Spanish-speaking school. Among the spaces where Spanish was not only supplemental, but became the main language of communication, were the Spanish-English bilingual classes, the interactions within English-medium classes, extracurricular school activities (such as Club Wake Up), and the official school administration. The bilingualism of these official spaces provided a unique environment for the ELC's language majority students to receive academic and social support that would otherwise be unavailable to them. On the other hand, while this accessibility supplied powerful benefits to the Spanish-speaking students, the language minorities were often excluded from these benefits.

Bilingual Classes and Spaces

The ELC offered bilingual social studies and math, intended not only to address content matter in Spanish but also to supplement English development. For many immigrant secondary students precariously lacking credits and running out of high school years to get them, bilingual classes were an important stepping-stone to fulfilling their graduation requirements. Teachers also testified that those intellectual and academic capacities with fewer opportunities to be noticed and nurtured within English-only classes could be recognized and cultivated in bilingual ones.

One example, not from one of the bilingual classes but from an activity in my own creative writing course, illustrates this phenomenon. We decided as a class to publish a school newspaper. Groups of students were assigned to interview teachers and students and to write stories based on topics of interest to them. In forming the groups, I tried to include at least one non-Spanish-speaking student in each group, and all instruction was given in English. But just logistically, one group remained composed of all Spanish speakers. Students were to use English to compose their interview questions, conduct interviews, and write and revise their stories, but I allowed for the all-Spanish-speaking group to draft their story and to conduct their interviews in Spanish, provided that they translated the interview questions, the interview notes, and the finished story itself into English.

The resulting difference between this group's and the other groups' stories would not surprise a bilingual teacher. While most of the stories covered their topics somewhat superficially, the group allowed to work in Spanish produced a story of notably greater depth and sophistication. As an example of the contrast, one group working in English wrote a story about the history of the school filled with mundane facts, such as the name of the first principal, the date that the school opened, and the differences in the school's schedule at its inception. In that story, the most abstract idea was a teacher quoted as saying, "She likes to teach students with heart and brain."

The group's story was not poorly written, and the students certainly stretched the limits of their language in conducting the interviews and putting together the story. But the group of students working in Spanish wrote a complex piece about the advantages and disadvantages of the school, collecting countervailing viewpoints about its academic merit, critiquing the lack of recreational activities for students, and suggesting connections between the challenges of immigrant life and the support offered by the school. While their story showed no greater sophistication in language, the four Spanish speakers could demonstrate a level of thinking much more difficult to attain through the more nascent discourse of the other groups.

The two bilingual classes that I observed, one an algebra class and one a U.S. history class, ran similarly to math and history classes that might be found in any high school but were conducted in Spanish. What separated these classes from the English-medium classes is that the students who were more academically motivated were also the "experts," the ones peers would seek out for help or who would answer a teacher's more challenging questions. In the English-medium courses, it was usually the students who had the most exposure to English, because of either their length of stay in the United States or their family and social situations, who became the "experts." Bilingual classes supplied an environment where both intellectual challenges and confidence building could continue for students, even while their English language was still in its beginning stages. For Spanish speakers, this was a vital and often unmet need. For the language minorities, it remained an unmet need in the early years of language development.

Club Wake Up

One drawback of the ELC's half-day program was that the extracurricular activities (student leadership, athletics, clubs) that usually contribute to life in school were nearly nonexistent in the ELC. After school hours, while other schools' gymnasiums and classrooms still bustled with activity, the ELC emptied as soon as the buses left. The exception to this inactivity was the group of students who gathered in the classrooms of Mr. Jesus Heredia and Ms. Mayra Lopez after school several days a week for Club Wake Up meetings. The club's 15 or so members and their teacher volunteers, who relinquished both time and authority to the students, organized dances, sports activities, field trips, fund-raisers, political action, and Valentine's balloon sales. For a group numbering just 5% of the school's population, their prolific organizing and uncompensated effort had an outsized impact on addressing the marginalization and exclusion from school activities that recent immigrants usually experienced.

Two of my Spanish-speaking interviewees, Miguel and Alma, were elected officers in the club. Although they were Level 3 English language development (ELD) students, both were still quite formative in their English acquisition. While neither was bashful by nature, both had moved quickly through Levels 1 and 2 and found themselves more reticent in Level 3, where many of their classmates had lived in the United States for twice or even three times longer. They seemed like quiet students in my class, and I might not have known differently had I not attended the early meetings of the club. Although they still lacked the language fluency to display their personalities and leadership abilities in the classroom, the club meetings, which were conducted in Spanish, provided a different space for them. They and the other members of the club had opportunities to exercise leadership, develop social and communal bonds, and enjoy respect and responsibility of a sort rarely given in classrooms. Perhaps Miguel and Alma wound up becoming high achievers in class as well as leaders in the club because they were simply highly motivated young adults. Or perhaps their leadership roles in the club put them in a position within the school community that inspired them to become high-achieving students. Either way, their participation in the club fostered a sense of ownership and conscientiousness about school life that was reflected in how they conducted themselves as students. As Miguel explained to me:

> In the club, I can express my opinions, express what I think. [We can talk about] the ELC—what is the problem, who is responsible, what we need to change or correct.

That's why we call it "Wake Up ELC!" A lot of students smoke marijuana, drink beer, gangs. . . . "Wake Up" means [changing] your life, making beautiful things, [and] playing sports.

Miguel described the alternative that Club Wake Up provided for its members as a space where students engaged in a level of thought and relationship rarely attained in their ELD classes.

Miguel's limited English only hints at the depth of thinking and purposefulness that the free use of his primary language facilitated when he was among the club members. He and the rest of the club's commitment and accomplishments would be notable from any teenagers, but they were even more remarkable coming from a group of newcomer immigrant students, who are often overlooked and treated to low expectations. The likely positive impact of this particular primary-language space illustrated the potential of these spaces to increase academic engagement and engender positive social development.

Yet, while the club's contributions were irrefutable, there remained another side of the coin. A few students, prompted by the teacher supporters, announced the club's inaugural meeting in every classroom and invited any and all to attend, though the invitation was given in Spanish. At the initial meeting, the attendees were all Spanish speakers save one, Jabby, who confided that she only felt comfortable going because of my presence. While the teachers and students made some effort to translate the conversation for us, I had some difficulty following the discussions, and Jabby was noticeably chagrined. She later admitted to me that she felt as though the club "was supposed to be for everyone but was really only for the students from Mexico."

Thus, while the club served the school as a vital and positive primary-language space, it also widened the chasm between the majority Spanish speakers and the non–Spanish speakers. This is not to say that the group caused divisions between students; on the contrary, activities organized by the club had built bridges and strengthened the overall school community. But what the club offered to Spanish speakers and could not offer to the other students amplified the *difference* between what the two groups experienced. What the club offered to students like Miguel in terms of providing a space for mature expression, responsibility, and engagement remained unavailable to students like Jabby.

Homerooms

Another of the formal primary-language spaces was the Homeroom program. Reintroduced during this school year, Homerooms were intended specifically as weekly, half-hour meetings to be conducted in students' primary languages. The Homerooms aimed to give students an opportunity to voice their opinions and needs, receive important information, discuss relevant issues, and build relationships in their first language. As a sanctioned space for primary-language use, the Homerooms would try to match teachers who could speak the first language of the students with a small group of speakers of that language.

Twelve Homeroom groups of about 15 students each were set up based on primary language, grade, and home school. Ten of those Homeroom groups used Spanish. One of the groups included students from India and Fiji, students who spoke Hindi, Farsi, and a few other languages; several faculty and staff facilitated that group. The other group included students from East and Southeast Asian countries, including Vietnam, China, Japan, and the Philippines. Even though the Homerooms were designed to allow students to develop a community in a primary-language space, the experience of Spanish speakers and non–Spanish speakers differed significantly. In the Spanish-speakers' Homerooms, facilitators led discussions and invited speakers to talk about gangs, toured home school campuses, and worked together on school service projects, among other activities. Although the Homeroom that I led did help students to understand graduation requirements, how the ELC's levels worked, and how their peers felt during each meeting, we were limited in the depth of our conversations; most of the students were in beginning levels of English, with as many as six different home languages among them. The school had grouped them together simply as the "East Asian" group. Given the different primary languages they spoke, building bridges of communication in our group was just as challenging as in any early level ESL class filled with students with different primary languages.

The official primary-language spaces afforded a unique and supportive environment for the Spanish-speaking students. For the non-Spanish-speaking students, the school may have offered a more supportive environment than their home schools would have. Nonetheless, a significant gap existed between the support provided by the official school staff for language majorities and that provided for language minorities.

SPANISH SPEAKERS PRIVILEGED IN UNOFFICIAL SPACES

I next found that in unofficial spaces, Spanish speakers had a higher comfort level as the language majority of the ELC compared with their language minority status in their comprehensive schools. However, the experience of the non-Spanish-speaker language minority was similar to their marginalization as language minorities in their comprehensive schools. Besides officially sanctioned primary-language spaces like Club Wake Up and bilingual classes, primary-language spaces for Spanish speakers also existed in the lunchroom and the informal socializing that happens between and within classes. In our interview, Martha, a Spanish-speaking student, told me:

> [The good thing about ELC] is that you can make so many friends in this school that speak Spanish to you, and the people don't talk about you so you can't understand them. You can understand what the people are saying.

When Martha explained why she preferred to remain at the ELC during lunchtime rather than return to her home school, she described the physical situation of the Spanish-speaking students in their home schools: largely grouping together in more peripheral and marginal areas of campus. In these spaces, the Spanish-speaking students at their home schools suffer all the insecurities and trials of being language minorities. In contrast, on the ELC campus, Spanish speakers routinely found reaffirmation of the value of their symbolic capital, their languages and music, their values and concerns.

These informal primary-language spaces were vital to the communal sense of the campus, but they were also haunted by specters of social marginalization. Students feeling disenfranchised by the American school system, instead of wiling away long hours with infantile but half-understood remedial English curriculum, may opt for unsanctioned spaces where their culture and language and even their intelligence is more valued. Such spaces even include street gangs, which can provide a kind of social support structure for young people experiencing multiple forms of marginality (Vigil, 1988). For those students, the school often ceases to be a channel of opportunity and becomes instead a meeting place or occupied territory, where truant students gather or gang insignias are scrawled on desktops. When I polled students about the most prevalent problems that exist in the ELC, among Spanish-speaking students "gangs" or "*pandillas*" consistently showed up among the top three. The mention of gangs was far less frequent from non–Spanish speakers. An abundance of social spaces, whether positive or negative, formed among the Spanish-speaking majority.

Within the school I also observed rare spaces where the primary language was not Spanish or English, such as a cluster of Vietnamese students lunching in a classroom or a group of Punjabi speakers playing basketball together. These spaces had characteristics that were common to language minorities in school settings. In fact, the primary-language spaces for the ELC's language minorities were just like the marginalized spaces for Spanish speakers in the home schools. When the language minority's primary language was too openly displayed, the students were often greeted with xenophobic taunts and looks. At other times, the primary languages and the cultures of the language minorities were appreciated and welcomed by the language majority students. Sometimes, however, their languages were trivialized or made into exhibitions rather than respected. Also common to the language minority groups was their dislocation to marginalized parts of the school geographically. Non-Spanish-speaking students who socialized together would sit on the far side of the cafeteria or in the least crowded walkways, away from the heavily populated thoroughfares.

Finally, in the rare places where language minorities were more vocal and their presence felt on the campus, they were voicing a self-expression of marked (nonusual) identity, in contrast to the unmarked (usual) case of the language majority. One example was the Diwali celebration held on the school campus, which several of the Indian students coordinated with faculty and family members. Food sales, dances, and cultural celebrations were conducted in English and Hindi, commemorating the Indian festival of lights. Even though India is the second-most-common nation of origin for the ELC's students, when ELC students and faculty were invited to attend the Diwali festival, the school announcements explained, in some detail, the activities and their purpose. I contrasted this with the activities put on at the school that were carried out in Spanish, which arose from a multiplicity of occasions and objectives, seeming to need no explanation. The language minorities of the ELC only became a strong cultural presence in the sort of exhibitionist way that "multicultural" celebrations are conducted in most schools, which often only further emphasize the marginal status of those minorities.

In summary, while the school's faculty and students shared a unique awareness of the struggles and needs of *all* language learners, the fact of the Spanish-speaking majority led to the presence of exponentially more Spanish primary-language spaces. These official and unofficial spaces can offer intellectual, social, linguistic, and academic support to students not found in other settings. However, these same supports were less available to the language minority students of the school.

SPANISH SPEAKERS HAD BROADER OPPORTUNITIES

My third finding was that the presence of primary-language spaces for the Spanish speakers offered them a broader range of social experiences and opportunities than was offered to their language minority counterparts. Importantly, this range of experiences was not always positive (e.g., gang membership, which could be detrimental to academic and social progress), but others helped these students board a fast track to success (such as an academically motivated friendship group). Thus, among the Spanish speakers, one might find the most accelerated English learners as well as those struggling the most, the most active in the social life of the school and the most withdrawn, the highest academic achievers and the lowest.

As members of the language majority, Spanish speakers oriented toward one another with a wider set of predesignated identity positions. In the broad landscape of the Spanish-speaker population, different student "types" grouped together. Although Spanish-speaking students may not have become future civic leaders or future gang members, their common language put them within reach of those groups. Many of those groups represented certain identity positions, whole sets of expectations, practices, and associations that were foisted on or adopted by students. In other schools, identity positions might be the stereotypically branded "jocks," "nerds," or "Goths." Students everywhere at all times are faced with identity choices that stem from the presence of these identity positions and often face social repercussions for trying to transcend or combine identity positions (Song, 2003). This also held true for Spanish-speaking students in the ELC, who found among the whole population certain roles and identities that they could choose from and were constrained by. Often, those choices and their consequences became a preoccupation of Spanish-speaking students at the ELC to a degree unfamiliar to the non-Spanish-speaking students.

Anecdotally, to see the negative side of this language majority status, one might contrast the experiences of Javier and Mentu. Javier, a Mexican student, missed half the semester suspended from school while he awaited an expulsion hearing because for several months since his arrival to the United States, he had been regularly threatened by gang members who were first pressuring him to join their gang and then later persecuting him for his refusal. One day, in self-defense, Javier brought a baseball bat as he walked to school and, trying to defend himself from the gang members, was picked up by police for fighting. Even as someone who was resisting the predesignated identity position of the gang member, Javier was judged and then pulled into a conflict based on his language and ethnic identity. Although Javier was cleared of charges and not expelled, the incident left its mark on his reputation and his experience of schooling, and doubtless on his sense of identity as well.

Mentu, an Indian student, was in his 2nd year at the ELC and had already passed through the first two levels of ELD. In Level 3, when his breadth of communication with the Spanish-speaking students finally allowed it, he became aware of the gang presence on the school. Out of curiosity, with no intention of joining any gangs, he frequently asked other students about them, noting the gang insignias often written on students' binders. At times, he joked about being a Mexican *cholo*, or gang member, an identity he had seen and learned about from his classmates. Once, a teacher caught him as he was drawing one of those gang insignias in some careless scribbling in his notebook during class, not intending to make any statement but simply imitating what he had seen around him. As he described to me, not at all defensively, "I wasn't trying to do nothing, I was just drawing something like what other people draw on their papers." Mentu was sent to the office, and after he explained himself, he returned to class with a warning to be careful what he wrote.

Mentu's jokes and the fact that he suffered no consequences for his gang-related writing point to his distance as an Indian student from an identity position widely understood by students. For Mentu and his classmates, the comedy of the jokes was in how inappropriately or strangely his cultural identity fit with a certain identity position associated only with Spanish speakers. In fact, when the non–Spanish speakers appropriated some element of Spanish-speaker identity, such as acting like a gang member or trying to interact socially with the more studious Spanish-speaking students, there seemed to be some recognition of the variety of identity positions available to Spanish speakers. On the other hand, in the interactions where Spanish speakers appropriated the linguistic or cultural identities of non–Spanish speakers, they did not base their representations on identity positions within the cultures and languages but on generalizations of the culture as a whole. Spanish-speaking students might imitate an East Asian language or harass Sikh students by associating them with Osama bin Laden, for example. While the non–Spanish speakers could see the various identity positions for the Spanish speakers, the Spanish speakers knew the non–Spanish speakers in a generalized way based on culture and language.

Interviews with students showed that they were aware of certain identity positions being acceptable for Spanish-speaking students. They were being pulled toward these various identity positions by social pressure. For non–Spanish speakers, those identity positions were not available to them; they had fewer social possibilities, but they also had fewer social pressures to conform. Thus, for the language majority Spanish speakers, there were more choices for who they would be in the school's social landscape: They could be the smart student, the social leader, the rebel, the outcast, and so on. The Hindi students were more likely to feel that they were pegged simply as a Hindi student. The Spanish speakers were provided with more social options, and at the same time they were also confined by more social expectations. The non–Spanish speakers often had space to shape their own identities and other students' perceptions of them.

LANGUAGE ACQUISITION VERSUS ACADEMIC PROGRESS

My fourth finding was that ELD level passing rates were an unreliable indicator of language acquisition disparities between the Spanish-speaking language majority at the ELC and the others who were language minorities in this setting; there were important differences between language acquisition and academic progress. The ELC provided classes for students designated in the first three levels of ELD in the district, from Beginners to Early Intermediate language learners. To move from one level to the next, students had to pass the Mastery Test given at the end of each semester. Students who passed the test, or who were promoted based on teacher recommendation, moved on to the next level; students who did not pass the test were usually given an opportunity to repeat the level and try to pass the next time.

The vast majority of students moved progressively from level to level, many of them repeating a level at some point. Because the district's high schools operated on a block schedule, where an entire course was fit into half a school year, the three semesters in which a student might pass from the first level through the third often did not provide enough time and exposure to English to prepare them to graduate from the ELC. While many students entered at the first level and passed from one level to the next without interruption, often these students had prior schooling in English or some regular exposure to English in their homes, such as via a relative with whom they stayed who spoke to them in English. Most students at some point faced the prospect of repeating a course they had already taken, starting the level over again and hoping to pass the next time. Some had to repeat levels more than once, or they found themselves repeating multiple levels.

Faculty members talked about the tendency of a greater proportion of Spanish speakers winding up as repeaters but had different explanations for it. Some faculty opined that it had to do with the presence of primary-language spaces because Spanish-speaking students were not forced to develop their English. Some pointed to the differing educational histories of students from other countries, noting that many students who had come to the United States from other continents (including from Spanish-speaking countries other than Mexico) had to have more resources to immigrate and were likely to be more highly educated and economically advantaged. Still another explanation was that more of the Spanish-speaking students felt comfortable in the social space of the ELC and thus sabotaged their own Mastery Tests because they did not want to leave the school.

Passing rates confirmed the differential. To take the example of one semester when the differences were even less pronounced than usual, 58% of the Spanish speakers had to repeat levels at some point in their histories, compared with 42% of the non–Spanish speakers. The difference was more observable when isolating those who had to repeat levels either twice or more, where 10% of the Spanish speakers had to repeat more than twice, in contrast to the 5% of non-Spanish-speaker multiple repeaters.

As I observed this pattern among students I interviewed and students I taught, I was compelled to examine the assessment instruments that the school used to measure language acquisition. Studying the Mastery Tests and how students performed on them confirmed that while the tests were a viable measurement tool for the academic language taught in ELD classes, they often held back students who had developed sufficient target-language communicative competence (Schmidt, 1983) but who lacked the academic proficiencies necessary to pass the tests. Therefore, many repeaters were more "fluent" than nonrepeaters—that is, if one defined fluency as the ability to comfortably comprehend, produce, and express ideas in interactional, spoken English. In reality, the Mastery Tests measured an array of proficiencies, such as familiarity with academic writing genres, decoding fluency, and knowledge of written conventions. Communicative language fluency and *academic proficiencies* (Cummins, 1996) were not distinguished in the Mastery Tests, which were intended to measure progression toward the Sheltered and then the non-ELD classroom. As a consequence, to pass from one level of ELD to another, students were required to master not only the English language but also the academic proficiencies embedded in the test questions.

Therefore, it was doubly misleading to conclude that Spanish-speaking students were inhibited in their language acquisition because they could rely on using Spanish so much. The first flaw in this explanation was that if the Spanish-speaking students in general were indeed picking up English more slowly than their non-Spanish-speaking peers, the Mastery Test would not be a good assessment of that trend, because passing the Mastery Test required academic proficiencies that were as much related to educational histories and socioeconomic resources as they were to language acquisition. Further, even if it could be proved that Spanish-speaking students were slower in their language acquisition (and this would have to be demonstrated with some measurement other than the Mastery Test), the prevalence of primary-language spaces could not be proved as the cause.

This was an important observation in my understanding of the impact of primary-language spaces on language acquisition. On the one hand, my interviews with students and teachers repeatedly surfaced the same intuition: Because the Spanish speakers can use Spanish all the time, they do not learn English as well as the other students. The preponderance of my observation notes and statistical data would bear out this conclusion. On the other hand, plenty of evidence suggested that the social supports available to the Spanish-speaking students aided in their language development. And as I mentioned in the previous finding, among Spanish speakers were both the fastest and the slowest learners of English.

By the year's end, a complete picture of how primary-language spaces affected students' language acquisition continued to elude me, but at least I found sufficient evidence to cast doubt on the usual measuring stick of language acquisition, which some interpreted in a way that dismissed the Spanish speakers as slower learners of English. Especially in the higher levels, the students who were more academically proficient were more likely to be promoted to the higher levels. Spanish-speaking students who could verbally communicate very well, but who had trouble sequencing narratives, organizing paragraphs, or identifying main ideas of informational texts, struggled to pass the Mastery Test.

These questions had heightened implications in the politics of school organization. When the school district that the ELC belonged to was beset by budgetary problems and needed cuts, the ELC often felt the pressure of being under the knife. Many questioned the worth of the program, sometimes basing their criticism on the real value of having a separate school for language learners. Did the program truly benefit its target population? Did the bilingual staff and the bilingual classes and the preponderance of non–native speakers actually *hurt* these students' chances of progressing in their language and schooling? Or did focusing a small school's resources and attention on the particular needs of these students keep them from "making it" out there in the English-saturated world they would have to face? Again and again, the leaders and the faculty of the school had to re-evaluate its mission and effectiveness.

RETHINKING MAJORITY/MINORITY LANGUAGES AND LEARNING

I carried out my research as an early attempt at critical analysis of the school's objectives, successes, and failures. I anticipated that the answer to those questions would be complex. If what was "good" for students could be measured with a simple multiple-choice test, then it would be easy to study whether the ELC was "good" for students. Simply send a random sample of students to a newcomer school like the ELC, and send another random sample to sink or swim in the home schools, and then test them to see how they do. But what would be on the test? Would it be a test of their critical thinking skills, provided in their first language? Would it be a test of their English language development? Would it be a test of how familiar they were with American culture? Would it be a test of how well they knew themselves, or how well they were able to retain the positives of their own culture while working toward American definitions of success as well?

For those of us who worked at the ELC, what was "good" for the students was never definite or easy to measure if we thought broadly about the well-being of students. With any aspect of a student's development, there were possible trade-offs. In terms of social development, being a language majority offered a wider range of possible identities to choose from, which could be positive or negative. In terms of academic development and language acquisition, being a language majority offered certain advantages and certain disadvantages that have to be weighed and addressed by the faculty and the students. Being a language majority created more daily situations where students were not compelled to speak English, thereby possibly inhibiting language development. At the same time, Spanish-speaking students who were motivated to develop their English language could find more resources and supports in the school, as well as situations where they could further develop their linguistic and literary proficiencies in their first language.

And what about what was "good" for the minority that remains a minority at the school, the non–Spanish speakers? Did it do them any good to be minorities twice over, first excluded from the English-speaking majority, then excluded from the Spanish-speaking majority? Or would a school culture that is mindful of linguistic differences offer a safer and more sensitive environment for these students regardless of whether they were in any majority? My interviews and observations indicated that non–Spanish speaking students harbored little if any dissatisfaction with the ELC program, perhaps never having had the opportunity to know anything else. Indeed, though they felt there were fewer resources for them than for the Spanish speakers, there were still more resources at the ELC than at their home comprehensive schools.

After carrying out this research, I did not have a definite thumbs-up or thumbs-down judgment about the school's worth. In the contemporary political culture, where schools are so often called up to prove their effectiveness and worth by test score improvement, the many dimensions of what schools provide are often dangerously reduced or ignored in the name of progress and accountability. Instead of returning with a determination of whether primary-language spaces help or hurt students, pursuing my question led to a complex array of stories, experiences, and group subcultures that begged not for judgment or approval but for sensitivity toward the nuances and struggles of adolescence, culture, and education. I could easily mount an argument for the merits of bilingual education, for the value of the ELC, and for the importance of the school to the district and community. There are opportunity costs that come with those benefits, too.

Recognizing these complexities as a researcher has sensitized me as a teacher to both the importance and impact of various types of collective social spaces, and simultaneously to the indeterminacy of how those spaces take meaning for particular students. Following students in and out of the classrooms and hallways, I was poignantly reminded of and struck by the variegated experiences of my own immigration, the way that despite traversing continents, this particular concrete sidewalk or that particular chalkboard became token reminders of familiarity or estrangement, intelligibility or mystification, security or danger. Keeping this in mind, I sought to create a classroom and support a campus where students could, individually and collectively, attempt to define and reconstruct spaces with their own labels, meanings, and possibilities. An early project in my classroom involved giving students cameras with which to take pictures of things they wanted to change in their neighborhood and writing descriptive, narrative, and argumentative pieces in order to imagine and bring about the changes they desired. My hope is that English becomes a language not of their marginalization but of their agency, side by side with their primary languages, a means by which they not only comprehend but also transform spaces, and that they transform spaces to be more inclusive not only of themselves but also of the many others with whom they share those spaces.

I end with an image. Students of all kinds lingered at the ELC. Long after they had left the school, whether they felt as though the school was a place where they could belong or just a place where they were less marginal, or perhaps even a place where they endured the hardest stages of their lives, they still lingered at the school if they could. When their home schools had days off, they would drift back to the ELC; the Spanish speakers, the Tagalog speakers, the Farsi speakers, the ones who were here for a short time, and the ones who remained for longer stints, all found a kind of refuge returning to the school. I often wondered why even the students who spent their first year at the school unable to communicate with teachers or with other students would still come back to visit often. My guess is that whether students are disoriented in a new world alone or disoriented in a new world with others, returning to the place where they first found some resolution, where they first found their sea legs in an ocean of unfamiliarity, reminded them that the challenges they face are not insurmountable. They have overcome them before.

CHAPTER 7

Chumpas, los Bilis, and *Peros*?

The Intersection and Collision of Language Communities in a Middle School Newcomer Classroom

Danny C. Martinez

During the 2001–2002 academic year, I was a first-year teacher at Valencia Middle School, a large school in an urban school district. During this year I taught 2 block periods of English as a second language (ESL) humanities in addition to a reading course for English language learners (ELLs). Every day I saw over 60 "newcomers," those categorized as English language learners (ELLs), specifically those who were recent arrivals to the United States and whose primary language was Spanish. I was only 23 years old and fairly new to the community, having moved from Los Angeles to the San Francisco Bay Area the previous year to begin the Multicultural Urban Secondary English (MUSE) program. Even after student teaching in the community previously, I still felt like an outsider. Despite the difficulty I experienced adjusting, my time at Valencia and in the surrounding community of Dolores powerfully shaped the work that I would do as a teacher for years after and continues to inspire my research and my work in teacher education. At Valencia I came to understand how language is intimately tied to who we are as individuals and that speaking the language of our families and communities is a *right* that as educators we must preserve for the children, youth, and teachers who enter our classrooms.

As I reflect on my first year of teaching, I still wonder why I was chosen to teach the "newcomer" group without a thorough evaluation of my own Spanish language practices. Was it because I was one of the few Latinos at the school, and it was assumed that I spoke Spanish "well enough"? The truth was that I was embarrassed by my *pocho* Spanish and feared that an administrator would *catch me* speaking it and fire me! I was also concerned that the Spanish I spoke would negatively affect student learning and derail their language development. I believed in bilingual education, and the school supported the notion that a student's primary language should be supported; however, I questioned my ability to teach my students simply because I did not speak Spanish with the proficiency I thought I needed.

While I was preoccupied with my Spanish language abilities, my students (and their families) were preoccupied with their English language abilities. They were experiencing, on a daily basis, pressure to speak English and they complained that their progress was slow. Their parents made it clear to me and other ESL teachers that they needed their children to learn English quickly to assist with translating and interpreting. In our own ways, we were all thinking about language. Our mutual attention to language, whether it be Spanish or English, became critical to my first year as a teacher, and I decided I needed to study the language practices of my students and myself, in interaction. This was especially true given the differences in our classroom language practices, something that many failed to notice. What fascinated me the most was how we dealt with what I call our linguistic "intersections and collisions." *Intersections* were moments when the varied language practices of our class intersected and introduced new meanings to words and phrases. *Collisions* were moments when debates emerged over the meaning of a word or phrase or when students offered corrective feedback to their peers or to me. The following question guided this study: How do the intersection and collision of languages (between students and myself as the teacher) create spaces for learning to emerge? This question was informed by the everyday interactions that I witnessed in my classroom, particularly classroom interactions where we shared our language practices with one another in ways that were not planned in official classroom spaces.

SOCIOPOLITICAL CONTEXTS OF LANGUAGE IN EDUCATION

Before my first year as a teacher, I was attuned to the debates around the language of instruction in public schools. I began teaching after the passage of California's 1997 Proposition 227, a voter-passed initiative that ended bilingual education in the state. Because of Proposition 227 the use of a student's primary language for instruction was severely limited through the requirement that schools implement a Structured English Immersion model for instruction, a model that immersed students into English without primary-language support. The district I taught in was not required to implement these changes because of a federal consent decree established in the federal *Lau v. Nichols* decision. This decision required the district to provide students with access to bilingual and bicultural resources for the languages spoken by students in district schools. Despite the consent decree, Proposition 227 led to English-only ideologies continuing to circulate.

During this time, California was leading the way in the standards movement, promising a framework of instruction that would facilitate the academic growth of all students. Administrators were calling for teachers to "teach to the standards." For teachers providing instruction to English language learners, this call indexed a demand to teach using English only, a move away from building on and using a student's primary language to support his or her development of English. At the federal level, bilingual education *was* still recognized, but it would take only a few years for the word *bilingual* to be erased from almost all federal documents (Gándara & Contreras, 2009).

EMERGING SOCIOCULTURAL PERSPECTIVES OF LANGUAGE, LEARNING, AND DEVELOPMENT

One thing I did know about *learning* was that an individual's language was a central tool that provided the necessary support for learning and development (Cole, 1996). In my lesson plans, I organized activities that allowed my students to interact with one another; I encouraged them to talk to one another using their varied language resources to make meaning. I was included in these conversations, modeling English for students and even speaking my *pocho* Spanish filled with "mistakes" that my students would consistently point out to me. While I worried about "getting caught" speaking *bad* Spanish, I eventually saw my "mistakes" as a model of the risks that language learners take when acquiring a new language. Students eventually took risks themselves, uttering new words and phrases laced with their *acentos* and common second-language-learner errors. Given my perspectives on the role of language, I was keen on listening to the language used in my classroom, and I quickly noticed a pattern of "intersecting and colliding" languages that caused tensions to emerge between and among the varied languages in my classroom.

In one particular class, with the suggestion from MUSE faculty, I provided students with a short understanding about how we acquire new languages, particularly since my students were frustrated with their English language development. First, I asked students to consider the importance of their languages to the varied communities to which they belonged. I asked questions like *¿Que pasará si no podrías hablar español con tu familia?* What would happen if you couldn't speak Spanish with your family? Before a discussion about this idea, students responded to the following question in their journal notebooks: *¿Como esta conectado tu lenguaje con tu cultura?* How is language connected to your culture? Elizabeth, a 7th-grade student from Nayarit, a state in Mexico, responded with the following journal entry.

Yo conecto el lenguaje con la cultura como algo muy importante
yo pienso que si dejamos nuestro lenguaje ya no nos re cordamos
de las culturas de nuestro país o de todas las tradiciones latinas y
vamos a querer aser otras culturas y tradiciones, y nes Yo creo que
Para aprender ingles nose nesecita dejar sue Idioma no las culturas o
costumbres THE END.

I connect language with culture like something that is really important
I think that if we leave our language we will not remember the cultures
of our country . . . all the Latin American traditions and we are going
to want to do other cultures and traditions, and I believe that to learn
English it is not necessary to leave your language or the cultures and
traditions THE END. (Elizabeth, January 29, 2002; transcribed as
written by student)

Elizabeth shared her belief that language is very important to participating in cultural practices, and if we leave our languages we will not remember the culture of our native country. Elizabeth's fears of cultural loss
were not isolated. Several students, despite their nascent understandings of
life in the United States, touched on the complex nature of what happens
to English language learners as they begin their socialization into various
English-speaking communities. Elizabeth also argued that if we (immigrants) lose our language and culture, ultimately we would begin to adopt
the language and culture of another group. Finally, Elizabeth stated that
she did not believe it was necessary to lose her own language and culture
in order to learn English. Here Elizabeth highlights a tension that some of
my students expressed. While my students had a goal to learn English, they
were concerned about losing their language and cultural practices as well
and wanted to figure out ways to prevent those losses.

Prior to asking this question, a number of students were being pres-
sured and encouraged by their families to stop speaking Spanish, or other
native languages, in order to learn English. Some parents and guardians had
already asked their children to stop watching Spanish-language television
and instead encouraged them to watch English-language programming, a
strategy consistent in immigrant families hoping to develop English fluency
among children. According to Wong Fillmore and Snow (2000), immigrant
students and their parents are routinely given the message that the home
language will only stump their English language development. "For parents
who do not know English at all, it is tantamount to telling them they have
nothing to contribute to the education of their children" (p. 12). It was
difficult to convince students and their families that their home languages
could help, rather than discourage, second-language acquisition. In considering Elizabeth's quotation above, I felt that my teaching *had* to take up

the tension she (and others) felt in learning English. I had to communicate to students and their families that their home languages were resources for learning English and that they *could* become bilingual and bicultural as they adjusted to their new lives in the United States.

Besides understanding that English language learners did not benefit from losing their primary language, I knew that continued development of their primary languages was necessary for their second-language development (Goldenberg, 2008). I decided to share with my students research on language acquisition to demonstrate that researchers believed that the best way to acquire a new language is through the use of an individual's primary language as a means of supporting their new language development (Wong Fillmore, 1991). However, the pressures to assimilate felt by my students and their families countered this perspective; therefore, a central concern during my first year of teaching was to promote a linguistically rich environment where languages were nurtured and all of us in the classroom were viewed as learners.

VALENCIA MIDDLE SCHOOL

Valencia Middle School's student body is 57.9% Latina/o, 19.7% Black, and 9.5% Asian, with the remaining racial/ethnic groups consisting of Filipino (7.6%), White (4.1%), and Native American (1.2%); 55% were English language learners. The surrounding community of Dolores was in flux at the time, and the demographics were shifting drastically because of gentrification brought upon by the dot-com boom, with the number of children in the community dwindling. With gentrification and rising rents in the neighborhood, few students at Valencia lived near the school, with some traveling on more than one bus to arrive.

The majority of my students had recently arrived in the United States, some with their entire families and others with few members of their family. A handful arrived on their own to live with relatives they barely knew. Overall, the "newcomers" in my class included 66 recent immigrant students in 6th, 7th, and 8th grade. They made up 31% of the entire ELL population at the school. The students came mostly from Mexico and El Salvador, with the rest from Guatemala, Nicaragua, Colombia, Peru, Costa Rica, Bolivia, and Panama. There were two Chinese females in my class, one whose family had immigrated to Panama from China and another to Mexico from China before migrating to the United States. Every student in my class was Spanish dominant, with a few who were already bilingual speakers of indigenous languages or Cantonese. Despite the dominance of Spanish, linguistic diversity still existed in my class, with each student speaking a variety and style of Spanish that they brought from their former countries and from regions in those countries. Despite the cultural and linguistic diversity of my students, many teachers viewed this group of students as a homogeneous group of Spanish-speaking "Hispanics" or Latinos.

DATA COLLECTION

My data come from field notes I wrote about key interactions in my classroom, specifically moments that reflected collisions and intersections of language among my students or between students and me. I jotted "raw" notes, regularly, immediately after classes to document moments where I witnessed a language collision or intersection. I attempted to approximate classroom discourse as closely as possible. I turned these raw notes into the field notes. I also used them to write periodic analytical memos. I extracted all moments when there was a collision or intersection of language practices and closely analyzed them. I looked particularly at how the intersection and collision of language related to the students' opportunities for learning in my classroom.

In the rest of my chapter, I will present three moments that highlight the intersection and collision of language practices and show some of their consequences. The moments I will discuss emerged naturally as my students and I participated in day-to-day classroom activities. It was a rule of thumb in my class that all participants, including myself, were learners. Anyone in my class could be an expert or novice at any time; these roles were dynamic and depended on what we were talking about.

The first example describes an interaction between a student named Adrian and me, on a morning before school started. It illustrates how language is ever changing and dynamic, as our languages collided when students and I borrowed and relied on different communities to appropriate certain words. The second example shows an interaction that took place during a classroom lesson where a traditional gendered language practice collided with the instruction in my classroom. This interaction shows how an instance of tension can facilitate learning in the classroom, while validating and bringing the language of a marginal community to the center, in writing, within the official space of the classroom. Last, I describe a moment that shows how the dynamics of expert and novice roles can lead to a collision of languages as members of more than one community intersected in an attempt to correct my own *pocho* language practices. Through these experiences, I have found that

- When there is a moment where the multiple language communities conflict, there is a space for learning that emerges.
- As this space emerges, a validation of language practices that may not be the official or standard forms of language spoken within the official space of my classroom occurs.

- When the unofficial student voices are brought to the center of the official classroom space, students engage actively in learning activities and also become the knowledgeable others, or the experts.

¿Es Tu Chumpa? Relying on Different and Dynamic Language Communities Outside of Class

Before class on a cold January morning, I had a conversation with Adrian, a 6th-grade student from Yucatán, Mexico. On this day, like many others, Adrian duped school security and ran past teachers, who demanded a hall pass from him, to make his way to the third floor, where my class was located. On this morning, Adrian and I engaged in an interaction that displayed for me how he and his peers were learning language from one another through their everyday interactions. On entering my classroom, Adrian asked me, "*¿Aye,* Martinez, is that your *chumpa*?" The following excerpt from my field notes captures how Adrian's role as a student/learner shifted, as *he* became the more knowledgeable person, since I had no idea what a *chumpa* was.

> Adrian came to me before class today and pointed to the bookcase in the class. "*¿Ey,* Martinez, is that your *chumpa*?" he asked. I had no idea what he was talking about. I never heard of the word *chumpa*, and I asked him, "*¿Que dijiste?*" (What did you say?) Looking quite surprised he responded, "*Te pregunté si esa es tu chumpa.*" Adrian pointed his finger in the direction of the room where several items could have possibly been a *chumpa*. Adrian was getting frustrated. "*¡Tu chamarra!*" he exclaimed, "your jacket, Martinez. *Tu sabes, así dicen los Guatemaltecos y los Salvadoreños, 'chumpa.'*" (You know, that's what the Guatemalans and Salvadorans say, *chumpa*). When Adrian said this, I began to laugh apologetically. "I'm sorry, Adrian, *nunca a oído yo esa palabra*" (I've never heard that word). Adrian's face seemed to show surprise yet interest at the same time. "*'Tu sabes Martinez, esos niños usan esa palabra, yo no se, pero así lo dicen, y ahora yo digo eso para que me intienden.*" (You know Martinez, those kids use that word, I don't know, but that's what they say, and now I say that so that they understand me.) (January 17, 2002).

Several elements in this interaction are interesting, including how throughout our conversation both Adrian and I code-switched (a pretty typical practice, especially during less formal conversations, but still atypical in some learning contexts). But what stands out here is the collision of languages, at the word level, that occurred in Adrian's use of the word *chumpa* to refer to a jacket, just as his Guatemalan and Salvadoran peers had done in his presence in the past. This collision was evidence that

Adrian had internalized a variety of Spanish that was not familiar to him prior to his interactions with his peers from Guatemala and El Salvador. In our interaction, Adrian was using his new knowledge of a word with me, ultimately teaching me another word for jacket that was similar to *chamarra* (jacket) or *abrigo* (coat) in Spanish. Adrian was surprised that *I* did not know what a *chumpa* was; however, he did not shy away from using the word. Instead, he used other words he knew in Spanish to help me understand the meaning of *chumpa*, scaffolding my own development of Central American Spanish.

After this interaction, I was interested in how Adrian first heard the word *chumpa* used by his Guatemalan and Salvadoran friends and eventually internalized this knowledge to become the knowledgeable one in our conversation. I was curious about the expanding lexicon that my students and I were developing. To help me understand this, the following charts illuminate how the development of one word, *chumpa*, might represent the language development of my students and myself with our classroom community. In Figure 7.1, I approximate the words that the participants identified in our interaction may have had for the word "jacket" or "coat" prior to interactions with one another, for example, before becoming part of the Valencia Middle School community. I mention these words as approximations since language is dynamic and individuals draw on diverse language practices, regardless of a shared racial/ethnic and linguistic community. However, these were the words mentioned with my interaction with Adrian.

After my interaction with Adrian, the words in my column grew by one, with the addition of the word *chumpa*. Figure 7.2 demonstrates this, in addition to other possible additions that all the participants may have had after interacting with Adrian. For the Salvadoran and Guatemalan students, Adrian could share words like *chamarra* (jacket) and *abrigo* (coat) with them. Adrian, of course, learned the word *chumpa*, a word that is used interchangeably for a jacket or a coat in Guatemala, and perhaps El Salvador.

While my interaction with Adrian was fairly short, it showed me how students were learning from their interactions with one another and with me, and expanding their knowledge of languages and their varieties. I found it hopeful to consider the power that students' home language had in our

Figure 7.1: Approximations of Participants' Knowledge of Words Used to Refer to a "Jacket" Prior to Interactions with One Another

Participants	Salvadoran/ Guatemalan Students	Adrian	Mr. Martinez
Words in each participant's lexicon for "jacket"	*chumpa*	*chamarra*	jacket
		abrigo	coat
		jacket	*chamarra*
			abrigo

Figure 7.2: Approximations of Participants' Knowledge of Words Used to Refer to a "Jacket" after Interaction Between Adrian and Mr. Martinez

Participants	Salvadoran/ Guatemalan Students	Adrian	Mr. Martinez
	chumpa	*chamarra*	jacket
	chamarra	*abrigo*	coat
Words in each participant's lexicon for "jacket"	*abrigo*	jacket	chamarra
		chumpa	*abrigo*
			chumpa

Figure 7.3: The Possibilities of Expanding Participants' Linguistic Repertoires

Participants	Salvadoran/ Guatemalan Students	Adrian	Mr. Martinez
	chumpa	*chamarra*	jacket
	chamarra	*abrigo*	coat
Words in each participants lexicon for "jacket"	*abrigo*	jacket	*chamarra*
	jacket	*chumpa*	*abrigo*
	coat	coat	*chumpa*

classroom. In my considering the possibilities, again, around our one word, *chumpa*, the chart grew even further. Figure 7.3 represents this expansion of participants' linguistic repertoire of words and their meanings.

Although this interaction occurred outside of "official" classroom time, it influenced my understanding of how students make meaning using their emerging and prior knowledge, expressed through their language practices.

In the following section, I address how these previous experiences intersect and collide with the "official" language of classroom instruction, and I consider what might have happened had Adrian been told that *chumpa* was not an appropriate or "correct" word, perhaps deemed to be unsophisticated because of its "colloquial" origins.

SON LOS BILIS:
TRADITIONAL LANGUAGE COLLIDES WITH INSTRUCTION

As an ESL humanities teacher, I had to integrate social studies into my ESL curriculum. In one of my teaching units about Columbus, the following experience occurred. I planned a lesson where I used a political cartoon from "Rethinking Columbus" by Bigelow and Peterson (1998). This cartoon depicts a White man dressed in a suit, pointing to a Latino family, a father, mother, and child, holding hands. The family is positioned to the right of the White man. To the left of the White man is a stereotypical image of a Native American wearing a fringed outfit and with braided hair with a feather emerging from the top. The White man is saying, "It's time to reclaim America from illegal immigrants!" The Native American man, with his hands crossed, is staring straight at the White man, telling him, "I'll help you pack."

For this activity, I employed a strategy called "reading the picture," where students were encouraged to make predictions and generate words or phrases that helped articulate the meaning of this cartoon without their reading the text. Initial responses from students included assertions that the family was *"Latina," "Mexicana,"* or *"Centro Americana"* and being kicked out of the country because they were undocumented immigrants. Some students shared their "reading" of the image suggesting that the Native American was going to help the White man get rid of the immigrants, while others viewed the Native American as an ally to the family.

When we began exploring specific characters, our conversation slowed down as we talked about the Latina in the image. Juanita stated that the Latina in the cartoon was *"gordita,"* or chubby. As I took note of this comment, female students made reference to popular media depictions of Latina mothers as overweight characters. Guadalupe exclaimed, *"En la pelicula de Amores Perros, la mama esta gordita!"* (In the movie *Amores Perros*, the mom is chubby). Susana added, *"En las novelas, algunas estan gorditas"* (In the soap operas, some [women] are chubby). As this whole-class discussion unfolded, the following excerpt from my field notes highlights the intersection and collision of language in the official classroom space. This time, what emerged was a distinctively gendered language practice that helped students articulate their concerns over the stereotypical representations of the chubby Latina cartoon character.

> *"¡Son los bilis!"* Sonia said excitedly. She repeated again, *"¡Los bilis!"* I did not understand what she was saying. When I asked her to repeat what she said again, other students joined her. I still did not know what she and other students were saying. Several other students joined in, exclaiming that *los bilis* was the main reason why some Latina mothers are overweight. *Los bilis*, for my female students, became useful to explain the physical weight gain caused by erratic emotions carried by a Latina mother. Many other students, when hearing what *los bilis* represented and meant, became cognizant and remembered hearing this word at some time. One of my girls said, *"¡Mi tía tiene los bilis! Subía de peso porque se preocupe de su marido, sus hijos y los biles!"* (My aunt has *los bilis*! She gained weight because she worries about her husband, her children, and the bills!). I learned that *los bilis* is one term

that explains the weight gain a women can experience, generally after marriage, because of family responsibilities. (February 2002)

Martha exclaimed that the Latina woman in the cartoon was chubby because she had *los bilis*. The introduction of *los bilis* into the official space of the classroom created a tension, as many students and I did not know the meaning. However, Martha's interjection brought other students, particularly female students, into the official classroom space to allow for a fruitful conversation about *los bilis* in relation to the topic of conversation, the Latina character in the cartoon.

In bringing the concept of *los bilis* into the classroom discussion, my students and I (again) became learners of a new concept that eventually would have multiple meanings in relation to the cartoon. Although the students were initially critical of how the Latina was represented in this cartoon, they used their own experiences and language practices to make some conclusions about why she would be chubby. *Los bilis,* according to my students, plagued this woman because she was stressed out, worried about her husband and child, and perhaps worried about their legal status in the United States. Our discussion about *los bilis* validated students' linguistic resources and cultural understanding of the their world, allowing my female students' tacit understanding of a medical concept to enter the official space in this literacy activity. While initial conversations about *los bilis* began with a few students talking to one another, bringing this discussion to the official classroom space allowed this linguistic collision to, again, foster a collective growth and expansion of linguistic repertoires. Had I not allowed such talk to occur, fruitful moments that, in this case, carried this activity to another level of understanding for many participants, including myself, would not have occurred.

This experience allowed me to consider the gender dynamics that can influence language practices. It was evident that the males in my classroom had not heard of this term, yet they were captivated by the explanations of my female students, laughing, and with a few males adding to this understanding. But the females in the class emerged as the more knowledgeable ones in this interaction. As the teacher, my role shifted to that of a novice, and I ultimately learned a new way of explaining a phenomenon that has not escaped me to this day.

¿Perros o Pero?

In another activity based on the same unit about Columbus, I previewed vocabulary for a book titled *The Untold Story*, which provided an indigenous Taino woman's perspective on the "discovery" of the Americas. This final example demonstrates what occurs as the teacher, the speaker of the official script within the classroom community, breaks the rules of the official space by failing to speak an official language "correctly."

There were many key words in *The Untold Story* that I believed my students needed to comprehend to understand the text. After writing several words on chart paper, I asked students to write anything they knew about these words with their group members. Students copied these words, translated what they could, and generated working definitions. Later, I brought my students' attention back to the official space of the classroom, to begin a whole-class activity.

After going through several vocabulary words, students asked for more precise translations for some of the words. When we discussed the word *viscious*, students wanted a more thorough understanding of the word, since their interpretation of the word as *vicio*, or vice, did not yield the meaning intended in the book. In my articulation of a definition I did not properly say *perro*, or dog; I failed to roll the *rr*. My field note explains two types of student reactions:

> Some students let out an "ohhh," while others quickly corrected me with shouts of *"perro,"* with emphases on the rolling *rr*. (March 11, 2002)

One group corrected my pronunciation, while the other group mistook my use of the word *perro* for the more vulgar use of the word, calling someone a dog, which sounds disrespectful in Spanish. When students blurted "ohhh" out loud, it was the usual indication that someone did something wrong in class. When I asked my students why the "ohhhs" were followed by laughter, Julio explained, "Mr. Martinez, *dijiste 'perro.'*" (Mr. Martinez, you said "dog"). Although I intentionally said *"perro,"* some students associated this word as the vulgar and inappropriate insult directed at someone. Realizing that I had crossed multiple language communities with my utterance, I became nervous, since I was also being observed by one of my professors. I was worried that I was "losing control" of my classroom, in front of another adult. My students, after correcting me (according to those who knew I pronounced *perro* incorrectly), and pointing out that I said an inappropriate word (those who laughed and later moaned, "ohhh!"), successfully reverted the role of the official classroom script. I was no longer expert. Here, students were successfully shifting expert/novice roles. Allowing students to "correct" me in my Spanish language afforded an experience where various languages intersected and collided in the official space of the classroom. It was within this space that I learned that my language practices, although accepted in many other communities, would be challenged. This challenge, however, resulted in a classroom community where all participants were expanding their linguistic repertoires.

CONCLUSION AND REFLECTIONS

As I revisit this research project, I am emotional and inspired by the memories of my first year as a teacher. The students in this class were new to the United States, and I was privileged to meet them and work with them for that year. I always worried about my success with them. Did I do enough? Did I mess them up? Did these students ever develop the English that the current standards frenzy requires of them? While I will never know the answers, I have come to understand, both practically and theoretically, that I was mostly concerned about creating real learning experiences for students and expanding what counted as learning.

The collisions and tensions that I experienced were spontaneous moments in classroom life that highlight the importance of understanding moment-to-moment interactions in our classrooms. I learned that many students in my class were able to learn from one another and from me, their teacher, *el mister*. We began to see *how* our varied language and literacy practices *counted* in our classroom.

Adrian's use of the word *chumpa* and the interactions that developed from this allowed him to assume the expert role, just as it did for the female students who introduced us to the notion of *los bilis*, and the rest of my students who corrected and chastised me for mispronouncing a word or saying an inappropriate word.

I worry about preserving such moments. In the years that followed, I was forced to use a scripted curriculum, without deviating, and to follow specific pacing plans while being observed by district-level "coaches" who enforced the implementation of curriculum. While I continued to insist that all languages should count in the process of learning, my work went against the grain. It seems important that what I learned during my first year continue to inspire the work of teachers of English language learners. The *right* of these, our most fragile children and youth in public schools, to use their linguistic tools in the service of learning needs to be preserved.

Authors' Dialogue on Complicating Culture

Jabari Mahiri

Sophia Sobko is infuriated by unsolicited, "simplified cultural explanations" of her students' struggles. She is often told that "they just don't care," "they aren't raised well," "it's all about what happens in the home," or some variation thereof. In addition to their not understanding the complexity of urban education, Sobko feels that people who make these kinds of comments don't see the enthusiasm for learning and desire to succeed that she has recognized in every one of her students. "Whether we are complicating cultural explanations, or the culture of a group, a school, or even a classroom," she noted, "it is important to be wary of the assumptions that we make and to give voice to the people we are speaking of. This is what I strived to do in my research during my first year of teaching."

Danny Martinez and Paul Lai echo Sobko's sentiments and further reveal how simplified cultural explanations carry over to diverse groups of immigrant students and other students for whom standard English is not the primary language. After his first year of teaching, Martinez moved to Southern California and began teaching high school English and ESL in a predominately Black and Latina/o urban school. From teaching experiences in both Northern and Southern California, he came to see that too many urban teachers and administrators failed to complicate culture, leading to static and problematic notions of race, gender, language, and literacy. He noted that his research as a first-year teacher helped him "shape a robust understanding of what *should* count as language and literacy for urban nondominant youth" and guided his work as a teacher "to disrupt static notions of culture . . . [and] particularly deficit ideas about Black and Brown youth."

In his subsequent teaching, Martinez found ways "to leverage the language and literacy practices of recent immigrants from Latin American countries, honor the hybrid language practices of Latinas/os born and raised in the United States, and build on the Black language practices of Black and Latina/o speakers." But these attempts ran counter to the "one culture, one curriculum mentality" he felt was pervasive in urban schools up and down the state.

Since Lai's first year of teaching, he, like Martinez, has worked consistently to maintain spaces where immigrant students can cultivate their primary-language proficiencies, their cultural ties, and their authentic adolescent identities, but he noted that his thinking on these issues has also evolved. "I came to recognize that spaces [that dispossess and marginalize youth] are accruals of legacies, discourses, and broader power relations, and now judge [the research in my chapter] as remiss in eliding more explicit discussions of race and racialization, class, gender, globalization, legal status, and other intersecting factors."

Additionally, Lai explains that "as a language teacher, I have become even more aware of how social context shapes language learning, making the presence and absence of certain kinds of spaces for language and identity development not only more significant but more complex as well." He warns against succumbing to a "paralysis of analysis" with respect to the "complexities of culture." He notes that "as a researcher I try to account for the layered influences on students' trajectories, but as a teacher, I seize the responsibility to work with the hopeful and creative students we serve to make a new world of their own." These considerations for complicating culture also capture the perspectives of Sobko and Martinez, and they are aptly summarized by Lai, who notes, "My concern is not only with the possibility of certain spaces, but with the creation of spaces of possibility."

Part III

CONCEPTUALIZING CONTROL

Prologue: Learning to Discipline Students to Internalize Their Discipline to Learn

John M. Scott

> Although I had been taught that (in theory) engaging, relevant curriculum would diminish negative behaviors, in practice this did not seem to be the case. As a first-year teacher, I have learned how truly important discipline is.
>
> —Nischala Hendricks

As teacher education programs take on the challenge of preparing new teachers to design effective lesson plans, integrate the latest technologies, navigate policy mandates, and honor multicultural student perspectives, perhaps no area of this preparatory work proves quite as contextually layered or amorphous as teacher control and discipline. Even the adoption of a standardized language around this crucial aspect of teaching, which ranges from classroom management to behavioral modification to disciplinary control, remains elusive and the subject of continued debate. Yet as the quotation above reveals, there is perhaps no more daunting moment than when the first-year teacher stands before a class of 28 students for the first time and tries to set in motion a body of rules, conflict resolution protocols, and behavioral practices in an effort to create a classroom culture where students feel safe and where learning potentials are maximized.

The three chapters in Part III conceptualize control through the lens of first-year teachers who problematize their preconceptions through observations and discoveries related to their work in order to construct well-managed classrooms that reflect their personal styles and strengths, adapt to their students' unique needs, and fit within the broader school culture. Each chapter differs in its specific focus and level of inquiry into classroom control. They are organized in this part from an examination of a restorative discipline process as a schoolwide disciplinary approach, to a classroom-level examination of the implementation of a new "progressive" discipline policy, to a close examination of a specific kind of classroom control issue, that of students' "yell-outs."

In all three chapters, notions of control and discipline are not framed as a teacher's desire to garner unflinching respect and exercise an authoritarian power and order over his or her students. Rather, each frames discipline as crucial to fostering a sense of school and class community, where respectfulness, compassion, and a sense of obligation to the well-being of the broader school culture are inseparable from student learning and success.

In Chapter 8, Eva Marie Oliver's study of her school's first "restorative discipline process" reveals key ways that this process helped resolve a violent conflict, but also a number of ways that the policy's implementation complicated the school's attempt to restore its culture and "heal" the two students involved in the conflict. Restorative discipline processes in schools are theorized within the larger framework of restorative justice that dates back thousands of years. Essentially, the theory is that all stakeholders affected by an injustice should have opportunities to discuss how they have been affected and also decide what should be done to repair the harm (Braithwaite, 2002). Three central concepts underlie restorative justice: that not only the victim, but also the community are affected; that the offender must make amends with both the victim and the community; and that the victim, offender, and community must collaboratively work to heal the pain that was caused (Zehr, 2002). This translates into education as a whole-school approach to discipline and building school culture (Charney, 1992; Hopkins, 2004), but it is not without critical problems in conducting the extensive process (Shank & Takagi, 2004). We see these considerations for an alternative approach to discipline play out in unique ways in the context of the small school community where Oliver teaches.

Nischala Hendricks's chapter follows Oliver's and offers a starkly contrastive approach to discipline and control. As a new teacher required to implement a strict, escalating set of discipline procedures, she wrestled with discipline practices that were just short of a "zero tolerance" approach. Despite the increase in the use of these kinds of procedures, there is little evidence that they either increase school safety or improve student behavior (Skiba & Peterson, 2000), and Hendricks's research reveals quite ambiguous outcomes of the approach at her school. Through a nuanced analysis of possible factors contributing to her seemingly paradoxical findings, she argues for ways to rethink this approach to discipline at her school.

In the final chapter of Part III, Rafael Velázquez Cardenas provides a microexamination of what he terms students' disruptive "yell-outs." Researchers like Gregory and Weinstein (2008) and Noguera (1995) argue that perceptions of disruptive behaviors may not be accurately interpreted or connected to the real causes. Through his diligent compilation of a list of such yell-outs, collected via observations of other classes as well as detailed weekly memos reflecting on yell-outs in his own classes, Velázquez Cardenas was able to construct a category system through which he identified and clarified the actual causes or motives for behaviors that have largely been misinterpreted. He did this by documenting both the frequency of particular kinds of yell-outs and the specific contexts or contributing factors of those yell-outs. He was thus able to demonstrate that, contrary to his initial beliefs that most yell-outs would fall under the category of defiance of teacher directives, he found instead that this kind of yell-out accounts for only 1% of all observed vociferous acts. Importantly, he found that the vast majority of student yell-outs either fell into the category of attention seeking or were reactions to peer provocation.

In each study, these teachers were able to use their findings to clarify what was needed to build toward truly effective discipline policies and practices. Also, in each of the three school settings, they found that to be successful, discipline procedures needed to work toward students' internalizing disciplined behaviors rather than discipline and control simply being imposed.

CHAPTER 8

Restorative Discipline

Healing Students and Mending School Culture

Eva Marie Oliver

On Monday, September 26, 2011, Rachelle and Maria, two female students in my 12th-grade English class at Excel Academy, met in Principal Thompson's office to discuss their online bullying of each other. But the conversation erupted into a physical fight so volatile that Mr. Thompson had to call for help to break it up. In a subsequent email to the entire staff, he wrote:

> In all honesty, this is the most toxic dynamic that I have ever experienced in education. The vile nature of the comments that the girls posted on Facebook [was] absolutely horrible. It is a conflict that has been raging for nearly [4] years now, and it just gets worse. The Facebook comments were made at the end of last year, and they were simply the most dehumanizing, humiliating comments that I have ever read. The girls ultimately sat down in my office with me this morning and during the mediation a fight broke out between the two of them.

The background to these young women's bullying of each other was tragically complex. Rachelle was a victim of incestuous molestation and rape, and Maria had lost her father at a young age and was scarred by his death. Unfortunately, these were the things that the two students addressed and attacked in their online bullying of each other to consciously cause pain where they were each most vulnerable. And they were truly damaged after a series of hateful comments were exchanged.

Mr. Thompson immediately suspended the young women for 5 days, revoked their graduation privileges (which included going to prom, attending the senior trip, and walking across the stage at graduation), and threatened to go through the Disciplinary Hearing Process for expulsion. Instead, in consultation with Ms. Ursula (an enthusiastic supporter of restorative discipline), he decided to organize our school's first restorative discipline circle (RDC) and set the date for Wednesday, October 12, 2011.

Advisors and other significant adults in the students' lives were invited to participate. In total, eleven adults, including myself, and one youth participant committed to attend the restorative circle to support the two young women. It was my first participation in a formal restorative discipline event, and my colleagues and the two students also allowed me to research this process as it unfolded.

RATIONALE FOR STUDYING RESTORATIVE DISCIPLINE

The Excel Academy staff voted to officially adopt a restorative approach to discipline for the 2011–2012 school year. The essence of this approach is that perpetrators of acts that hurt others and thereby negatively affect a school's climate or culture must be able to admit and accept responsibility for what they have done and be willing to do things that are collectively decided to help repair the harm and restore the culture. Reading Amstutz and Mullet's (2005) book, *The Little Book of Restorative Discipline for Schools: Teaching Responsibility, Creating Caring Climates*, piqued my curiosity about this process because the goals applied "not only to those involved in or affected by [a student's or group of students'] misbehavior, but to the larger educational community as well" (p. 10). I imagined the positive effects that this approach to discipline could have on our school, which was already working to build a strong school culture. Also, both students were in my class, and though I did not understand the full extent of their altercation, I wanted to be an advocate for both of them. So I volunteered to participate, and also to study the potential benefits and drawbacks by exploring the following research question: How does the restorative discipline process facilitate or complicate students' ability to restore their place in the school community and culture?

BACKGROUND AND SCHOOL CONTEXT

Excel Academy is a small public school located in Northern California. Its mission, as noted on the school's website, is "to dramatically interrupt patterns of injustice and inequity for under-served communities in [the city where the school is located]. Through transformative learning experiences focused on the health and science fields, students are engaged in learning and skill building needed to succeed in college and their chosen careers." It has 270 students enrolled: 83% Latino/Hispanic, 7% African American, 7% Asian, 1% Filipino, 1% Native American, and 1% White. Approximately

63% of these students are English language learners, and more than 91% qualify for free or reduced-price lunch.

As a new humanities teacher and youth developer at Excel, I felt that the school was clearly committed to helping students grow intellectually and emotionally. For example, to support students' cognitive, emotional, and social growth, it specifically taught Habits of Work, Habits of Mind, and Habits of Life in each grade and across subject areas. The first two focus on study skills and skills for cognitive growth, respectively, while the final one focuses on developing "emotional literacy," by promoting love of learning, integrity, fearlessness, and empathy.

COLLECTING AND ANALYZING DATA ON RESTORATIVE DISCIPLINE

I used qualitative methods to document and analyze the first restorative discipline process at Excel. This included participant observations and videotaping of the RDCs, formal and informal interviews, and the collection of official school and other documents about the restorative discipline process.

Participants

Three major categories of participants in the restorative discipline process were the two focal students; their five key advocates; and seven "culture keepers," whose roles are explained below.

Focal Students. Both Rachelle and Maria are Latina women who have attended Excel for all 4 years of high school. They have never been friends, and during freshman year, Maria accused Rachelle of stealing her boyfriend. This allegation was not actually true, because Rachelle had her own boyfriend at the time. But since then, these two students have refused to sit next to each other in classes, or work together, or generally acknowledge each other's presence. Only weeks before their physical altercation, both young women separately met with me and informed me that it would be good to keep them apart if I wanted to avoid drama. I initially worried that they were taking advantage of my "new teacher" status. After their fight, however, I realized they had not been exaggerating their animosity toward each other.

Key Advocates. There were five key stakeholders in the restorative discipline process: Principal Thompson, Ms. Ursula, Ms. Smart, Ms. Hawthorne, and Ms. Martin. As an alternative to expulsion, Mr. Thompson asked Ms. Ursula, the former program director of the school's extended day program, to facilitate the process. This included preparing the two focal students and the adult participants to understand the norms and agreements for engaging in the restorative discipline circles, creating agendas for the circles, and facilitating during the circles. Ms. Smart, Rachelle's advisor, had the role of being Rachelle's advocate, while Maria's advisor, Ms. Hawthorne, was Maria's advocate. Finally, Ms. Martin had the role of helping both students complete any restorative activities prescribed by the process.

Culture Keepers. Mr. Acuña, Ms. Bell, Mr. Guzman, Ms. Barrett, Ms. Nuval, Bianca, and I were the other seven participants. Maria asked that Mr. Acuña participate beause he was a mentor to her. Ms. Bell and Mr. Guzman are youth developers whom Ms. Ursula asked to participate in the process because of their work with the extended day program even though they had limited contact with Rachelle and Maria. Ms. Barrett volunteered to participate in the process because she taught Rachelle and Maria when they were freshmen and had a long-term relationship with both young women. Ms. Nuval is considered by all students and staff members to be the "mother of the school" and is commonly referred to as Mama Vanessa because she is able to build a relationship with almost every student prior to his or her graduation. Both Rachelle and Maria often went to Mama Vanessa for advice and comfort throughout their years at Excel Academy and, therefore, wanted her to be a part of their circle. Bianca, Maria's best friend, was there to be Maria's peer support. Finally, I volunteered to be a part of the process because both Rachelle and Maria were students in my 6th-period Introduction to College Writing class during the first semester and also Maria was a member of a young woman's empowerment group I started called RAW (Real Ambitious Women). Therefore, I wanted to be an advocate for both of the young women.

Data Collection Procedures

My data collection centered on the two RDCs that were the key events of the process. I took extensive field notes during these discussion circles, and in addition to documenting what was said, I described the visual aspects of the room, such as the norms, agreements, and agenda written on the board and how people were seated. I also reviewed further documentation of the RDCs in the form of two DVDs by a researcher at the University of California, Santa Cruz, who videotaped our circles as part of her general research about our school. After both circle discussions were completed, I formally interviewed eight of the participants: the two students (Rachelle and Maria), Bianca (Maria's peer supporter), Ms. Smart (Rachelle's faculty advisor), Ms. Hawthorne (Maria's faculty advisor), Ms. Barrett (Rachelle and Maria's freshman teacher), Ms. Ursula (the RDC facilitator), and

Principal Thompson. I recorded and transcribed each of these interviews, which were prompted by the following questions asked of each interviewee:

- What were your expectations of the restorative discipline circles?
- What were your perceptions of the restorative discipline circles?
- Was there anything about the process that disappointed you?
- Was there anything about the process that gave you hope?
- What surprised you about this process?
- How do you think the time lapse between the two meetings affected the process?

Additionally, I conducted several informal interviews with all 14 participants, from September 2011 through February 2012, and recorded their responses in my teaching logs.

I also collected all the documents and paperwork used during the restorative discipline process, including the Action Plan for Restoration and the follow-up notes from Ms. Martin and Mr. Thompson's meeting about the restorative activities. Finally, I saved all the email correspondence that took place between the participants from September 2011 to March 2012.

Data Analysis

My data analysis process had three distinct phases: coding all my data for patterns and themes, developing and populating key categories based on the themes, and analysis within and triangulation of data across the key categories to arrive at my findings. In the first phase, I added to the notes that I took during the restorative circles by comparing what I had written with what I saw when watching the video recordings of the two circles, making particular note of facial expressions, body language, gestures, and eye contact.

I collected all the documents related to the restorative process (e.g., the Action Plan for Restoration and emails between the participants). I highlighted and annotated these documents. Next, I highlighted and annotated the transcriptions of all my formal interviews. Based on the highlights and annotations, I began to take notice of particular themes that were coming out of my data. I kept track of these themes by writing analytical memos. I divided each analytical memo into three categories: interesting information, great quotes, and things I wondered about that might need further investigation. Last, for each informal interview that I conducted, I wrote a critical memo in my teaching log where I would describe the event and analyze its significance to my study.

In the second phase of data analysis, I developed the themes that came out of all my "cooked data" into three categories: what happened before the restorative circles, what happened during and between the restorative circles, and what happened after the restorative circles. I used constant comparative analysis to evaluate what I actually saw and heard during the restorative circles and the experiences and reflections of the participants. I then did some reflective writing about key considerations that were emerging in each of the three categories.

In the third phase of analysis, I further worked the data in the three categories by using a binary code to delineate processes that *facilitated* the students' ability to restore their place in the school culture and processes that *complicated* the students' ability to restore their place in the school culture. This process led to clear findings that directly linked to my research question.

Position of the Researcher

The line between researcher and participant was challenging to navigate because I was invested in the success of both students, as their teacher and coach. When I learned that the young women would be going through the restorative discipline process, I volunteered to be one of the adult participants. After taking copious notes during the first circle, I realized that something truly researchworthy was taking place and decided to be a participant and researcher for the remainder of the process. In order to do this, I had to define clear boundaries for myself between participating and researching.

IMPLEMENTING THE RESTORATIVE DISCIPLINE PROCESS

Prior to the first restorative circle, Rachelle and Maria met with Ms. Ursula and Dr. Martin to prepare for the process. They were informed of the norms for talk and behavior in the circle and that they were responsible for writing reflections afterward. On October 12th, 2011, the adult participants had a brief meeting to discuss the process of conducting the RDC before the young women arrived. Then Ms. Ursula invited Rachelle and Maria into the space and began the process. The agenda was as follows:

Introduction
    Introduction of group members
        State your name.
        In one word, explain how you are feeling right now.
    Explanation of process
        Restorative discipline is a different way of dealing with
            discipline issues.
        Review entire agenda.
    Questions about the process

Review social norms
  Discussion about the norms that the young women developed
    Nobody speaks twice until everyone speaks once.
    Everybody must show respect toward participants.
    The process needs to feel productive.
    At any time, the young women can use the safety word, *room*,
      and the process will stop.
    No one in the room can bring up what happened between the
      two young women.
    The friends of participants will not mug (look) or speak
      negatively about the young women.
    All members must make a commitment to nonviolence and to
      respect school norms.
    All members must trust the process.
  Whole group must agree to social norms.
Talking
  Why am I here?
  How do I feel?
  What do we need to restore the culture?
Appreciations

The group of 14 participants agreed to meet for an hour and a half and quickly moved through the Introduction section of the agenda. However, there was 15 minutes of discussion about one of the requests made by the focal students that "no one can bring up what happened between the young women." As a result, the fifth agreement was changed to "All members will keep the conversation about what [generally] happened, not the details of the event."

Then the discussion changed to each participant answering the question "Why are you specifically here?" The general sentiment expressed by the adult participants was that they were there because they cared about the two young women. As Principal Thompson noted, for example, "This work is incredibly deep to me. . . . When you guys hurt, I take some of that home with me. . . . I want you all to be more whole than [you were] when you came to me [to talk about the Facebook issues]." The young women's reasons for being in the circle were a bit more specific. Rachelle explained that she was there to resolve the conflict with Maria and to fix the culture that they broke, while Maria explained that she was there to acknowledge the mistakes that she made and to show the group the changes that she was ready to make.

Interestingly, responses of the participants to the second question, "How do I feel?" (about the bullying and fight between Rachelle and Maria) ended up taking the remainder of the allotted time for the meeting. Of the 11 adult participants, six expressed feelings of *disappointment*. Mr. Thompson even stated, "This was one of the top five darkest moments of my teaching career. . . . Both of you went so deep into nastiness that it scared me." Three adults expressed feelings of *confusion*. Four expressed feelings of *guilt*. Mr. Thompson explained that he felt guilty because he believed that the physical altercation would have never occurred if he had talked to the young women separately about the Facebook bullying first. Four expressed feelings of *betrayal*, including Ms. Ursula, who said, "You both embody who [Excel] students could be, and you betrayed that." Two expressed feelings of complete *disgust* at how the young women treated each other. Ms. Barrett said, "I'm embarrassed, sad, and disgusted that you attacked each other as women!" To Ms. Barrett's comment, both young women had visible reactions: Maria looked down and Rachelle began to cry. Finally, five adults expressed feelings of *hopefulness*. Most notably, Ms. Nuval explained, "You two can grow from this experience and hopefully come to some sort of resolution . . . and learn from this experience."

The student participants said very different things. Maria expressed that she felt very different from how she had when the fight occurred—more mature. "I wouldn't have handled it the way that I did. . . . It wasn't worth it. . . . I regret it a lot." About the online bullying, she commented, "I told [Rachelle] that I could never get into her shoes, but I do feel bad about it because I could never feel what she felt. . . . I didn't even think about how she would feel; I just said [those things]." Through tears, Rachelle expressed her feelings of deep hurt, guilt, regret, and remorse. She apologized to Maria and then to Ms. Barrett for letting her down. Finally, she said, "I want to resolve everything."

Because these first two questions took so long to address, Ms. Ursula decided to end the circle in the middle of the process. She explained that the circle would continue the following Wednesday and that the participants were not allowed to talk about the event until the next meeting. However, the second circle did not take place as scheduled, and it became clear that interrupting the process had caused its own problems. For example, Ms. Barrett wrote in an email to everyone on Thursday, October 13, "I have felt incredibly raw since yesterday and I am on the verge of tears today. I really appreciate this process, but I wish we'd been able to complete it in one sitting rather than leave these emotions so exposed. Hopefully, nothing will set me off into a crying jag today."

There were other obstacles also, such as finding a time when all the participants could make the next meeting. Finally, we ended up scheduling the follow-up meeting on Wednesday, October 26—two weeks after the first circle.

The agenda for the second restorative circle was the following:

Introduction of participants
Review norms
Talking
    What do we need?
Follow-up plan
    List of items for the action plan
Appreciations

Three members from the first circle (the principal; Maria's best friend, Bianca; and Rachelle's advisor, Ms. Smart) were not able to make the second circle. After reframing the process, doing introductions, and reviewing the agreements, the participants reflected on what they needed for true restoration and healing to occur. After going around the circle two times to brainstorm restorative activities and get the young women's feedback, the group created an Action Plan for Restoration that would be passed on to Mr. Thompson for approval that addressed each of the school's habits of life—love of learning, integrity, fearlessness, and empathy. Ms. Guzman commented, "I want to see actual ways that you guys can embody our culture. . . . I want clear steps to demonstrate your love for our culture."

Dr. Martin volunteered to draft the requirements that the group came up with into the official Action Plan that spelled out restorative activities for which the two students would be held accountable. After appreciations for the process were shared, the RDC concluded, and the following week, Dr. Martin got all the participants to sign the final plan. From October 26, 2011, to March 15, 2012, I followed up with the circle participants and also worked closely with Rachelle and Maria on their restoration activities.

FINDINGS

After 5 months of data collection and analysis, I found three major ways that the first restorative discipline process worked to resolve the conflict between Rachelle and Maria and facilitated restoring their place in the school culture. There also were four key complications. Consequently, I report my findings in the two categories of "Aspects of Facilitation" and "Aspects of Complication." The safe space that the format of the circles created, the preparedness of the students and teachers, and the authentic and organic creation of the students' Action Plan for Restoration mitigated the conflict and facilitated the students' in restoring their place in the school culture. Alternately, the communication with teachers (especially around scheduling and time commitments), the time lapse between the two restorative circles, and the implementation of and accountability for the Action Plan for Restoration all worked to complicate the two students' restoration in the school's culture.

Aspects of Facilitation

A Safe Space for Complex Personal/Social Issues. The format and formal elements of the restorative circles were conducive to creating a safe place for honest communication where participants could clearly identify those who the process termed "oppressors" and "victims" in the situation. Maria's friend Bianca summarized this aspect of the RDCs when she said, "Everything was well organized. Everybody took a chance to speak. Everything was well coordinated. I think it was successful."

Both the order and flow of agenda items as well as formal elements like the agreements and norms contributed to the development of a safe place where difficult conversations entailing highly emotional issues could occur. Bianca's response in an interview captured this. She said, "When I was in there, it was like really tense. Like everything—everybody's words were really like—really deep, really emotional. And, I think that that got to both of them. The things that they ended up saying to each other—they were really meaningful." In other words, Bianca believed that Maria and Rachelle were able to get to a place of "meaningful" healing and empathy only because the RDC promoted honesty from all participants. Additionally, Ms. Ursula, the facilitator, continually reminded participants of their responsibility—to restore the aspects of the school culture that the young women had violated. These factors made the restorative circles productive, focused, and safe.

In addition to the process providing a safe space for all members, it is also designed so that everyone has an equal voice regardless of position, age, gender, ethnicity, and socioeconomic status. These conditions are key for restorative discipline to be able to be transformative rather than merely punitive. As Principal Thompson explained,

> Once we started [the process], I was like, this is going to push them
> . . . to reflect in a way deeper than I could get them to by myself,
> sitting in my office, or if I'd gone a traditional route. . . . I mean . . .
> the level of dialogue [needed] was not going to happen unless there
> was a body of people sitting there kind of holding them accountable.

The principal recognized that restorative discipline was going to be more transformative for Rachelle and Maria because it would give them the opportunity to reflect in a way that is not fostered in traditional discipline. As facilitator, Ms. Ursula was largely responsible for making sure that this deep reflection happened. Mr. Thompson even commented, "I trusted [Ms. Ursula] to . . . create a space—an environment—where kids are in a deeply reflective place, where they're trying to get in touch with their core issues as to why they're acting in a particular way. [When we're in a place] that gets us to deeply reflect about who we are, I think is how people change."

The formal element (or agreement) that most participants commented on was "nobody speaks twice until everyone speaks once." This agreement was important for ensuring that the space was safe and equitable for all members. As Ms. Ursula described, "There's not like crosstalk because crosstalk . . . tends to create in our Western culture—oppression. Because we are not—we haven't been trained to talk to women or children correctly, right? And, so when we have traditional crosstalk, then it comes already with the lens of oppressive factors." Although the young women were considered the "oppressors" in the restorative circle because they violated the school culture, they were also young women of color who needed to be protected from other oppressive factors, such as ageism, sexism, and racism. So Rachelle's and Maria's abilities to have authentic voices were both fostered and protected by the agreements.

Ms. Ursula was impressed by how well the participants upheld the circles' agreements, and she attributed much of the success of the process to this fact. She said, "What was great to see is when we put these norms [down] and people embody the norms, then they're starting to transform what a conversation can look like—that is, to remove the historical factors of oppression." The embodiment of the agreements by all participants created the safe space, which led to the honest and deep reflection that made the restorative process successful for Rachelle and Maria. Ms. Hawthorne noted, "I really like the structure . . . and formality. . . . I felt that the lack of 'crosstalk' forced me to be a better listener. Instead of thinking about how I was going to respond to the other group members, I found myself sincerely listening to what they were saying." The video recordings supported this in that they showed participants sitting up, leaning toward whoever was speaking, and giving eye contact, indicating attentive listening.

In addition to creating a safe space in the RDCs, enacting the agreements created opportunities for deep reflection and honest communication. Therefore, participants could actually express how they felt about the "oppressors" and why they felt that they had been victimized as a result of the young women's actions. This included participants expressing feeling of disgust, betrayal, and disappointment without Rachelle and Maria feeling attacked and being able to agree that it was the overall school culture that had been victimized. For example, Ms. Ursula candidly told the young women, "[As a result of your fight,] the school was victim, not either of you."

Therefore, participants were able to require that Rachelle and Maria demonstrate commitment to each of the four "Habits of Life" in order to restore the school's culture and their place in it. Since they admitted what they had done at the beginning of the process, they could move beyond being defensive to agreeing on what they needed to do to help. Maria shared this awareness during the second restorative circle when she said, "I need to think about myself *and* other people too. I'm a careless person, and I've realized that that is bad."

Participants Prepared to Enact the Process. I found that extensive preparation allowed participants to effectively enact the RDCs such that authentic healing and creative problem solving occurred. First, Ms. Ursula and Dr. Martin spent time with the young women prior to the meetings to help them to reflect on the fight and their mutual, longstanding animosity as a foundation for creating agreements that could lead to restoration of the school's culture. The adults I formally interviewed all commented on the students' thorough preparation. For example, Ms. Smart stated, "I thought they did a good job coming up with agreements and norms. I thought that was really cool, um, to create a safe space. And, I like how they met with the girls ahead of time." Similarly, Ms. Barrett said,

> I definitely expected [the girls] to come into the room, you know, kind of their arms crossed and scowls on their faces and just sort of staring at each other, or—or avoiding eye contact completely. . . . So I was really surprised when they walked into [the first circle]. They seemed like the were at a good place. . . . I give kudos to [Ms. Ursula and Dr. Martin] for talking to them and getting them prepared for that process.

Ms. Hawthorne felt that the preparation helped the two students be truly ready to restore/heal themselves and the school culture. She explained, "[The girls] already came to the table with a lot of regrets and like readiness to see from the other person's perspective, and I believed it. It felt genuine when they talked about like how it would be like to be in the other person's shoes. . . . It felt cathartic, and it felt productive." In short, the adult participants recognized that the young women's preparation partially led to the success of the circles. Ms. Ursula also appropriately prepared the adults prior to the first RDC. When interviewed, they all expressed that they were clear about how the circles were going to work.

The clear structures for participation in the RDCs facilitated authentic healing and problem solving. For example, both young women were required to come to the circle with written reflections that addressed each of the questions on the agenda. While both relied heavily on their reflections at first, they eventually relaxed and allowed a healing process to take place.

Ms. Smart noted that "[At first, Rachelle] just kind of stuck to what she had written down, but, um, after everyone like kind of opened up and just stated being honest, I noticed that she kind of veered away from what she had written down, and, you know, was really honest and personal about her response, which was, I thought, really good."

Similarly, Principal Thompson commented that when Maria entered the room for the first circle, her arms were crossed and her body posture was rigid. However, as the circle proceeded, she uncrossed her arms and her body visibly relaxed, allowing her vulnerability to come to the surface. Mr. Thompson also recognized Rachelle's increasing vulnerability during the first circle, saying, "I would say that [Rachelle] went about as far as I thought she could go . . . which really meant that for the first time—not the first time, but one of the few times and definitely the [most public time]— I've never heard [her] show vulnerability to that level." Had the participants not been as prepared as they were, this honesty, openness, and risk-taking may not have been possible.

In addition, being prepared for the RDCs allowed for creative problem solving. During the second circle, members reflected on what they needed in order to restore the aspects of the school culture that the young women had violated. The group drafted an Action Plan for Restoration that was passed on to Principal Thompson for approval. Creativity and openness were essential to the development of these restorative activities. All participants commented positively about creation of the Action Plan for Restoration. Most notably, Ms. Barrett said,

> I was surprised by how organic it really did feel because I knew the questions ahead of time and that we were going to have to say what we needed, what we wanted, and a possible solution. And, I remember thinking, I don't really know. So it was really interesting that I found myself saying that I felt they should do a Facebook project. . . . So it was really interesting to see that in that space I was able to process and think about things. . . . It actually went a lot deeper and was more authentic than I expected.

Equally impressive was the young women's ability to advocate for what they needed to achieve restoration. Both young women, but especially Rachelle, were able to articulate what they could and could not do in the name of healing and restoration. This self-advocacy can be directly correlated with the fact that the young women came into the meeting prepared with ideas (some vague, some more concrete) of restorative activities to which they were willing to commit.

My research clearly showed that the thorough preparation of all participants about the inner workings of the restorative circle process led to the creation of a place where true healing and creative problem solving could occur. All participants were ready and willing to take emotional and intellectual risks because they thoroughly understood and trusted the process. After the two RDCs were completed, Maria detailed how the process had worked for her by saying, "I used to feel uncomfortable being in the same room with her, and right now, I don't. . . . Um, what she said when she apologized and when I apologized, it made me feel like okay, I can do this. I guess it was just what she said and how she wasn't mad or she didn't look at me wrong. It was just—it made me feel better." Similarly, Rachelle noted, · "Me and [Maria] don't have anything against each other anymore. We don't mug—we smile. We can be together in a group."

I witnessed this change in their relationship in my class. On January 17, 2012, I wrote the following critical memo in my teaching log: "Although [Rachelle and Maria] do not work together in class, they are much more comfortable around each other. . . . I no longer see them shooting bad looks across the room. Furthermore, the tension [in the classroom] truly seems to be gone." In seeing the two students after the restorative discipline process concluded, Principal Thompson noted,

> To be able to see both girls like kind of in a shared space together both happy, not necessarily engaging with one another, but definitely coexisting—and coexisting in a way that was different than before . . . The fact that [Rachelle] could be in a space joking and laughing and talking and have [Maria] also have a smile on her face was like wow, that's like we've definitely done something here.

In this way, the school's culture was restored because the young women appeared to have come to an understanding and acceptance of each other. The toxic tension that had existed between Rachelle and Maria (and their friends) for more than 3 years dissipated, and this definitely improved the culture and climate of our small school.

The Action Plan for Restoration. The final major finding regarding things that facilitated restoring the two students was linked to the Action Plan for Restoration that was co-created and how it was closely followed by them. It was developed in such a way that both students clearly understood the essence of what they needed to do to restore their place in the school culture with very little adult intervention. Ann Hawthorne, Maria's advisor, summarized this aspect of facilitation well when she said:

> With very little prompting from [the adults], I thought [the girls] came up with some good suggestions, um, for what they needed to do . . . [for their Action Plan]. . . . I expected maybe to hear some

more parroting of like what the adults in the room were saying, and it seemed like they had really thought about it and had like, you know, smart empathetic things to say, which felt good.

Essentially, the Action Plan required Rachelle and Maria to work on a project together that would demonstrate their commitments to the four habits of life that were central to the school's culture. To demonstrate love of learning, they had to write an extensive reflection. They had to continue to work with therapists on anger management to demonstrate integrity. Additionally, they were required to work together on a public project outside of class to demonstrate fearlessness and also show forgiveness and be neither violent nor disrespectful to each other to demonstrate empathy.

The requirements of the Action Plan were arrived at organically in the RDCs. Because I was taking notes, Ms. Ursula asked me to search for recurring themes that would become the basis for the two students' restoration activities. For example, Ms. Barrett had said that she needed to see the young women "embody the culture of [of Excel] outside of the walls of the school." She even added that she needed to see the habits of life embodied on Facebook. Participants also indicated that they needed to see the two students demonstrate empathy. I added that in addition to the students learning to work together in my class, it would be good for Rachelle to join RAW, my young women's empowerment group. Maria was already a member. Importantly, the adults wanted to see the young women take agency in and ownership of their restoration. Dr. Martin explained, "I need the [Action Plan for Restoration] to really come from what you both say. What are you willing to do?"

The group committed to supporting the young women as they made their way through the restorative activities outlined in the Action Plan, and it turned out that the adult support became crucial to completing the required activities. Initially, rather than exhibiting agency, both young women needed a great deal of prompting from Ms. Ursula to begin the restorative activities. Up until late January, for example, they had done very little beyond continuing in counseling and doing some reflective writing. Yet in my follow-up interviews, I found evidence of true feelings of forgiveness in both young women. For example, Maria said, "I feel good that I said sorry. I don't regret saying it. And I know I'm not going to because I know what I did was wrong." About Maria's apology, Rachelle commented, "She actually apologized. I didn't think that was going to happen. . . At least it was something."

Additionally, both students eventually were able to demonstrate empathy for each other. For example, Rachelle noted that her biggest disappointment in the restorative discipline process was how the adult participants "looked at [Maria]. . . . I felt bad for her. . . .The teachers were so disappointed in her because of what she wrote about me." Although not quite as passionately, Maria demonstrated a feeling of empathy for Rachelle when she said, "I think that if we work on a project, I feel like that will—that's gonna get us not close, but I guess [it will help us] understand each other." So there was evidence that the young women arrived at a place of forgiveness and empathy that put them on a path to healing, and they ultimately completed those aspects of the restoration activities with almost no adult intervention. However, by January 2012, they had not completed any of the other major projects required in the plan.

This changed at the beginning of the second semester. Rachelle and Maria started working on a Facebook project together. They built a "like" page to talk about online bullying and other important women's issues such as teen dating, violence, and rape and linked other helpful websites to their page. They became so excited about their joint work on the Facebook project that they asked me to convene a meeting of all the participants of the RDCs to report and demonstrate to them what they had done. The group met on March 27, 2012, with only two members absent.

From all the activities connected to the Action Plan, everyone involved acknowledged Rachelle's and Maria's work and commitment to restoring their place in the school culture. Ms. Ursula said, "The young people were incredibly not just forgiving, but willing to be accountable. I learned that . . . I mean seeing the amount of forgiveness that both did to each other in the sense of truly saying, 'Okay, I'm gonna let this one go. You said something nasty, but fine. We're gonna work together.'"

Aspects of Complication

Problematic Communication with Adult Participants. I found that communication with teachers (especially around scheduling and time commitments) worked to complicate the restorative discipline process. The communication throughout the process was chaotic at best beginning right after the pivotal incident of the fight. For example, Ms. Smart said, "There wasn't clear communication to participants about, um, specifics of the problem, which I think everyone needed to know. Like if I'm gonna be in this circle and I am going to try to come up with some expectations for these girls, then I need to know what the problem is."

Also, because of problems with communication and scheduling, not all the participants could attend the second circle, which negatively affected the results. It was challenging and frustrating to find a time when all 14 members had 2 free hours. Ms. Hawthorne said, "For all of us adults, it was like a nightmare to schedule, and it was kinda breeding, I think, resentment between people—of all those email conversations and stuff. So, it just felt like negative because of the logistics, which sucks. . . . That shouldn't have been the focus." As frustrations grew, the emails became even more candid, direct, and brusque.

In an attempt to lessen the apparent tension, Principal Thompson made a joking comment in one email, saying, "I think we need a restorative circle for the restorative circle." Since the adult participants were the "protectors" of the school culture, their participation and "buy-in" were very important to the success of the restorative process, and the problems with communication definitely worked to complicate and reduce the effectiveness of the restorative justice process.

Significant Time Lapse Between Restorative Circles. The restorative process took much more time than originally anticipated. As a result of the above-mentioned scheduling complications, the group was not able to have a timely follow-up meeting after the first RDC, and this negatively affected the overall process. Although the participants were emotionally exhausted at the end of the first RDC, it was clear that the next meeting needed to happen quickly because immediate work was needed to address the rawness and vulnerability that had been created. So when 2 weeks passed before the group could meet again, people in the circle felt noticeably different and a bit awkward. As Ms. Hawthorne explained,

> I was disappointed that it got stretched over 2 weeks. . . . Because I feel like it's easier for adults to like get back into certain places, but it takes kids, especially these kids, longer.

Key Participants Missed Follow-up RDC. Because of the scheduling problems, three participants in the first RDC (the principal; Rachelle's advisor, Ms. Smart; and Maria's best friend, Bianca) were not able to attend the second one.

Without these three, the second circle had a significantly different feel and tone. Principal Thompson knew so much about the young women and their situation, and without him, the space and the level of reflection changed. Moreover, those absent were not able to help craft the Action Plan. Suggestions were not a part of the Action Plan, so when they eventually signed it, it didn't reflect their potential input had they been present.

Disagreement over Action Plan Accountability. As the second circle ended, there was disagreement between the adult participants about who (if anyone) should hold the students accountable for completing the requirements of the Action Plan for Restoration. Consequently, the lines of accountability for the students were not entirely clear as they worked on their restorative activities. For example, during follow-up interviews in February

2012, both students' advisors were unclear about what the young women had actually accomplished.

Some adults, including Ms. Smart, were hesitant to get involved because they were unsure of their roles in this phase of the process, while others, including Ms. Hawthorne, did not get involved because they wanted the young women to hold themselves accountable in completing the restorative activities. Additionally, the young women were just as lost as their advisors, and being unclear about whom they were accountable to in demonstrating their completion of the required restorative activities added complications to their process of restoring their places in the school's culture.

DISCUSSION AND IMPLICATIONS

As I observed and participated in the restorative discipline process, I felt that it was transformative. I had never seen adults and youth come together like this to promote students restoring themselves to positive places within the school's culture after they had violently violated it. I also found that the process helped both young women to heal emotional and physical wounds that they had inflicted on each other over a period of years.

Interestingly, Ms. Ursula reflected, "I don't think that adults have the same capacity for forgiveness as young people. So, I learned that yes, that muscle [of forgiveness] is still very fresh in young people, and I don't think we use that in school as a tool enough. So I learned that [restorative discipline] keeps the muscle being celebrated and healthy." This aspect of restorative discipline is what I found most unique and beautiful about the process. In short, the fundamental elements of restorative discipline provide schools and teachers with the opportunity for both healing students and mending classroom and school culture.

On the other hand, it is important to note that Rachelle and Maria's restorative circles were the only two that happened at Excel Academy during the academic year by the time of this study. The aspects of complication detailed above are the primary reasons why I believe the process is challenging to replicate, even in a small school. The circles took a great deal of time, emotional energy, communication, and adult support. However, my research led me to two suggestions that could make restorative discipline more sustainable for Excel Academy specifically.

Single-Session Restorative Circles

First, all restorative circles need to be done in one sitting. The goal should be to complete the circles in 2 hours; however, all participants should commit to up to 3 hours for the process. Ms. Barrett recommended this by saying, "I would really advocate for us revising the idea that we do it in one sitting," and every one of the participants I formally interviewed echoed this suggestion. Importantly, if the process had been completed in one sitting, then two of the aspects that complicated the young women's restorative process would not have occurred—the problems of communication between adults after the first circle and the significant time lapse between circles.

Adult Responsibility for Accountability

A second suggestion is that after creating the Action Plan for Restoration, one adult participant be assigned to regularly check in with the student (or group of students) who violated the school culture throughout the process of completing all the restorative activities. While several adult participants wanted Rachelle and Maria to be primarily accountable for the completion of their restorative activities, I found that this is not a realistic goal for high school students. As teachers, we know that adolescents need scaffolds to complete new tasks and to learn new ideas. Restorative activities are no different. Rachelle and Maria clearly needed significant support throughout the process in order to feel successful in its completion.

Additionally, the responsible adult should communicate the students' progress to all the adult participants on a regular basis. The awareness of progress or problems in the completion of Action Plans would allow adult participants to better support the restoration process after the circle closes. Despite these considerations, however, the first restorative discipline process at Excel Academy did mend the school's culture and provide true healing, empathy, and forgiveness for both Rachelle and Maria.

CHAPTER 9

Examining the Effectiveness of "Progressive" Discipline Policies

Nischala Hendricks

LOOKING FOR A DISCIPLINE STRATEGY THAT WORKS

Throughout my student teaching experience, I was quick to realize that across diverse classroom contexts, classroom control was an essential part of being an effective, influential teacher. Although I learned early on in my preservice coursework that an engaging, relevant curriculum would diminish negative behaviors, in the field, the challenge of promoting the kinds of positive behaviors conducive for a respectful and successful learning environment appeared more complex than merely a matter of curriculum. To be sure, negative behaviors are motivated by many things beyond the effectiveness of a lesson and include such factors as challenging home lives, special needs issues, and boundary-testing. Classroom control was not a central topic in my teacher preparation program, but in my first year as a teacher, I learned how important a role successful discipline policies play in determining the overall quality of learning.

When I began teaching at East Bay Vocational High School, the decision about regarding classroom control was not left up to me. During the summer before my first year, the 9th-grade vice principals elected to institute a new "Progressive Discipline Policy." This policy was intended to foster collaboration and interventions with students across subject areas by creating interdepartmental houses where new and veteran 9th-grade teachers could work together via weekly meetings to address behavioral and discipline-related issues. By formalizing a space for collective decisionmaking, the policy intended to facilitate teacher communication in maintaining a consistent set of expectations for teachers and administrators around disciplinary protocols and actions.

The longer-term goal of the policy, like that described in Chapter 8, was to generate a new school culture fueled by a collective approach to discipline. But this approach was very different from those of restorative discipline policies. It was hoped that a consistent and equitable implementation of the discipline policies, targeted at the incoming cohort of 9th-graders, policies that became "progressively" more severe, would provide a systematic approach to control that ultimately would instill in students discipline that they would carry through their high school years. It was also hoped that this approach would serve as a model for future cohorts of students.

In general, the Progressive Discipline Policy is implemented more for addressing minor negative behaviors and tardiness. Such minor negative behaviors—referred to as "lightweight infractions"—are definitively outlined in the policy and include things like failure to bring required materials to class, being disruptive, using profanity, and eating or drinking in class without permission. The policy also outlines protocols for more severe student transgressions—referred to as "severe infractions"—that bypass the progressive policy steps and result in an immediate referral for a meeting. The policy documents provided by the vice principals explained that severe infractions include but are not limited to such things as physical fighting, bullying, drug or weapon possession, threats to staff, and refusal to give over a cell phone.

The steps toward action outlined in the Progressive Discipline Policy include a five-step protocol for a "lightweight infraction." The first step is a verbal warning from the teacher. If the warning does not solve the problem, the second step is an informal conference. This conference is intended to provide an opportunity for the student to reflect on his or her actions and for the teacher to reiterate that if the behavior continues, more severe consequences will follow as set out in the discipline policy. The third step in the policy involves a phone call home, which provides an opportunity for the parent or guardian to reinforce behavior expectations in another context. Sometimes the call home is also used to negotiate outside-of-school consequences and incentives, such as warning the parents that their child would be serving an after-school detention if his or her behavior continued. At this point a teacher may also choose to send the student to a colleague's classroom with a reflection sheet. The reflection sheet is supposed to highlight the negative behavior and provide an opportunity for the student to gain perspective on the situation. If the problem is not yet resolved, the fourth step is an after-school detention. Finally, if that too fails, step 5 is a referral for a meeting with the vice principal for an administration-level behavioral intervention. Referrals would continue throughout the marking period until the system would finally reset back to zero for all students at the end of each marking period.

Although this policy at first seemed very strict and rigid to me, I was also glad to have a plan in place with a clear protocol for action that was consistent across the 9th-grade faculty, especially given I was working in a context that was quite different from that of both schools I had worked at previously as a student teacher. As a new teacher eager both to become a productive member of the school community and to please my administrators, I was optimistic that such a protocol would help me develop strategies for classroom control and ultimately help my students succeed.

SCHOOL CONTEXT AND STIGMAS OF THE ENGLISH/DRAMA CLASS

East Bay Vocational High school is located between two racially and economically diverse neighborhoods, and while students from all over the district attend the school, the majority live in either of two areas in the city. Interestingly, the school's career-oriented academies draw students from both public and private school backgrounds. In recent years, African American enrollment has decreased and White enrollment has increased. According to the school's 2010 WASC (Western Association of Schools and Colleges) report, 1828 students were enrolled in the 2011–2012 school year. Of those students, nearly 40% are African American, 20% are White, almost 20% are Asian, and less than 20% are Hispanic. The report also noted that half the students at East Bay High qualify for free or reduced-price lunch.

As a diverse urban school, East Bay High strives to meet the unique needs of a large population of students. The school emphasizes in their mission statement the cultivation of a respectful and safe school community in which *all* students will have access to rich curriculum that will help them to reach their fullest potential, and that *all* students are expected to graduate with the academic, social, and vocational skills needed to succeed in college or career training.

As in so many schools, however, achievement gaps persist in math and English between Latino and African American students compared with their White and Asian counterparts. One approach to ameliorating this problem has been to detrack students and create more heterogeneous classes for all 9th-grade students. As students move into the higher grades, though, it becomes more and more difficult to facilitate this kind of detracking, and even in the 9th grade, detracking is limited by the range of math and reading levels with which students enter high school.

In the 9th grade, students have a choice between two blocked humanities classes: English/California studies or English/drama. Although one might expect English/drama to be a popular choice, the course has developed a negative reputation over the years as a class that did not promote students to high-caliber (honors and Advanced Placement) classes in the 10th grade. Compounded by the fact that the class was originally designed for increasing engagement among low-performing students, parents and students alike have come to categorize the block as designated for low achievers.

Unsurprisingly, given the overrepresentation of African American and Latino students in such classes, my English/drama class was less heterogeneous than most other classes, with nearly 40% of my students having been placed on an "in danger to dropout" trajectory—a label designated by school administrators—and come to high school with sometimes extensive records of middle school misconduct, academic struggle, and absenteeism. Given the stigma of the English/drama class and the over-representation of students of color in at-risk situations, I felt that a focus on this particular class would be beneficial for understanding both the actual and perceived effectiveness of the policy, as well as for developing a comprehensive picture of how well policy objectives and procedures aligned with actual disciplinary processes and results.

RESEARCHING MY IMPLEMENTATION OF THE POLICY

In an effort to gain a more nuanced understanding of the ambitions and goals of the project, as well as gain insights into the effectiveness of the policy (both broadly across the 9th-grade faculty and in my own practices), I conducted a semester-long research study that drew on interviews with the vice principals who set the policy in motion, two student surveys, six focal student interviews, categorized discipline charts, and my own reflective journaling.

I focused my inquiry on my afternoon English/drama class, a 2-hour block after lunch, because my preliminary observations revealed that afternoon classes seemed to be have more issues related to discipline and student behavior than morning classes. This might have been the result, in part, of factors such as afternoon sleepiness, carryover frustrations from morning classes, or a restless anticipation for the end of the day.

For the focal students, I tried to select high-achieving, average-achieving, and low-achieving students to illuminate whether or not the policy was more or less successful relative to a student's previous academic performance. I also tried to focus on students who fit the typical paradigm of low academic achievement accompanied by poor behavior, but also students who did not fit this paradigm, such as those with high academic achievement but with multiple disciplinary infractions.

HOW I ANALYZED MY DATA

The corpus of my data collected over both marking periods of fall semester included interviews with administrators, student surveys, focal student interviews, teacher reflections, and a detailed account of all the disciplinary infractions and the subsequent protocol measures taken to address the infractions. I began to work the data by first calculating both the nature and the frequency of student infractions that I assessed in my English/drama clsss using a discipline chart I created that was organized by categories.

Next I analyzed the two sets of survey data to get an initial understanding of how students responded to the implementation and administration of the Progressive Disciplinary Policy over time. After transcribing the student and vice principal interviews, I developed a set of thematic codes to organize and understand how they perceived and reflected on the policy. I also used these insights gained from the interviews to determine the perceived success of the policy compared with its actual effectiveness in mitigating behavioral infractions as well as to reveal aspects of the policy that were working and those that required rethinking or refining. I then used my journal logs, teacher memos, and recorded observations to more fully contextualize or complicate the themes and patterns that emerged through the coding process.

FOUR MAJOR FINDINGS

Ultimately, I arrived at four major findings related to the effectiveness, both perceived and actual, of the Progressive Discipline Policy:

1. Overall, the policy did not diminish negative behaviors over the course of two marking periods, as the total number of infractions increased from the first to the second. This included both an increase in the total number of infractions as well as a dramatic increase in the number of students who received referrals (from only 2 in the first marking period to 13 in the second marking period).
2. The first two levels of the policy protocol (the teacher warning and the informal teacher conference) seemed to have the most impact on improving student behavior, though this impact varied in relation to the type of infraction.
3. Contrary to the evidence, students and administrators perceived that negative behaviors had diminished, and most students (69%, according to the second marking period student survey) believed that the Progressive Discipline Policy was fair.
4. While there appear to be conflicting intentions behind some of the policy initiatives and practices, administrators and students agreed that consistency is key to a successful discipline policy.

PUTTING THE TYPE AND FREQUENCY
OF INFRACTIONS IN CONTEXT

Through my careful documentation of each infraction in my classroom and the subsequent protocol steps taken to address them, the chart I created for type and frequency analysis enabled me to compare infractions across both marking periods included in this study. First, the chart revealed a significant increase in infractions, spiking from 95 in the first marking period to 131 in the second.

The most frequently occurring negative behaviors included such things as talking during silent work, throwing paper balls, using profanity, "play" fighting, and eating in class, while other singular incidents included throwing a pencil at another student, wearing a mask (after several requests to remove it), imitating a student with severe special needs in a mean-spirited way, and leaving the classroom before being dismissed. These lightweight infractions were mostly addressed either by way of a verbal warning or an informal teacher conference (steps 1 and 2 of the protocol), though I also observed a dramatic increase in the number of referrals made for a formal conference between the offending student and the relevant committee of teachers/administrators (step 5). This number spiked from 2 referrals in the first marking period to a total of 14 in the second, including fours cases where the same student received two referrals.

With only two marking periods of data, it would be difficult to make the claim that the jump in infractions and referrals was the result of the failures of the Progressive Discipline Policy to improve student behavior and accountability. First, it is possible that student behavior had remained essentially the same across both marking periods, but after one semester of becoming more accustomed to the policy as well as becoming more consistent in addressing behavior issues in my class through the protocol steps, the increase in incidents could have been a product of my becoming more rigorous in my disciplinary approach.

In the two student surveys, I tried to gain an understanding of whether or not students felt that, across the two semesters, I had become stricter in enforcing protocol measures by asking students to rate my strictness level. However, survey results revealed that the exact same number of students felt that I was "very strict" in the first marking period compared with the second marking period. And only two more students expressed that I was "strict" in the second marking period. Thus, while it is still possible that I did indeed increase my vigilance in monitoring and recording infractions, students did not perceive this in relation to my level of strictness.

A more likely explanation for this increase might be found in what teachers in the school referred to as the "honeymoon period" and notions of boundary-testing. The *honeymoon period* refers to the first few weeks of the school year, when teachers generally found that the number of discipline-related incidents was consistently low, particularly among the 9th-grade students. But for any number of reasons, behavior tended to deteriorate (or at the very least fluctuate) over the course of the year.

As students begin to feel more comfortable in their new classes, they begin boundary-testing to see if the teacher will hold them accountable for the expectations, rules, and discipline policies enacted at the beginning of the year. In my class, students were likely testing my follow-through in observing and documenting their infractions as required under the discipline protocol, and whether or not these early steps (warning, informal conference) would ultimately lead to formal referrals, detentions, or calls home. Regardless of the degree to which this honeymoon period and boundary-testing would have affected the increased number of infractions from the first to the second marking period, acknowledging such possible behavioral trends and finding more nuanced explanations of changes in behavior is an important aspect of reflective teaching practices and is crucial for the effective installation, management, and enforcement of a classroom discipline policy, including the Progressive Discipline Policy.

ADAPTING PROCEDURES AND CONSEQUENCES TO HELP IMPROVE BEHAVIOR

Determining the relative effectiveness of each protocol step and intervention is difficult because of the numerous contingent factors that can influence the data. For one, an interview with Mr. Radcliff (the 9th-grade vice principal) and survey data from students revealed much different perspectives about which steps were most effective for addressing negative behavior. Even among the students, there was variation in the survey data from one marking period to the next.

According to the first marking period student survey, step 1 was most likely to cause students to change their negative behavior. In the second marking period, students responded that step 2 was most likely to inspire change. More than half (57% in the first marking period and 56% in the second marking period) of the students agreed that the warning and teacher conferences were the consequences most likely to help moderate and improve their behavior. Given the similarities between steps 1 and 2, such as both steps being handled by the teacher within the classroom and falling within the broader category of "warning," I found it crucial to look more closely at why students regard these steps as most important for modifying behavior.

The theme of "warning" surfaced in nearly a quarter of the open-ended reflections across both sets of surveys. Some students reflected that they had not earned a single warning all marking period. Other students explained that their classmates' behaviors changed after the latter receiving warnings in steps 1 and 2. And some students wrote that they earned fewer warnings or that they hoped to earn fewer warnings. These comments were interesting because they prompted questions about the semantics of the policy, specifically how students viewed the meaning of *warning* in relation to the pending consequences. It appeared that students were initially confused about whether or not a warning was indeed a documented infraction and another step forward in the protocol, or if it was signaling that a future infraction would result in another protocol step. For instance, when writing a referral that included a detailed description of each of the five infractions one student received, on more than one occasion, the student argued, "But you didn't tell me that that was an infraction!" This ambiguity around the language of "warning" in the protocol and in my own enforcement of the policy quickly became a point of the policy that needed addressing and modification.

It was therefore important for me to be able to enforce the protocol procedures with clarity and in accordance with the values and strategies that I was developing as a first-year teacher. I first felt that I needed to loosen the rigidity of the protocol in order to be a flexible and compassionate teacher, as I intended to be, going into my first year. I began by issuing what I termed *pre-warnings* as a way to avoid formally beginning the protocol process with a step 1 "warning," in particular for circumstances where I believed students were making a conscious effort to modify their behavior but still struggling to meet the classroom behavioral standards as quickly as the protocol demanded. These pre-warnings took various incarnations from requests to pleas. I would sometimes find myself telling students, "If you don't stop talking, I will give you a warning." However, this only really resulted in more confusion about when a "pre-warning" formally became a "warning." And I quickly found that this strategy was doing more to complicate and confuse the process than it was serviceing a flexible and compassionate approach to discipline.

Behavior expectations soon became foggy, and this presented difficulties for me when I did have to document negative behavior, such that students would use my intended flexibility against me and argue that I had not given another student an infraction for the same offense. These struggles forced me to re-evaluate my values around discipline and reassert a firm disciplinary stance by making a point to reestablish my fidelity to the policy.

Still, despite these early challenges and my own continual modification of the protocol in my classroom, interviews with six focal students confirmed the survey data in that these students continued to regard the first two steps of the protocol as most effective in changing behavior and in that I was consistent in my follow-through in upholding the standards of the policy. In my interviews, three out of the six focal students agreed that the first two levels would diminish negative behavior. One student explained his perspective on the teacher conference: "After you talk to somebody, nobody wants you to call their parents." For this student, the warnings served as a threat that a more severe consequence would follow, and this generally worked to curb negative behaviors. Another student remarked:

> Warning one and two, it's like you know that you are going to get in trouble if you do something else. You know you are going to regret it—serious trouble. One and two are just telling you to be prepared for what's coming up.

Once again the difference between the warning (step 1) and teacher conference (step 2) appears somewhat blurred, but the sentiment is the same insofar as students believe that they should modify their behavior before the consequences become more severe as per the steps outlined in the Progressive Discipline Policy.

My interviews with administrators, however, revealed a slightly different attitude toward the effectiveness of certain policy steps. Mr. Radcliff, for example, shared an opinion that was generally consistent with the students as far as perceiving the first two steps as similar kinds of warnings. He explained:

> I think that they [the levels in the policy] get progressively effective. I think that the first couple of steps are somewhat abbreviated; you know you're just kinda warning a student.

Although the notion of the initial steps being warnings stays the same, Mr. Radcliff seems to rely on the more formalized discipline processes outlined in steps 3 through 5 to be most impactful and effective in mediating student behavior. However, I found that the warnings, which raised the possibility of further consequence, seemed to be the most effective steps in the protocol for improving behavior, whereas when students reached steps 3 through 5, there tended to be more of a continuation of the behavior and subsequent consequences. It is possible that, as an administrator, Mr. Radcliff's opinions are informed more by his interactions with the students at the more formalized levels of the protocol and miss the impacts the policy makes at the classroom level.

One aspect of the policy where there appeared to be a consistent desire for protocol modification among administrators and students involved addressing, disciplining, and ultimately mitigating student tardiness issues. Whereas according to the discipline chart for my focal class, some negative behaviors decreased while others stayed relatively the same or increased across the two marking periods, infractions related to profanity, "play" fighting, and yelling decreased. Tardiness and infractions related to talking, electronics, not sitting in one's assigned seat, sleeping, and eating did not diminish.

In some cases negative behaviors increased. The protocol procedures for addressing tardiness in particular, however, seemed at times counterintuitive to fixing the problem because the multiple conferences that resulted beyond step 2 infractions required that the student miss more class time, instead of leading to finding opportunities for students to make up the class time they had already missed because of lateness. Mr. Radcliff explains:

> I think that we need to work on the tardy piece. . . . We recognize that it is not good to continue to have students miss more class time; they have already missed some by being late. Sending them on a referral compounds it. But we still want to have consequences. We still want to have documentation in the student's record.

Clearly, managing tardiness is a complex task, not just in terms of addressing it from a consequences perspective, but also because I have found that tardiness is sometimes a behavior that is out of the student's control. For instance, students receive infractions for being tardy when they do not have reliable transportation to school or their parent does not write them a note for being late.

In another vice principal interview, Ms. Whitman agreed that managing tardiness was something that needed attention and revision. She reflected, "I think that I would like to take—I know it's crucial—but I think that I would like to take out tardies. We are less effective." Instead, she suggested tardiness be addressed at a schoolwide level rather than through classroom intervention. Currently, there is a schoolwide policy regarding tardiness; however, the truancy officer charged with administering this policy is overworked and without help in ensuring that the entire body of 2,000 students is held accountable for tardiness. Because consistent tardiness can be a factor (or at least occur adjacently) with other kinds of infractions, adjusting the protocol and finding effective measures to properly address the issue could also lead to more consistent student behaviors in other areas and help improve the overall effectiveness of the policy.

PERCEPTIONS OF POLICY EFFECTIVENESS AND FAIRNESS

Despite statistical evidence to the contrary, students and administrators perceived that negative behavior had diminished from the first marking period to the second. One initial explanation for this incongruence could be related to the aforementioned notion of the "honeymoon period," where perception was shaped by the anticipation that infractions historically increase in the second marking period, and so the policy had helped to at least temper this inevitable increase. In interviews, both vice principals expressed the opinion that negative behavior had diminished. Student reflections from the class survey reported positive gains in students' recognizing and addressing negative behavior. Additionally, focal student interviews reinforced the notion that the Progressive Discipline Policy had helped students to improve their behavior. As for the vice principal interviews, Mr. Radcliff noted during his second interview with me:

> I have seen some gains in individual students that I needed to address more frequently in the first marking period and I think that I am addressing their behaviors less in the second marking period.

This seems to be a significant improvement considering that the policy had been in effect for only two 6-week marking periods. However, Mr. Radcliff was more hesitant to claim that the policy had been effective for all students. He stressed the importance of consistently implementing the policy over time. On the other hand, Ms. Whitman highlighted that she was not seeing as many students on a referral as she had in the first marking period. She added, "I think that the problems that we are having with students is cutting down some." Although somewhat generalized and lacking rigorous explanation, these interviews are important because even though they are only perceptions, they are valuable in that the vice principals are observing the policy effectiveness from a schoolwide perspective, whereas my own observations and records were limited to my own classroom. However, administrators and students alike may have inflated perceptions of the policy's effectiveness for any number of reasons. For the vice principals specifically, since they chose to institute the policy, they may be expressing some bias in declaring its overall effectiveness.

Regarding perceived effectiveness from the students' perspectives, in both marking period student surveys, responses reflected sentiments that the policy had helped them to change their behavior. For example, one student wrote, "In the 1st marking period the Progressive Discipline Policy helped me improve my behavior because once Ms. Hendricks gives me a warning it doesn't happen again." Even more frequently in the second marking period students wrote about how they perceived the policy as effective for addressing and deterring negative behaviors. They wrote not only that it helped them to control their own behavior but also that they noticed how it helped their classmates to improve their behavior. Another student shared, "I can tell from others that it works well with them." It seems that students, over the course of the two marking periods, became aware of the impact of the policy on themselves and their classmates.

Interviews with focal students reinforced this sentiment. One of the high-achieving well-behaved students reflected:

> At first, I thought that a lot of people would be sent out of the classroom for no reason. After a while, I realized that people stop doing things so they don't get sent out. I agreed that it worked.

Even after just a few months, it appeared that students were buying into the policy and thus expressing confidence in its effectiveness. Again, the reflection above is especially interesting in light of the fact the number of referrals (students "sent out") actually did increase significantly in the second marking period. Another student explained that "any child know [sic] that they can change, they have to get better or face the consequences. It's kinda forced upon 'em." Although less supportive of the policy as a whole, this student shared the perspective that students are in fact changing their behavior.

Finally, an average-achieving student with a history of negative behavior looked back on his experience with the policy. He said, "Back then, like I used to get in trouble a lot—those first two marking periods. Now it's like nothing. I really haven't got a consequence for a while." This reflection supports Mr. Radcliff's assertion that there are strong examples of individual students having made gains in terms of improving their behavior.

Perceptions of policy effectiveness were accompanied also by a feeling that the policy was fair in addressing and disciplining negative behaviors and infractions. According to the second marking period survey, 69% of students responded that yes, they did consider the policy to be fair, a 12% increase from the first marking period survey. This increase from the first to second survey indicates that as students became more accustomed to the protocol, and as I improved in my own practices in consistently adhering to the policy procedures, students began to view the policy as more fair.

Perceptions of fairness extended beyond a view of the policy generally but also included fairness across genders. On the surveys, I posed the question of whether or not policy affected one gender more than another because my previous research and experiences had led me to believe that male students endured harsher consequences for infractions than did their female peers. Across the two surveys, however, students responded consistently (56% and 55%, respectively) that they felt the policy was administered fairly across genders, a somewhat surprising finding for me given my prior research and experiences.

To gain a more nuanced understanding of why students found the policy to be fair, I asked students to explain the Progressive Discipline Policy in relation to their previous middle school experiences. One of the focal students provided a particularly compelling perspective:

> I think that this one is more fair because at my old school they didn't really have a policy. But all they did was like if you do something—it was like unreasonable—like if you do something you're gonna get in trouble. Like if you was playing around like talking to your friend, they are gonna take it too seriously. They don't like give you a chance to explain. They just go straight to calling parents and stuff. And like this one gives you a chance to change and understand what you did wrong.

This thoughtful response was somewhat surprising because I experienced a few conflicts with this student during the marking periods over my enforcement of policy procedures. In the first marking period survey, he reflected that the policy "did not help me at all." However, in this testimony, he expressed a deeper reflection on the processes at work in the protocol. The fact that he emphasized the importance of giving students a chance to explain seemed particularly poignant and illustrative of a tangible benefit of the Progressive Discipline Policy and its emphasis on creating multiple channels of communication between teachers, administrators, and students through the referral conferences. In mentioning the importance of allowing students to reflect on their behavior through the protocol process, the student concludes not only that the policy is more fair than his previous school's apparently absent policy but also that the protocol procedures can help students recognize and correct behaviors accordingly.

Despite the many positive remarks from students about the fairness of the Progressive Discipline Policy, there were also students who were openly critical of it for various reasons. During the first marking period, one student wrote, "The policy didn't really do anything but I think it's unfair because I think we should start over on warnings everyday." Interestingly, while his opinion about resetting the policy each day remained the same from the first to the second semester, the student did not characterize the policy as unfair in the second marking period. This student's desire for a fresh start each day were echoed in some of the other surveys, along with other complaints about the policy, such as being "wrongfully punished."

Three out of 30 students in each marking period reflected that they had been wrongfully punished. One of the students responded that she had been wrongfully punished on both surveys. This student commented that "it helped but not really because we would get levels for unnecessary things and sometimes it wasn't us." This student might be identifying some of the challenges I encountered in both trying to be flexible in approach to the policy while also upholding the rigidity of the procedure, but also the difficulties teachers generally face in carefully monitoring every infraction while still trying to conduct a lesson. Another student explained, "I think that you guys should be less strict about it because sometimes you give us strikes when we didn't do anything."

This reflection expresses another crucial dilemma teachers encounter while trying to establish positive classroom behaviors: Teachers and students hold conflicting views and expectations about what constitutes appropriate behaviors in the classroom and a clash ensues between what teachers perceive to be fair and reasonable and what students deem just.

The policy's fairness was also challenged by two of my male focal students who criticized the rigidity of the policy. One of them, a high-achieving student who had already received two referrals from me, responded:

> I don't really think that it is fair because I feel like what we get in trouble for is really minor things and to be marked down as strikes is not good. I feel like we should have more strikes or like more drastic things to earn a strike.

Similar to how some of his classmates responded on the survey, this student resisted buying into the rigid nature of the policy. Although the policy clearly articulates the offenses as "lightweight," the student remained unconvinced about the merit of some of the consequences in relation to the severity of the behavior. He seemed unconvinced that such an emphasis and energy should be placed on changing such trivial behaviors. Despite my best efforts to explain to students how small disruptions in the learning process can quickly accumulate and create more serious problems for the classroom culture, most adolescents seem not to grasp this concept, or at least understand it to the point of consistently avoiding negative behaviors. This could be the result of where the students are developmentally and their struggle to be able to consistently look beyond their own immediate interests and desires.

Ending up on different sides of an issue with a student can happen with frequency and can even make addressing discipline issues in a fair way difficult. In an interview with a male student who felt wrongly punished from an infraction, the student reported, "One time I got in trouble and like the girl hit me and like I guess you got kinda confused about what really happened and it was on me." Immediately, I felt bad that I had punished this student without understanding the situation completely. However, knowing this young man's behavior history from my class, I began to probe further into the details of this incident, and a clearer sense of what had happened began to form in my memory. He continued:

> I think I was just like—it seemed like a joke the way I was handling it because I was like running around from her and like she tried to throw

something at me. But then like I thought that I didn't deserve to get in trouble for that because like she was trying to do something to me.

Right away the altercation between the two students was clear in my mind. I recalled speaking to both students about their behavior and explaining to the young man that there are appropriate and inappropriate responses when another student is antagonizing him (running around the classroom screaming not being one of them). Whether or not the student ultimately agreed to the fairness of his punishment, our conversation in the interviews did help in generating an opportunity to communicate to the student appropriate ways to conduct oneself in the classroom as well as how to respond to situations of peer antagonism. Although it did not remedy the past incident, the conversation helped the student either avoid such behavior in the future or, at the very least, understand better and accept why he was being punished for his behaviors.

FINDING CONSISTENCY IN A PLAN THAT WORKS

As I began this study, I thought that it would be especially important to understand the intentions behind the creation of the policy. Not only was this information important to me as a researcher; it was significant to me as a teacher who would be implementing it, as I wanted to feel some ownership over a discipline policy that I would be upholding on a daily basis. Whenever possible, I try to have clarity around what I am asking my students to do and why, both in terms of the academic goals of the class as well as in regard to classroom control and behavior management.

To gain this understanding and to see how other members of the school community understood the intentions and workings of the policy, I drew on my interviews and surveys to develop a diverse picture of the policy. First, I interviewed Mr. Radcliff. Mr. Radcliff was adamant about the fact that teachers must implement this policy with consistency and that this approach would lead to student buy-in:

> If a teacher will use this policy consistently, I think that over time the students recognize its fairness. And that's really important because inevitably you do need students in some way to buy-in to your school, your policy, your procedure and they need to see value in it. And they need to see that it is consistent—that it is not just applied to them but that it is applied to other students.

Prior to working as a vice principal, Mr. Radcliff had taught at East Bay High for more than 10 years. His emphasis on the word "consistency" here emerged for me as a key theme for implementing and maintaining a successful discipline protocol. Given that my previous findings suggest that 9th-grade students were concerned with and often had difficulty grasping the fairness in the behavioral management process, I wanted to make it a point to develop consistency in my own practices, to help make the process as transparent, understandable, and most important, consistent in helping students in the future recognize or take responsibility for negative behaviors.

Part of my responsibility as a teacher lies not only in making my expectations for good behavior clear initially to the students, but also in using the referrals and conferencing steps of the protocol to open up new channels for communication to help students understand both the consequence of the infraction and how the infraction could be avoided in the future.

My interview with Ms. Whitman reinforced the notion of having diverse school members, from students to teachers to administrators, all involved in the process and on the same page. She also shared an aspect of the intentions behind the policy that was particularly relevant to me as a first-year teacher:

> [The policy was designed] especially for new teachers so that they'd have something in place—that it would give them teeth in their discipline and they could jump right in and have a good policy and everyone's on the same page.

This notion of "teeth" is significant because the policy is something that is backed by the administration, which means that there is support outside of the classroom. Ms. Whitman continued to explain how the policy had been something that she had used when she was a physical education teacher at a local middle school. She used the policy to provide documentation and consequences for students who were not dressing for PE. Ironically, Ms. Whitman claimed, "I never had a discipline problem." Therefore, the origins of the policy were not related to classroom control but rather a recurrent issue of a lack of participation and of forgetfulness and lack of preparedness for class.

Ms. Whitman shared how her colleagues struggled with discipline and wanted to bring in an expert to give them a schoolwide system. She told me that the system cost more than $30,000 and that it was clearly not a good fit for her school context:

> It is crazy—it's just crazy. That is not a program for a school that has a large number of African American students because it's a program where the teacher keeps saying, "I understand but . . . blah, blah, blah." For African American kids in most family's households [they] teach that if I tell you to do something, I want it done, not six times

later. "I understand but you need to get that done . . . I understand but
you need to stop . . . I understand but"—*nooo*. Nobody in their right
mind is gonna let a kid go six times for one infraction before they
move on it.

I noted how Ms. Whitman stressed the importance of having the policy or program meet the unique needs of the school context. However, I
also found it interesting and somewhat contradictory that our Progressive
Discipline Policy was similar to that which Ms. Whitman critiqued in that
both protocols were not equipped to address negative behaviors quickly and
directly. The five-step protocol process actually appeared to share some of
the qualities of the six-step program Ms. Whitman described.

Ms. Whitman went on to explain how the administrators follow a consistent protocol. However, she quickly contradicted herself and complicated
this assertion. She said that "between the two of us [Mr. Radcliff and herself]
we know exactly what is gonna happen next." She explained what would
happen on each referral to an administrator. But along the way she added,
"Sometimes I do, sometimes I don't." This statement led me to believe that
at the administrative level, it is possible to be flexible and make judgment
calls, though this can in turn compromise the rigidity necessary for maintaining a consistent and transparent behavior management protocol.

This seeming lack of consistency at the highest level also became a point
of contention and frustration for teachers, who were asked to forgo such
flexibility in actualizing the policy in their classroom. In an informal discussion with a colleague, I shared that it was sometimes difficult to decide
which behaviors warranted an infraction. The teacher responded that students should receive an infraction for any behavior that does not meet the
teacher's expectations. She added that this is why we must be crystal clear
and consistently vocal about our expectations, as well as consistent in the
way infractions are documented and remedied.

As for the students' perspective, one focal student provides an important
insight into thinking about the issue of consistency, which she agreed was
vital to a successful policy:

I think that if the teacher is like more strict then the students will listen
more. 'Cause I have some teachers that constantly threaten students
but the students keep doing it 'cause they know that the teacher won't
do anything about it.

In this case the student seems to understand that being strict and consistently holding students accountable for their behavior is both fair and effective. I was impressed by the maturity of this student's perspective. Although

most students may not express that they want their teachers to be strict out-wardly, I believe that on some level, a consistent approach that holds them accountable is actually comforting and reassuring for them.

IMPROVING PRACTICES AND RESOLVING CONTRADICTIONS

Despite its fairly limited time frame and scope, this study has helped to illuminate the complex nature of classroom control and the amount of ef-fort, commitment, and experience needed to implement a highly structured, administrator-initiated approach such as the Progressive Discipline Policy.

Through the reflective practices of my teacher research, I learned that consistency and buy-in are essential for the success of a discipline policy, but that at times flexibility and compassion also need to play a role in maintain-ing a healthy and productive classroom culture, even though it would seem at times that structure and flexibility fly in the face of one another. Clearly, there is no magic solution to ameliorate the challenges of classroom control, particularly among students already stigmatized as being low performing and "at risk." Yet there remain prominent examples of teachers who have minimal problems establishing an orderly, respectful learning community and who appear to masterfully balance seemingly opposing ideas on how to mediate student behavior.

I strongly believe that methods of classroom control must be tailored to each unique classroom context. Regardless of the type of strategies or policy a teacher adopts for managing his or her classroom, however, I firmly believe that in order to be successful, a teacher must be consistent in how he or she both establishes the expectations and enforces those expectations on a daily basis. This study has revealed to me that consistency is the foundation for a fair and equitable approach to discipline. Students and administrators alike need to know that a discipline policy will be committed to being just, as will the teacher implementing it, and in the best academic and social interests of all members of the school community. As Mr. Radcliff expressed in his inter-view, student buy-in is essential to any aspect of a successful school culture, particularly regarding disciplinary issues and changing behaviors.

Unfortunately, consistency is easier said than done. Over the course of this study, I struggled to be consistent with holding students to the very high standards for behavior outlined by the policy. I found myself feeling sympathetic toward the various motivations behind my students' negative behaviors. As I got to know my students I came to appreciate more their daily struggles inside and outside the classroom, and I wanted to give them a break or show them some leniency, mostly to show them that I cared. I committed myself to an understanding of the fact that their lives were hard and behavior management was more than just following the rules, but in the process, I was also compelled to make some inconsistent decisions that compromised my pursuit for consistency.

In addition to trying to be aware of and compassionate toward my students' struggles beyond my classroom, there were also practical challenges to following through consistently with policy procedures, particularly when this required me to momentarily disengage from the act of teaching to record an infraction. In the middle of my lessons, I would have to take time away from teaching the whole class to conference with students about behavior. And I would inevitably end up sacrificing the 5-minute passing period to catch up on these conferences. Thus, I could go hours without a moment of rest for myself while still trying to find time to actually make detailed notes about the infractions for each of the referrals.

These time commitments to upholding the discipline policy were not confined to only the school day, either. After school, I would have to call parents, hold detention, and write emails following up on administrative consequences. Some weeks I would spend more than 3 hours calling parents about negative behavior. And if I did not stay on top of making these calls, I felt that I could not proceed in giving students further consequences because this would be in direct violation of the policy procedures. Although it became easier and the conversations more abbreviated over time, calling parents was very hard in the beginning. I would brace myself for the inevitable yelling that would ensue when I made these parent calls. The predominantly African American parents would often keep me on the line while they called their child over. The parent or grandparent (usually mother or grandmother) would proceed to reprimand and sometimes humiliate the child in a loud and intimidating tone. I dreaded this part of the call, but I dreaded even more the possibility of yelling that was directed toward me.

I had a few experiences with parents that made me aware of how different the school's expectations for behavior were compared with the parents' views. In a couple of instances, parents yelled at me because they were upset about getting so many phone calls regarding their child's behavior. Since all the core teachers had also implemented the policy, a parent could get upward of three calls a week about their child's behavior.

Therefore, when I was the second or third teacher to voice a similar complaint to them, some parents became very agitated. Also, I had an encounter with a parent who was upset because I had made a call regarding her daughter's negative behavior and she did not believe that the behaviors warranted such a consequence. The mother argued that it was a waste of her time to receive such a call and that it was not fair to the student to get in trouble for such minor offenses. The mother's sentiments here echoed responses in the student surveys and focal interviews where they found the punishments for what they deemed to be trivial behaviors both unfair and unnecessary.

Conversely, I learned that some parents were upset because I had waited until the third negative behavior before placing the call. On a handful of occasions, parents demanded to know why I had waited until the negative behavior had gone so far, not knowing that I was merely following the steps outlined in the protocol passed on to me by my administration. Some parents requested that I call them during class at the moment that I observed the infraction. I had to explain to these parents that I could neither call them during class nor on the occasion of every infraction, per the mandates of the protocol, but also because of practical constraints.

Although I do believe that it is important to get parents involved in upholding the expectations at school, it does not always have the desired impact. Some parents were very effective in getting students back on track with behavior. Other parents had little to no impact. Therefore, one place in the protocol that could benefit from great flexibility would be around parent phone calls. For instance, if a parent is consistently ineffective in terms of supporting his or her child to help modify negative behavior, and if the parent seems disinterested in or even hostile to this process, it makes sense to limit communication with him or her and search out alternative mechanisms to help correct the behavior.

As a first-year teacher, I most certainly wish that there were more definitive solutions to issues of classroom control. However, I do know that there must be a balance between structure and flexibility. The Progressive Discipline Policy is highly structured, which presents some advantages such as developing the necessary consistency for being an effective classroom manager.

On the other hand, this structure can be very rigid at times and prevent a teacher's making context-specific decisions that require some flexibility within these structures. Like most aspects of teaching, classroom control is not black and white with a standard key of actions to take. There persist significant gray areas that need to be navigated and negotiated by teachers, students, and administrators.

I believe that teachers should be supported and empowered to develop their own strategies and styles for navigating the behavioral norms and disciplinary procedures of their own classrooms. While schoolwide policies can help in creating some consistency and give teachers, and especially new teachers, some much-needed guidelines for helping to develop a healthy learning context for students, teachers must also be supported in adapting, modifying, and changing these protocols and policies to address the uniqueness of each situation.

CHAPTER 10

"Why You Gotta Keep Muggin' Me?"

Understanding Students' Disruptive "Yell-Outs" in Class

Rafael Velázquez Cardenas

Students' unsolicited vocal commentary or outbursts, what I have termed "yell-outs," are verbal behaviors that disrupted the learning and sense of community in my classes. Yell-outs are audible statements directed at another student, at the whole class, or at me specifically. I am a 7th- and 8th-grade teacher at King, an urban middle school in Northern California. I teach students who are considered below basic or far below basic in English language arts. I strive to have everyone be respectful of our classroom community and emphasize that students must listen to one another. Yet many students would still yell out during class in ways that were often spontaneous and meant to be harmless but also could reflect hostility toward others.

As a new teacher, I was concerned about these yell-outs that began happening in my classes on the very first day of school. Of course, I have worked to stop them by having discussions with the whole class and with individual students as well as implementing other discipline procedures. Yet across my classes some aspect of this verbal behavior would still occur almost every day. Some students would blurt out comments that actually made connections to our class discussions. For example, I might have called on a specific student to answer a question, and another student would yell out the answer. Although this demonstrated some level of engagement and excitement to share ideas, it also took away an opportunity for another student to participate. Additionally, students have yelled out comments indicating frustration with others like "Oh my God! That's *so* easy," or "How do you *not* know this?" Worst yet were verbalized insults directed toward other students that created toxic and potentially explosive situations.

It became clear that most of the students who exhibited this behavior were also struggling academically, and I wanted to understand more about why yell-outs were happening in addition to how to better mitigate them. What were the different types of yell-outs, and what was really attempting to be expressed? How were these verbal behaviors different from those of quiet students or those of students who were academically successful? These initial questions, and my need to get control of these disruptive behaviors, were what motivated my study of student yell-outs. Eventually, I focused my study on the following research questions: What characterizes the nature and range of student yell-outs in class? And why do student yell-outs occur?

MY SCHOOL AND CLASSROOM CONTEXT

King is a middle school with 25 teachers and about 700 students in 7th and 8th grades. The student ethnic demographics are 70% Hispanic, 10% African American, and about 20% other (including South East Asian, Pacific Islander, Asian American, and Caucasian students). The overall school culture is focused on student personal development and high academic expectations. It has slowly been increasing in its Academic Performance Index scores and strives to set a culture that will enable further improvement.

King is recognized as the flagship school of its district. The principal and vice principal constantly reiterate the goals of "building a school of champions," through weekly announcements, posters, meetings with target groups, and information in a bimonthly newsletter. These constant reminders and pressure are a reflection of the school administrators' drive to meet the API scores of 800 and to change the negative culture of schooling that resonates in the city where the school is located. Furthermore, the principal and supporting staff strictly enforce student discipline and constantly remind students of the school's high expectations for academics and behavior.

At King, teachers meet at least twice a month in their departments and also twice a month as an entire staff. The school also has many opportunities for students to get involved in a range of activities that attempt to build a positive school culture through collaborations between teachers and students.

I teach two sections of strategic 7th-grade English and one 8th-grade class of Intervention INSIDE English (which is an intensive literacy intervention course). My courses serve students who are considered below basic and far below basic in English language arts, determined through the California State Test (CST) and other standardized tests. My two sections of strategic English have students who are close to proficiency based on the CST. But students in my 8th-grade INSIDE class are considered far below basic.

I focused my research on student yell-outs on my INSIDE class. It meets for 2 hours every day, once in the morning during 1st period and again during 7th period. The school requires that I use a highly specified curriculum as a basic guide for instruction, but my principal also encourages me to develop and use other learning resources because she feels that the basic curriculum is not rigorous enough, although I am encouraged to use the benchmark readings whenever possible.

I have 22 students in my focal 8th-grade INSIDE class: 11 females and 11 males, 18 of whom are Hispanic, one who is Pacific Islander, two who are South East Asian, and one who is Filipino. Although it is designated as an 8th-grade class, there are also eight 7th-graders mixed into it. Many of these students expressed feelings of low academic esteem at the beginning of the year and occasionally said that they were not smart. I have also dealt with a lot of hostility among these students—some caused by rival gang members being in my classroom together.

Additionally, the students of this class travel together throughout the day because the majority of the intervention students have been tracked into the same classes. This tracking has been both a problem and a support for the community of our classroom. From the beginning of the year, I have emphasized the importance of having a strong community and peer respect in the classroom, but it is something I am consistently dealing with.

MY COLLECTION AND ANALYSIS OF DATA ON YELL-OUTS

My objective was to gather data that would provide information on the nature of vociferousness for my class and to illustrate the cause of the yell-outs. The methods for collecting this data were as follows.

Methods of Collecting Data

Daily Notes. To get direct quotes of the yelled-out comments, I carried a notepad for a little over 3 months and took notes of instances of yelling out whenever possible. I tried to capture the context, the date, and who made the comment as well. These daily notes provided me with a daily record of comments from my classroom and who was yelling out.

Audio-Recorded Interviews. I conducted interviews of the most vociferous students, two female students and two male students, to provide a gender balance, and asked the following questions:

Why do you yell out in class? Which classes do you yell the most in? What does the yelling do for you? Why do you choose to do it? Are your yells ever distracting? Would you say these yells ever help the class?

Furthermore, I supplemented these recorded interviews with several informal interviews in which I asked similar questions. This tool was used to understand why students yell out and to understand their self-perceptions of yell-outs.

Weekly Logs. I reflected on my daily notes once a week and compiled a weekly log of incidents and comments that stood out to me. I tracked the vociferous comments and any insights on why students yelled out. The weekly logs enabled me to recall incidents of the week and gave me a record of student comments that allowed me to see patterns and the role that yell-outs have in the classroom.

Class Observations. To get a deeper perspective of the vociferous students, and their yell-outs, I observed the most vociferous students in other classes. Using my prep periods, I was able to see the students in their 2nd- and 6th-period classes and was able to take notes on their vociferous comments as well as the context of their comments.

Student Work. I collected written samples of student journal responses that asked students why they yell out in the classroom. This enabled me to get an individual answer from different students about vociferousness in class.

My Approach to Analyzing Data

In order to analyze my daily notes, I first read all the written notes. Then, I began to reread the same notes while using a different-colored pen to write down any ideas or patterns of interesting information in the margins. Additionally, I highlighted any notes that I found interesting or revealing of patterns.

Furthermore, while I highlighted and wrote marginal notes, I also began to create an index based on what types of comments were yelled out. As I read through the different comments, when I felt a comment was different in its "intention," based on the context of the comment, who yelled it, and what was said, I created a category and a name to identify it. I continued this process and took note of what page I found these comments on. Finally, I reread the highlighted, noted, and indexed notes and tallied the amount of times each comment was made in order to find the frequency of each type of comment.

Similarly, I used marginal notes, highlighting for the student written journals, and the classroom observations in order to find patterns in the data. I was also able to index the classroom observations to find who the vociferous acts were targeted to.

Next, for the audio-recorded interviews I listened to each interview several times and transcribed notes on the students' answers. After writing down the notes I reviewed the interviews to find more detailed patterns. Similarly, I reread my notes from the informal interviews and tried to detect any common answers or ideas that stood out.

FINDINGS ABOUT THE NATURE AND CAUSES OF YELL-OUTS

After analyzing my data, several patterns began to emerge, and I arrived at three major findings.

Finding 1: There are several different types of yell-outs that occur with widely varying frequencies.

In this section, I describe the nature of the yell-outs. After carefully reviewing my daily notes, I noticed 15 different types of yell-outs. In order of least frequent to most frequent they were the following:

- Comments expressing defiance of teacher requests
- Comments about the class
- Comments about student feelings or emotions
- Announcements of possible conflict with peers
- Comments about the teacher
- Comments about discipline or commands
- Comments directed to other students
- Comments about gang issues or confrontations
- Comments clarifying work or class
- Comments about other students
- Comments about personal needs or personal requests
- Comments about self
- Comments about work or topics
- Comments to the class
- Comments to the teacher

Types of Yell-Outs

In the analysis, I had a bit of difficulty separating the different types of vociferous acts, but after several reads of the data, I was able to detect the different nature of the yelled-out comments. The vociferous comments in *defiance of teacher requests* occurred in the first months of our class and included comments like "No, I'm not going to be quiet!" from Natasha after I told her that I needed her to stop talking while I was giving instruction. Another student expressed her refusal to stay after class by saying, "I'm not staying for shit!" On a different note, *comments about the class* were vociferous acts that would reflect our class, our routines, or class expectations. These yell-outs occurred throughout the year and included comments like "What? We were louder in Mr. A's class and we never had any homework!"

The yell-outs about *student feelings or emotions* generally expressed what students were feeling. I would hear students yell out, "I don't want to go to the damned dentist" or "I don't feel very good" to show the way they felt; sometimes specific comments like "That poem almost made me cry" were also yelled out. Next, *announcements of possible conflict with peers* seemed to be comments that announced possible conflicts and were forms of warnings that were announced to the general class or the teacher. For example, when there were tensions between two students in our class, one of the students yelled, "Somebody better tell that boy to stop looking over here." Similarly, I have heard comments like "Let her say something. I'll beat her [up]." When I created a new seating chart, a student yelled, "I don't want to sit there, I don't get along with *paisas*!" to express his dislike of recent immigrants and a possible conflict.

Comments about the teacher mostly expressed comments about me and how students felt about me. When I asked students to stop talking during a quiet work period, students yelled out, "You are the only one who tells us to stop! You are always bugging us!" Students also make expressions like "Mr. V looks like the Foot Locker guy in Southland Mall!" and "You're messed up, you called my moms."

Another category of yell-outs, *comments about discipline or commands*, were vociferous acts that were made to question discipline of students in class or to question a teacher command. When I asked a few students to stay after school because of gang writing on desks, one student yelled out, "I'm telling my mom, that's messed up." Similarly, after I sent a student out for throwing a ruler, another student yelled in her defense, "It's not her fault, [the other student isn't] supposed to call a girl that!" On a different note, *comments directed to other students* were comments that students yelled directly to another student or group of students. For example, when a student would not stop disrupting this class with his talking a student yelled out, "Shut up, Kenneth! He needs you to stop." Students also made expressions like "You are always trying to act hard!"

The yell-outs about *gang issues or confrontations* included vociferous acts where students vocalized problems involving gangs or had confrontations because of gang tensions. In our class two students' tensions were building and one student yelled out, "Call me a scrap again!" as he walked toward the other student. Comments like "Why you gotta keep muggin' me?" were also made.

Yell-outs *clarifying comments about work or class* were comments that were yelled out to get more information about the work our class was doing or to clarify assignments. For example, students yelled out, "We have to write on that!?" and "Can we write about dogs?" when I presented a writing project. Similarly, when we were reading part of a play a student yelled out, "Are we going to do some questions or what?" to try to understand what the assignment would be.

Another category of yell-outs was *comments about other students,* where students yelled out comments about other students without directing them to the commented-on person. For example, during a stormy day, one student yelled, "This one kid was walking in the rain!" Additionally, when a student of our class had been absent for a few days, a student announced, "Maria has a 15-day suspension!" On a different note, the category *personal needs or personal requests* included comments where students yelled out their needs or asked for something that they needed. During a standardized test, one student asked, "Can I take my test in ISD?" wanting to be at the In-School Detention to avoid distractions. Other comments included yell-outs like "Can I move over to that group?" and "Can you charge my phone, Mr. V?" along with requests for using the restroom and drinking water.

The yell-outs *comments about self* were vociferous acts where students would share something about themselves. For example, when I finished giving instruction on a writing assignment a student yelled out, "Ohh, I get this!" Furthermore, when I tried to place a student with a group he yelled out, "I can't [even] work with myself!" Other comments that have been heard are "I got an F in history!" and "I never read. How do you expect us to read?!" Additionally, in terms of academics I have noticed that these yell-outs have generally been negative comments.

Comments about work or topics included comments that referred to the assignments and activities that we did in class. This included a range of questions like "Is this book for the smart people?" and comments like "This is boring!" and "I want to keep talking about this!" In addition, when our class was working on a difficult assignment a student yelled, "This sucks—I don't get this!" On another note, *comments to the class* were yell-outs that were meant to be directed at a general audience and included comments like, "Did anyone see the game? I went to the Raiders' game yesterday!!" and "What date is it?" Similarly, when we did an activity for the Day of the Dead celebration a student yelled out, "Who celebrates the dead?!"

Finally, *comments to the teacher* included questions and acts of vociferousness directed at me. For example, during a whole-class activity as I was writing notes for the class on our board a student yelled out, "Mr. V, why did you teach? Did you want to sell drugs?" There have also been comments like "I wasn't here, you are trippin', Mr. V," and "Did you see my new clothes, Mr. V?" Additionally, during our assignments students also often yell out comments like "Mr. V, can you come check my poem?"

Frequency of Vociferous Acts

Over the 3 months, I recorded 228 vociferous comments. According to the yellouts recorded in the teacher log, 56 fell into the category of "comments to the teacher." In terms of the least frequently yelled-out comments, in the category "defiance to teacher requests," I recorded 2 out of 298 comments.

According to my indexing, and my count of all the comments yelled, the students demonstrated more vociferousness in comments to the teacher (about 19%), followed by comments generally announced to the class (about 15%). The next most frequent comments were comments about the work (about 12%) and comments about self (about 11%). On the other hand, the least frequent yell-outs were made in defiance of teacher requests (less than 1%), contrary to the literature in education that suggest that defiance is the most common reason for vociferous acts. The next less frequent comments were made about our class in general (about 1.5%).

Most vociferous acts that disrupt the class are interpreted as defiance, but in my class I saw off-task behavior as questions and comments to the teacher and to the class and to share thoughts about our assignments and about themselves. This challenges the research of classroom behavior. As a new teacher, I found that this disruptive behavior was more commonly a way to seek attention, not one caused by disobedience.

Interestingly, after reviewing the data, I noticed that the majority of the vociferous acts were made by the 8th-graders in our mixed classroom.

Finding 2: The majority of yell-outs directed to other students were triggered by students and by subtle and less audible comments.

I was surprised to find that many of the yell-outs directed to students were prompted by other students. I had not considered that the vociferous students may not have initiated the disruption but may have been the louder student in the situation or discussion. In other words, the yell-outs directed to other students were most often a response to an initial comment or action that was not as vocal or clear. These outside observations allowed me to see that the majority of yell-outs in other classrooms were made in reaction to other students. I also noticed a difference in whom the yell-outs were targeted at, based on the sex of the vociferous students. Although these yell-outs, which are student-directed yell-outs, were not the most frequent ones in my data, it was interesting for me to find that these types of comments were commonly provoked.

In my interviews with the students, I heard similar comments that illustrated the need to yell out caused by other student comments or actions. When I interviewed Nancy, I asked her why students yell out in class. She responded by saying that "[students who yell] get frustrated. For example, if Kendrick was bugging me I have to yell it out, or else they will do more!" Nancy's comment demonstrated that her vociferousness toward another student was prompted by the other student's initiating action.

Similarly, Luis wrote in his writing journal that he yelled out "because they talk [insults at me]" and that other students will "say something stupid to get me mad."

During observations, I noticed a similar pattern. I was able to make observations of students during my two prep periods, 2nd and 6th, and was able to observe Nancy, Oscar, Kendrick, Natasha, Edwin, Ruben, and Brandon. In my two classroom observations of Nancy and Natasha I noticed that they were often yelling out in response to under-the-breath comments of other students. Natasha yelled out 17 comments during these observations. Five of these comments were directed at the teacher, 1 was directed to the general class audience, and 11 were made in response to other students. Six of these comments were yelled as a response to what other students either said or did to her. When a young man made a low-volume comment about a girl and hinted at Natasha, she responded by yelling out, "What!?" and to another young man, "Shut the %#&* up." Similarly, when Nancy showed Natasha a bloody bandage, Natasha yelled out, "*Eeww!*" In these observations, the majority of her vociferous acts were being prompted by other students.

Similarly, Nancy made 15 vociferous comments during my observation. One comment was directed at the teacher, 4 were directed at a general audience, and 10 were directed at other students. Among these comments to other students, Nancy yelled out seven times in response to comments and actions of other students. These yell-outs included telling students to "turn that off!" and yelling, "It looks evil . . . I don't care," when others would make noises or comments to Nancy.

Further, while the young men whom I observed were not as vociferous toward other students, out of the three yelled-out comments, two were prompted by less audible comments from other students. These comments told other students to "shut up," and asked a student why he was "telling people."

Additions to Finding 2

After reviewing my observation notes and both formal and informal interviews, I noticed the fact that the female students in my study demonstrated more vociferous behavior in reaction to the comments of other students. Many of the call-outs to other students, in the classroom observation, were made by young women to young men. Furthermore, Melanie and Nancy both pointed out the need to be vociferous when being bothered by other students, and in these cases bothered by young men. It seems like the young women whom I observed were being harassed more often than the men and were reacting with vociferous acts.

> **Finding 3:** The most frequent reasons for yell-outs are students' seeking attention from the teacher, the class, or other students.

Through my notes and journals I began to notice that many students made vociferous acts to gain attention. This idea first came to me from one of most vociferous students, who in an interview directly answered that students yelled out because they might not get the attention that they needed. The student interviews, written work, and recorded notes of vociferous acts support that student yell-outs are a way to get attention.

This finding of wanting attention is justified by the most populous yell-outs recorded in the daily notes: comments to the teacher, to the class, and about self. If a student was seeking attention, a comment to the teacher would ensure that the whole class heard what was being said, as it was directed to the facilitator of the class, where most of the student attention was. Comments to the teacher was the most common category of yell-outs in my class, followed by comments yelled out to the class. This vociferous act also demonstrated attention-seeking behavior as the yelled-out comment was directed at the attention of the whole class. Finally, the comments about self were expressing to the class something personal and trying to engage the class with that person's comments. Over half of the comments (about 57%) were made to the teacher, were made to the class, were about work, or were about the student him- or herself.

As I reviewed the interviews, I noticed that several students mentioned that vociferous acts are made in order to get attention. When I interviewed Nancy, she said that students yelled out because "they get frustrated. For example, if Kendrick was bugging me I have to yell it out, or else [he] will do more!" Here Nancy emphasized, with an example, that if she didn't yell out to get the teacher's attention, then she would continue to be harassed. The vociferous act was then being used as a way to both express frustration, and to stop harassing students by gaining the attention of the teacher.

On a different note, Nancy also expressed that students yelled out "because teachers don't pick us!" As soon as she mentioned this, Kendrick, the second student in the interview, agreed with great emphasis. Similarly, Natasha expressed that students yelled out because "probably some of them don't get enough attention. Like when they're raising their hands, you don't pick on them—so they just call out." Furthermore, when I followed up on her comment about attention, I asked Natasha if she meant attention at school, at home, or with friends, she responded that she meant all of them. I found it interesting that one of my vociferous students felt that not getting enough attention at home, with friends, and at school was tied to yelling out in class.

Furthermore, when I asked Oscar why he yelled out in class, he answered that it was because "sometimes [students] are not listening, and I have to yell out. Sometimes I'm telling them something and they are not paying attention, so I have to yell out." Oscar expressed using his yell-outs as a way to get the attention of other students.

Several of the students echoed this finding in their journals. A student who had been vociferous wrote, "I want to yell all [the] time in class so I can get in trouble, so the teacher can sent me out." He expressed yelling to get in trouble, and even to sent out of the class, which in a classroom draws the attention of all the students, as well as the teachers who deal with finding a place to move this student. He continued by saying, "I yell out some funny word and it make[s] everybody in my class laugh," demonstrating awareness of the effects of his actions.

Complications to Finding 3

Although many students mention that vociferous acts are a way to seek attention, I found it interesting that some students also mentioned that they did not know why they yelled out, or that it was influenced by who was in their classroom. Several students responded in their writing, "[Because], I don't know. 'Cause I feel like it. It's just a thing, that I like talking." I also heard Melanie echo this idea by saying, "It's just natural" in our informal interviews. In addition, during the interviews two of the most vociferous students mentioned that they also yelled out a lot because they had many friends in the class. On the other hand, another student mentioned that she frequently yelled out because she did not get along with people in our class. These comments sparked my curiosity about how the class composition also affects student vociferousness, as well as what makes students believe that their yell-outs were natural.

REFLECTIONS ON WHAT I FOUND REGARDING YELL-OUTS

When I began my research, I was hoping to seek ways to better support students who were struggling academically, and struggling within the school system. I originally wanted to do research on the tensions between students in my tracked Intervention INSIDE English class, which were very frequent at the beginning of the year. As I began to carefully observe the interactions in class I noticed that the struggling students seemed to be the most vociferous. I hypothesized that these vociferous acts would most frequently be comments of conflict, or insults, as I had witnessed several signs of tension during our first weeks of class.

I also thought that these yell-outs were only ways to create distractions and avoid difficult work. After conducting this research, I now see that although vociferous acts of defiance, insults, gang tensions, and confrontation do occur, the most frequent vociferous acts are those that seek attention. I also learned that yell-outs were positive and used for more than distractions, as some students used them to deter harassment or as a way to gain attention.

This project has enabled me as a first-year teacher to better understand why students may frequently yell out in class. Understanding that students may be seeking attention or reacting to the provocation of other students, I have been made more aware of the space that I create for students to express themselves, to share their thoughts, and to be noticed as integral parts of our classroom community. This has also made me conscious of the smaller actions and comments that may cause vociferous acts and has prompted me to find solutions to these issues. On another note, I have become more aware of the actions that the young men take in my class, in that they may be harassing young women students or making them feel uncomfortable to the point that the female students yell out.

Authors' Dialogue on Conceptualizing Control

Jabari Mahiri

Eva Marie Oliver, Nischala Hendricks, and Rafael Velázquez Cardenas all conceptualize classroom control as being predicated on caring, consistent, and respectfully communicative relationships with students that guide them toward higher levels of self-reflection and self-control. Based on his first-year research and subsequent years as a middle school teacher, Velázquez Cardenas notes that having caring conversations with students along with explicit instructional dialogues regarding the content being learned promotes more focused academic discourse and less disruptive talk in his classes. Hendricks adds that "without this respect and care, it is nearly impossible to cultivate classroom control."

Yet Hendricks also feels that no matter what the overall approach to discipline is, the students' perception of fairness and consistency are key. "I have found," she noted, "that the slight differences in the policy do not have a great impact on perceptions of fairness from students . . . [but] both students and staff struggle when various teachers approach the policy inconsistently." She believes consistency is important to adolescents because of their developmental preoccupation with justice and further that notions of justice may be especially important for students of color, who are more likely than other populations to have experienced injustices firsthand.

Oliver learned from her research that the restorative discipline process is itself difficult to control. Her study taught her that "it's a lengthy and emotional process that must incorporate a number of 'culture keepers' and student advocates in order to be successful." Yet she reports that she feels that her research pivotally "informed my classroom management style and the way that I interact with students. For example, part of the way that I now conceptualize 'control' is that students should be active participants in the norming process of their classroom. When students feel like they have agency [in the discipline process], they are more likely to respect the classroom agreements and accept responsibility for their mistakes."

Importantly, all three authors ultimately conceptualize control in terms of processes and policies that facilitate students becoming metacognitive about their behavior and adherence to classroom and school cultures. As Oliver aptly put it, "Without the metacognition, punishment is purely punitive. . . . With metacognition, punishment can be restorative because it gives students the opportunity to reflect on and learn from their mistakes."

CHAPTER 11

Reflecting on Urban Teaching Then and Now

Synthesizing the Power of Research by First-Year Teachers

Katherine K. Frankel and Jabari Mahiri

> Doing teacher research positioned me differently in relation to the work
> I did as a beginning teacher. Rather than viewing the problems a new
> teacher faces as a set of insurmountable hindrances, fodder for lunchroom
> commiserating, or the jurisdiction of technocrats, I was apprenticed to make
> problems the object of reasoned and rigorous inquiry. This set the tone for
> my teaching career. I could circumvent office politics and forgo despair, and
> instead apply an action researcher's mindset to teaching's vexing questions
> and issues. Name the problems. Find others to think reflectively together
> about them. Gather data. Conjure interventions. Rinse and repeat.
>
> —Paul F. Lai

As the work of the teachers in this book demonstrates, and as Lai eloquently explains, researching one's practice is a way to have agency as a new teacher, to turn problems into possibilities. But action research is not an easy thing to do, particularly during the first year of teaching. Consequently, the objectives for this final chapter are to delineate the benefits and challenges of conducting rigorous research during the first year of teaching and, in so doing, to further demonstrate the importance of action research to teachers. We take a novel approach to these objectives by again bringing the voices and insights of our nine chapter authors into a simulated dialogue about these issues.

From their current vantage points as educators, we asked the teachers to respond in writing to six open-ended questions related to the content and processes of their research as well as their perspectives on their preparation and subsequent experiences teaching in urban classrooms. We coded the teachers' responses using a descriptive coding technique (Saldaña, 2009). These codes were subsequently collapsed into larger themes. Through this process, we were able to synthesize the teachers' perspectives on the benefits and challenges they experienced as well as identify key analytic tools they developed while conducting action research. As a result, these teachers are brought into a vibrant discussion on what teachers need to know and be able to do in order to be successful in urban schools, and what teacher preparation and professional development programs need to do to ensure teacher effectiveness. Together, these insights illuminate how others might critically engage their practice in the early years of teaching and throughout their educational careers.

CHALLENGES OF BEING A TEACHER WHILE THINKING LIKE A RESEARCHER

In doing teacher research, the greatest challenges were also the greatest affordances. Research forced me to take a step away from the immediate and frantic needs of the classroom and to look more deeply and also more broadly at the learning and the practices in my classroom.

—Julia R. Daniels

One of the greatest challenges, beyond time, was to take on the identity of a researcher while trying to feel confident in my new emerging identity as a teacher. At moments, I was unsure how to be a teacher, and at others, I was unsure about how to be a researcher.

—Danny C. Martinez

As these teachers attest, one of the most significant challenges they encountered in their first year of teaching was navigating the demands of learning to be researchers at the same time that they were learning to be teachers. This dual learning process—which required that they assume multiple, at times conflicting, roles in the classroom and consider their practice through the lens of a researcher as well as a teacher—challenged them to be more analytical, critical, and reflective toward their pedagogical work.

The researcher lens, as distinct from the teacher lens, provided all nine new teachers with a different perspective through which to view their work in the classroom. It was a way for them to examine, critique, and reflect on their classroom practices. Depending on the type of research they undertook, the researcher lens led different teachers to different insights about their practice. For some, the researcher lens was a way to view problems and apparent failures as objects of inquiry; for others, it was an opportunity to step back and examine their classroom practices in a larger context and from a broader perspective. Finally, the researcher lens assisted some teachers in listening to and acting on the voices and perspectives of their students. Whatever the focus of their inquiry, all nine teachers viewed their research experiences as a reminder that they are always learners as well as teachers. It is this basic tenant of their pedagogical work—combined with the analytic, critical, and reflective tools of inquiry they developed as researchers—that, we argue, is a key to their effectiveness in the challenging urban contexts in which they teach.

VIEWING PROBLEMS AND FAILURES AS OBJECTS OF INQUIRY

> Researching the progressive discipline policy allowed me to focus on the aspect of teaching that I was immediately preoccupied with knowing more about and eventually remedying. Engaging in the research process allowed me to be a bit more patient with myself because I realized that I could play the role of observing and describing the situation before I had to jump to any conclusions about how to fix it. When I sat down in a coffee shop to comb through my data or draft sections of my research, I was able to detach myself from some of the intense emotions that regularly plagued my teaching practice.
>
> —Nischala Hendricks

> In my first year of teaching, as in my second year of teaching and in my current teaching, I struggled to help every student succeed, and I suffered when someone did not. My research was a way for me to examine more strategically, and react less emotionally, to what I perceived as "failures" on my part.
>
> —Sophia Sobko

For some teachers, the researcher lens was a way to identify problems or perceived failures, understand them better through examination and analysis, and then make changes to their practices in light of their findings to better serve themselves and their students. This was the case for Hendricks and Sobko. Although Hendricks looked at the intended and unintended consequences of her school's progressive discipline policy while Sobko sought to understand her students' perceptions of academic success and what underlay behaviors that seemed to contradict their academic goals, both teachers found that conducting research provided them with a more systematic and less emotionally charged way to understand something they had identified as problematic.

For Lai, the researcher lens was more than a different perspective; it was a way to combat "learned helplessness," to carve out a space for personal agency in his role as a teacher:

> I have come to believe the reason becoming a teacher researcher is so important in induction years is that beginning teachers face a huge number of dilemmas and problems, and while mentor colleagues and coaches, professional development trainings and workshops, and books and conferences provide vital growth opportunities, they can also foster a learned helplessness in teachers, a sense that someone out there somewhere holds the keys to evidence-based best practices and student-learning data metrics. Approaching our professional practice as teacher researchers counters that helplessness by equipping teachers with the mental tools of critical inquiry, data collection, and analysis.

In his research, Lai employed these tools of critical inquiry and analysis to better understand the diverse experiences of English language learners at his school and to gain insight into how he, as their teacher, could more effectively assist them as they learned English.

For Oliver, the researcher lens was a way to view her successes as well as her failures as objects of inquiry so that she could understand what it was that led to those outcomes and make adjustments accordingly:

> I don't allow something to simply work in my classroom; instead, I force myself to inquire about why it worked and how I can replicate that success. Similarly, I investigate why lessons go wrong in my classroom so that I can avoid making similar mistakes.

This attention to finding out why something works was evident in Oliver's research. Although Oliver found that her school's restorative discipline process was effective, she also investigated the ideologies that undergirded the process and contributed to its success and then considered how this knowledge might inform conflict resolution in her own classroom. For each of these teachers, the researcher lens was a way to critically and systematically investigate problems and perceived failures, as well as successes, with the ultimate goal of improving their practice and, in turn, better serving their students.

CONSIDERING CLASSROOM PRACTICES IN A LARGER CONTEXT AND FROM A BROADER PERSPECTIVE

For some of the teachers, the researcher lens was also a way to assume a broader perspective and longer-term view of the immediate work of their classrooms. Daniels, for example, reported that the researcher lens helped her to put the daily requirements of being a teacher into a larger context:

> The immediacy of teaching means that I could always be doing something that needs to be done right away: grading papers for tomorrow, planning for tomorrow, making a parent phone call about something that happened today. Researching my own classroom forced me to look beyond the next day and to think about the arc of my teaching over the course of a year. Sometimes looking up from the moment and thinking about where you want to go and what you want to try allows you to see more clearly and with greater insight. Research forces the researcher to take a broader view and perhaps a slightly wiser perspective.

In choosing to research Socratic seminars, Daniels was able to look beyond the immediate planning of the seminar itself in order to also think about how that seminar fit into the larger "arc" of her teaching over the entire school year.

Argentieri described the benefits of her research in similar terms. She credited the research project with giving her "a grand context and social purpose for my daily work," adding that it "kept my eye on the prize, which was ultimately to push boundaries of possibility in the classroom and to stand for the students' lives" during that first year. This perspective was particularly important for Argentieri, whose research centered on her implementation of an alternative curriculum that was initially met with great resistance by students as well as other teachers and school personnel.

Taking a different perspective, Nicola Martinez's research encouraged her to consider her teaching in the context of the other courses offered at the high school and gave her insights into how to make connections between her course material and what her students were learning in their other classes. By studying her school's project-based learning approach, Martinez had the opportunity to "think more deeply about the notion of critical thinking across subject material." Her research led her to rethink how she taught novels in her English class. She redesigned the English curriculum so that her students could compare a character in the novel *Like Water for Chocolate* to a historical figure they were studying in global studies. Her goal in designing this new curriculum was to "continue the learning process of critical analysis of subject material across academic disciplines."

For Daniels, Argentieri, Nicola Martinez, and others, the researcher lens was a way to take a step back and consider both the larger context and the longer-term goals of their daily work in the classroom. In this respect, the researcher lens served a purpose similar to that of the teachers who used it to look at problems (and successes) more critically. Through systematic inquiry and reflection, teachers used the researcher lens to view their work in the classroom from a perspective that was qualitatively different from how they viewed their work in their role as teachers.

LISTENING TO STUDENTS

For teachers like Velázquez Cardenas, Sobko, and Danny Martinez, the researcher lens also afforded a different perspective, but in these cases the specific focus was on listening to the voices and perspectives of the students themselves. In his investigation of students' "yell-outs," for example, Velázquez Cardenas remembered that he "began to listen to what was being said and why so that I could understand what was really happening in my classroom." Similarly, Sobko noted that "the beauty of my research . . . was that the methodology I chose to use required me to sit down one on one with a few students and truly listen to them." For each of these teachers, listening to the voices of students and attempting to understand their perspectives directly informed what happened in their classrooms. Sobko, for example, saw a direct link between her research, which required that she carve out the time and space to listen to her students, and their improved performance in her class:

> If I remember correctly, all my focal students did better their second semester than their first, and I wonder if this happened in part because I got to know them better through the interviews. I stayed in contact with my focal students the following school year and to this day I feel that I got to know these students better than many of my other students. If only I could have channeled all the time I spent fruitlessly worrying about my students or making assumption about them into sitting down with them one on one and truly listening to them! I am still struggling to find ways to do this when teaching a class of 30.

By listening to her students, Sobko helped to challenge and refute the inaccurate assumptions that she had made about them. This was an affordance of the researcher lens that Velázquez Cardenas highlighted as well:

> The teacher research gave me the ability to hone into the intricate details of my classroom and the student voice. This helped me take in many pieces of information before making any assumptions. In addition, the research enabled me to focus on one large question, while keeping me in the state of inquiry. This state of mind kept me from rationalizing with common lunchroom theories and dominant discourse that tends to blame students and their communities.

For Velázquez Cardenas, the researcher lens was a way to challenge his own assumptions about his students while also countering the larger structures and discourses within which he and his students operated.

Incorporating student voices in research led to their incorporation into the classroom as well. Danny Martinez attributed his research project with helping him "realize that students must talk, in ways that are organized around the content" and, consequently, "organize learning in ways that always allowed students to talk to one another, and to organize whole class activities in ways that made as many students comfortable to use their diverse language tools to contribute to discussions." Velázquez Cardenas remembered similarly dramatic shifts in his pedagogical approach as a result of his research project:

> I began to question how to guide the students' voices into academically productive conversations. I have learned to be more aware of the factors that I control as a teacher (classroom setup, curriculum, student expectations, and teacher-student dialogue). I have also tried to infuse more student voice and opinion in our classroom instruction while coaching students toward productive academic dialogue. In addition, I now ask more questions when conflicts arise in my classroom before assuming anything.

For all the teachers in this book, the research they conducted during their first year of teaching helped them to develop a researcher lens and an inquiry-oriented stance toward their work in their classrooms. Although each teacher focused his or her research on a problem or question that was unique to his or her specific classroom and school context, for all these teachers the research instilled in them a foundational understanding that teaching is an ongoing process of exploration. Put differently, all these teachers see themselves as learners as well as teachers.

TEACHERS AS LEARNERS

Whatever the topic of the research, at its core teacher research is about learning. While the "teacher as learner" concept is particularly salient during the first year of teaching, it is a perspective that these teachers have carried with them as their careers in education have progressed. We argue that their research experiences during that first year gave them the opportunity to hone the tools of analysis, critical thinking, and reflection that are key to being a learner as well as a teacher.

For many teachers, the research they conducted during their first year served as a model for how to be critical and reflective in their future work. Oliver explained how her early experiences as a "metacognitive" teacher researcher continued to shape her work as a teacher:

I am constantly critically evaluating my practice, my classroom culture, our school culture, and our school policies. This metacognition encourages me to always be very present as a teacher because I always want to be ready for the next learning experience.

Danny Martinez also saw the teacher research project as an opportunity to practice being "reflexive"; through his research, he realized that he still needed to refine his teaching, despite what he thought he already knew about "social justice, radical teaching, and critical pedagogy." He discovered that "teaching was an art, and at times, I closed myself to learning the practice of teaching because some of what we were being taught did not have a 'critical' perspective." At the same time, Martinez and Lai both called attention to the fact that the teacher-as-learner concept also, and necessarily, applies to teacher-student relationships: Martinez noted, "Urban teachers must have the ability to listen and observe what their students are already doing," while Lai explained, "Teachers in urban schools must learn to be continually students of their students." Indeed, the ability to be critical and reflexive is so important to Argentieri that she highlighted it as one of the essential factors for success for teachers in urban schools:

> Teachers in urban schools need to be able to place themselves in environments that will consistently challenge and support their own growth as educators. We no longer have the luxury of replicating the educational techniques, content, and context that we experienced ourselves in school. We need to be able to be authentic about what isn't working and stop pretending that how we are teaching in classrooms and old ways of measuring success are effective when sometimes they really aren't.

The teacher research projects that these teachers completed in their first year of teaching challenged and supported them to grow as educators. As Argentieri articulated, it is this ability to continually learn and grow that is vital, because success is not a static concept or ability. It must be constantly refined and rethought over time and in context.

CONNECTIONS AMONG TEACHER RESEARCH, PREPARATION, AND PROFESSIONALISM

Conducting research during the first year of teaching gives teachers a unique opportunity to hone the tools of analysis, critical thinking, and reflection and to adopt an inquiry-oriented stance toward their practice. A key component of an inquiry-oriented stance, one that these teachers believe should be a part of all teacher preparation programs, is ample opportunities for reflection and dialogue. While these types of opportunities were explicitly built into the MUSE MA/credential program and associated MA teacher research projects, the teachers highlighted the importance of strong relationships—with students, with other teachers and school personnel, and with the larger community—to ongoing opportunities for reflection and dialogue beyond the first year.

During The First Year of Teaching

For the nine contributors to this book, reflection and dialogue are key components of maintaining an inquiry-oriented stance toward one's practice. As part of their teacher research projects, the teachers wrote in logs daily as a way to reflect on their teaching and research. They also met regularly with a cohort of other first-year teachers in the MA thesis seminar in order to discuss what was happening in their classrooms and their schools during that first year. As Oliver explained, "The combination of writing about and discussing my challenges and successes as a teacher helped me to grow immensely during that first whirlwind of a year." Argentieri also highlighted the importance of the weekly seminar during her first year of teaching and observed, "Moving theory to practice and back to theory, discussion, research and writing is an excellent model."

These teachers believe that the opportunities for ongoing reflection and dialogue that were built into their MA/credential program should be a component of all teacher preparation programs. Hendricks discussed the importance of reflection to teachers' initial and ongoing growth as educators and the role that teacher preparation programs should play in empowering teachers to be reflective learners during their first year of teaching and beyond:

> It is important for a credential/MA program to empower beginning
> teachers to be true to themselves, to not be afraid of growing and
> changing, and to always be reflective. As teachers enter the field
> it becomes increasingly important to be reflective. As a teacher,
> particularly in an urban school, your students, families, colleagues,
> and administrators constantly test you. So it is essential to hold on
> to your integrity. Furthermore, I am often my own worst critic and
> when the job at hand is so challenging, being reflective can help me to
> know what I am doing well and what I can do better. Taking time to
> give myself credit for the things that are working is important because
> there are times when no one else will.

In addition, Sobko noted the importance of dialogue in teacher preparation programs, arguing that ongoing effectiveness in the field of education depends on a teacher's ability to discuss as well as reflect on the problems and questions that he or she identifies in his or her classroom and school:

Programs need to give young teachers copious opportunities to dialogue about real situations, concerns, and problems that occur in the classrooms in which they are student teaching or observing. The more that credential or master's students can participate in conversations about problems like the ones we researched our first year, the better able they will be to serve their students and the less isolated they will feel.

These teachers agree that opportunities for reflection and dialogue should be built into all teacher preparation programs. The research projects that they completed during their first year of teaching facilitated these types of opportunities and were a model for how to engage in critical inquiry beyond the first year.

Beyond the First Year of Teaching

The teachers found that a key way to continue to engage in sustained reflection and dialogue—and to maintain an inquiry-oriented stance toward their teaching—was to build relationships within their classroom and school communities. Teachers identified three different types of relationships—relationships with students, relationships with other teachers and school personnel, and relationships with the larger community—that they believe are critical to successful teaching in urban schools.

First, teachers highlighted the importance of listening to and learning from their students in order to know them better and understand how to teach them best. Nicola Martinez, for example, emphasized the need for teachers to develop "authentic relationships with their students in order to create and implement relevant and contextualized curriculum" as well as "a positive classroom community." This emphasis on a relevant curriculum stems from her own high school experiences, where she remembers a distinct lack of connection between "novels written mostly by middle-class, White men" and herself and her peers, the majority of whom were "youth of color from various income levels":

> I recall countless conversations with my friends regarding the decontextualization of these works of writing, that these novels had no relevance to their lives and that the texts that they chose to read pertained to the realities they were living daily.

Sobko also highlighted the importance of listening to students as a key component of being a successful teacher in urban classrooms:

> The first step to being "successful" in urban schools is believing in one's students regardless of their lives outside of the classroom, and

sometimes in spite of their behavior. The second step is listening to them, giving them a voice in the classroom, and making every effort to know them. The better we know our students, the better we will know how to teach them.

This emphasis on building relationships with students is such an important component of successful teaching that it was at the core of many of these teachers' research projects. However, as Sobko observes, knowing one's students is a multistep process, one that can be accomplished only through mutual respect and ongoing dialogue.

In addition to building relationships with students, teachers highlighted the need to build relationships with other teachers and school personnel, which they argue is important for student learning as well as teachers' ongoing professional growth. Nicola Martinez noted the importance of teacher collaboration in designing curriculum that is aligned and interconnected, while Oliver focused on teacher collaboration as a way to determine "how to best support students with very different needs." Velázquez Cardenas added that an equally important aspect of building relationships between teachers and other school personnel is to foster a school culture in which teachers hold each other accountable and grow together through reflection and dialogue:

> Teachers need to have the voice and knowledge to productively, confidently, and kindly challenge the dominant discourse of their peers, supervisors, and staff in a school so that the community of adults can work together to ensure that schools are truly centers of education and personal development for the students. If teachers want to best support the effectiveness of urban schools they will need to build a community of like-minded people and allies who at the very minimum can be reflective of their practice. Furthermore, it is important to also build networks with other teachers in order to maintain a critical lens and sustainable environment for educators to continue supporting student *and* teacher development.

For Velázquez Cardenas, relationships between teachers are important because they create a structure through which to support one another while also holding one another accountable as learners and teachers. From his perspective, this has the dual benefit of supporting student learning and well-being as well as teacher growth and professionalism.

Finally, teachers also emphasized the importance of building relationships with the larger community of which their classrooms and schools are a part. Danny Martinez commented on the importance of these relationships in terms of the "transformative work of urban teachers," [which] is not only measured on the test scores of their students, but also on the commitment we make to the communities in which we teach. To work from within means that we are developing relationships with parents, that we are tapping into the strengths of our students.

Although Martinez focused on relationships with parents as a hallmark of what he calls "working from within," the type of work that he describes extends beyond simply knowing students and their parents to understanding the cultural, linguistic, and social contexts in which they live and learn within and beyond school. It is through this type of work that an inquiry-oriented stance, with its emphasis on reflection and dialogue, is critical, particularly when students' realities are not necessarily the same as the realities of the teachers who teach them.

NEGOTIATING CULTURAL, LINGUISTIC, RACIAL, AND GENDERED IDENTITIES IN URBAN SCHOOLS

Teacher training programs that train teachers to look at themselves and analyze their own actions and identities in the classroom are essential. This isn't about creating guilty teachers who spend hours bemoaning their own short fallings; rather, it's about cultivating teachers who are acutely aware of their tremendous power in the classroom and take responsibility for that power.

—Julia R. Daniels

Credential/MA programs should enable educators to question their ideologies, their practice, and their purpose as educators in their position.

—Rafael Velázquez Cardenas

Opportunities for reflection and dialogue are important for all teachers. In urban schools these opportunities are often filtered through stark power differentials in contexts where cultural, linguistic, racial, and gendered differences are negotiated on a daily basis. Indeed, many of the teachers who contributed to this book emphasized the important role that reflection and dialogue play in their attempts to counter the systemic silencing of their students, who, in the urban contexts in which they teach, are predominantly students of color. At the same time, some of them also called attention to the occasions on which they themselves were silenced as a result of insufficient opportunities for reflection and dialogue among other teachers and administrators at their schools.

All the teachers emphasized the importance of working with their students to create classroom spaces in which they and their students could grapple with difficult questions about culture, language, race, gender, and privilege. For Oliver, Daniels, Hendricks, Argentieri, Sobko, and Lai, this meant confronting the concept of privilege head on with their students and discussing how their experiences as White women or as a Chinese American man (in Lai's case) shape their identities and the positions of power they hold in the classroom and in larger society. As Sobko observed, "As a White teacher teaching primarily students of color, it was my responsibility to talk explicitly about race; it seemed unthinkable to not talk about race." Although each teacher approached discussions about privilege in his or her own way, at the core of each approach was a commitment to honest reflection and dialogue for both the teacher and students.

More specifically, and in keeping with the "teacher as learner" perspective they all highlighted as an essential affordance of adopting a researcher lens, these six teachers explained that talking explicitly about race meant unveiling and interrogating their own questions and uncertainties in dialogue with their students. As Lai explained:

> I think it was because I couldn't help but be honest, reflective, at
> times even confused and contradictory about the implications of my
> racial identity and of Whiteness in front of them, working out those
> entanglements as part of my own existence as a person of color, a
> citizen, a reader of texts, et cetera. I think maybe that helped make
> space for their own assertions of pride, doubts of betrayal, subversions
> of performance, and gray silences about their own racial and ethnic
> identities.

The questions that Lai asked himself as a Chinese American male—"What does it mean to [my students] that I'm a Chinese American male teacher? What does it mean to me? What does it signify culturally, politically, personally?"—were ones that he shared with his students, and this set the stage for them to think through these issues and concerns for themselves and in dialogue with one another. Argentieri also recounted how sharing her personal experiences with her students was a way to position herself as a learner as well as a teacher:

> I consistently challenged myself to be an ongoing learner and to delve
> into (versus avoid) issues of race and class. I crossed identity bridges
> with my students easily by sharing my own struggles, family issues,
> and challenges as a young person, and I was as real as I could be about
> the social dynamics of society and the inequities in the system.

Likewise, Oliver explained how she strives to create a classroom environment in which she and her students "each bring our own experiences to the table as equals." Similar to Lai and Argentieri, she shared details about her past so that together she and her students could discuss the "silenced discourses of our society—bias, ethnicity, gender, sexuality, poverty, and immigration." For each of these teachers, awareness of privilege shaped their pedagogy and required ongoing reflection and dialogue on the part of themselves and their students.

At the same time, other teachers like Daniels drew attention to the fact that being aware of difference and privilege is only a part of what is necessary in order to engage across difference:

> I believe that an ideal teacher for underserved and marginalized students understands firsthand an experience of marginalization, and the resilience necessary to combat that marginalization. I believe that relationships across difference—all relationships that bridge powerful divides of race, class, sexual orientation, language, gender, and culture—require significant analysis and skill in order to be genuine, meaningful, and productive. More specifically, I believe that within the student-teacher relationship publicly naming the existence of difference is a necessary but insufficient condition for those relationships' success. Every day, I question how to use and think about my race in the classroom. I know that it matters, and that I must give my students space to articulate how much and in what ways it matters to them.

Daniels noted in particular the lack of "resources or structures to recruit the teachers who would be the most meaningful or most effective for my students." Oliver made a similar observation, pointing out that often the acute lack of teachers and administrators of color at her school is "silenced or ignored."

For teachers like Danny Martinez and Velázquez Cardenas, who identify as men of color, and Nicola Martinez, an Armenian American woman, the challenges of teaching in urban classrooms are equally daunting, though distinctly different from those described earlier. Although discussing privilege was also an essential part of their work as teachers, they approached the topic from perspectives that changed the nature of the discussions in significant ways. While Lai and the five White women contextualized their approach from the perspective of teachers who are different from their students, Danny Martinez, Velázquez Cardenas, and Nicola Martinez called attention to the benefits and challenges of working predominantly with students who come from communities similar to their own. Nicola Martinez, for example, observed that her background, which she described as part Middle Eastern and part White, resulted in "racial ambiguity—my peers and the youth I taught had difficulty categorizing my race." This ambiguity, combined with her experiences growing up in a "socioeconomically diverse school and neighborhood community," meant that she learned how to "code-switch between and among groups." She explained that she drew upon these experiences and used them to provide "relevant and contextualized curriculum for my students."

Taking a different perspective, Velázquez Cardenas reflected on what it means to be "a man of color, who grew up in the city where I now teach" and the "often inexplicable effect I can have on some students." He acknowledged that this "position of power" in which he senses that he is often "observed carefully" by students, parents, other teachers, and administrators comes with a great deal of responsibility. Specifically, he explained that he struggles to balance providing students with English content such as "metaphors, similes, and grammar," while also making them aware of "the systemic issues that make it difficult for our students to succeed":

> I try to incorporate ideas that I learned in ethnic studies or in college courses because I feel that students should not wait until college to get very engaging questions, theories, and explanations of their world. I mainly strive to teach interpretation skills and to present current events so that students can begin to read between the lines of text and to see how current and past decisions affect their reality.

Danny Martinez struggled with a similar conflict as he sought to counter required school curricula with his own pedagogical approach:

> As a teacher of color, I was fundamentally aware of how schools attempted to socialize nondominant children and youth into dominant ways with words. This alone became a challenge for me when I was hoping to honor the valued home and community practices of these youth.

Although Martinez sought to incorporate his students' home and community experiences into his classroom as a way to combat their historic absence from school, he faced resistance in this endeavor that in turn contributed to his own silence.

Like Danny Martinez, others remembered feeling silenced themselves as a result of identities they brought to their work as teachers, even as they sought to foster reflection and dialogue around these issues in their classrooms. Argentieri, for example, recounted one of the challenges she faced as a White woman teaching in an urban school:

The biggest challenge I faced as a White teacher in general was my relationship with a school administrator who assumed my prejudice/ ignorance as a White person, without taking the time to find out who I really was. I experienced a bias in the way that I was treated, and how I was spoken to. Perhaps this was a blind spot in his scope, and perhaps he had not learned about his own sexism enough to own it. He actually talked down to me in front of students and disempowered my authority.

Martinez also recounted experiences that raised questions for him about his identity as a Chicano male and a teacher of color. These experiences highlight some of the unique challenges that teachers of color face in urban schools. Despite the fact that he "truly believed [his] Spanish to be horrible," Martinez explained, "I often questioned whether I was hired for the teaching position because I was a brown face to put in front of a classroom of all brown kids who didn't speak English." Moreover, as a Chicano teacher working mostly with White teachers, he "felt silenced during faculty discussions where White-dominant ways with words dominated conversations" and where he was "repaired" for "some of [his] common 'ESL' slips." He remembered that "as a male of color I would sometimes hold back comments fearing I would be seen as the angry Chicano male. I should have been the angry Chicano male more often."

Martinez explained that experiences like these precluded him, as well as other teachers at his school, from engaging in the kind of reflection and dialogue that play such an important role in teachers' growth and professionalism. Paradoxically, however, these experiences also shaped his emerging identity as a Chicano teacher:

> Part of coming into my identity as a Chicano teacher was my own unwillingness to reach out, to ask for help, and to collaborate. I was stubborn and did not believe I could learn anything from White teachers. I believed only I knew what was best for the youth in my class. While I take some responsibility for this, I had many reasons to be angry during my first year. I was angry when I overheard teachers whispering or talking very loudly about my students. I found myself shutting the door to my classroom most of the day, eating lunch with students, and mostly organizing with the one other ESL teacher, a White woman who spoke better Spanish than me, and who the students loved. I might have been a better teacher this year if I would have made an effort to collaborate and speak to other teachers. I might have been much less angry if I had allowed myself to learn from other teachers, at least the ones who loved teaching and were teaching powerfully in their classrooms. Yes, even the White teachers.

During his first year of teaching, Martinez did not benefit from the kind of supportive relationships with teachers and school personnel that many of the other teachers highlight as such an important part of their ongoing growth. However, he did engage in a research project that allowed him to learn more about his Spanish-speaking students and the many different cultural and linguistic practices in which they engaged and that he found went unacknowledged under the "ESL" label. His research was a way to give voice to his own and his students' cultural, linguistic, and racial experiences in and out of school.

In reflecting on his experiences during that first year of teaching, Martinez regrets that he did not speak out more often against what he saw happening to himself and his students at his school. We argue, however, that Martinez's teacher research project, like many of the research projects that first-year teachers undertake as part of the MUSE MA/credential program, was a way to begin to combat the systemic silencing that too often occurs in schools, and particularly urban schools. His research allowed him to take a problem—the pervasive, deficit-oriented perspective many teachers had toward the Spanish-speaking students at his school—and examine it from the perspectives of his students, thereby unveiling the complex cultural and linguistic practices in which his students engaged as part of their daily lives.

THE BENEFITS OF TEACHER RESEARCH

Taken together, these teachers' reflections highlight many of the benefits of conducting research during the first year of teaching. First, teachers who conduct research cultivate an inquiry-oriented stance toward their practice that shapes how they view problems and possibilities in their classrooms and schools. It comes as no surprise to us that all nine of the teachers who contributed to this book continue to identify problems and imagine solutions to teaching's most vexing questions and concerns.

Second, teachers who conduct research understand that being a teacher is as much about learning as it is about teaching. According to these teachers, opportunities for reflection and dialogue are critical to being a learner as well as a teacher. These types of opportunities were built into their MA/credential program, and the teachers reported that they continued to seek them out beyond their first year of teaching through the relationships they developed with students, other teachers and school personnel, and the larger communities of which their schools were a part.

Third, teachers who conduct research hone the tools of inquiry, data collection and analysis, critical thinking, reflection, and writing that will assist them in their future careers. All nine teachers emphasized the importance of engaging in dialogue with their students about issues of equity and privilege and viewed it as a critical part of their jobs as teachers. The tools that they used in their research were ones that they could draw on with their students in order to discuss cultural, linguistic, racial, and gendered issues in a productive and mutually beneficial fashion. For these reasons, we believe that all teachers enrolled in MA/credential programs—and not just those who intend to teach in urban schools—should have the opportunity to conduct rigorous research during their first year as a way to develop a critical researcher lens through which to view, reflect on, and ultimately improve their work in classrooms.

References

Achinstein, B., & Ogawa, R. T. (2011). *Change(d) agents: New teachers of color in urban schools.* New York, NY: Teachers College Press.

Amstutz, L. S., & Mullet, J. H. (2005). *The little book of restorative discipline for schools: Teaching responsibility, creating caring climates.* Intercourse, PA: Good Books.

Annenberg Senior Fellows. (2000). *The promise of urban schools.* Providence, RI: Annenberg Institute for School Reform at Brown University.

Anyon, J. (1997). *Ghetto schooling: A political economy of urban school reform.* New York, NY: Teachers College Press.

Anyon, J. (2005). *Radical possibilities: Public policy, urban education, and a new social movement.* New York, NY: Routledge.

Applebee, A. (1996). *Curriculum as conversation.* Chicago, IL: University of Chicago Press.

Ballenger, C. (2009). *Puzzling moments, teachable moments: Practicing teacher research in urban classrooms.* New York, NY: Teachers College Press.

Barron, B. J. S., Schwartz, D. L., Vye, N. J., Moore, A., Petrosino, A., Zech, L., & Bransford, J. D. (1998). Doing with understanding: Lessons from research on problem- and project-based learning. *Journal of the Learning Sciences, 7*(3–4), 271–311.

Bartlett, L., & García, O. (2011). *Additive schooling in subtractive times: Bilingual education and Dominican immigrant youth in the Heights.* Nashville, TN: Vanderbilt University Press.

Bell, S. (2010). Project-based learning for the 21st century: Skills for the future. *The Clearing House: A Journal of Educational Strategies, Issues and Ideas, 83*(2), 39–43.

Bellanca, J. A., Fogarty, R. J., & Pete, B. M. (2012). *How to teach thinking skills within the common core.* Bloomington, IN: Thinking Tree Press.

Benson, H. (2000). *Socratic wisdom.* Oxford, England: Oxford University Press.

Bigelow, B., & Peterson, B. (Eds.). (1998). *Rethinking Columbus* (2nd ed.). Milwaukee, WI: Rethinking Schools.

Blumenfeld, P. C., Soloway, E., Marx, R. W., Krajcik, J. S., Guzdial, M., & Palincsar, A. (1991). Motivating project-based learning: Sustaining the doing, supporting the learning. *Educational Psychologist, 26*(3–4), 369–398.

Bourdieu, P. (1973). Cultural reproduction and social reproduction. In Richard Brown (Ed.), *Knowledge, education and cultural change* (pp. 71–112). London, England: Tavistock.

Braithwaite, J. (2002). *Restorative justice and responsive regulation.* Oxford, England: Oxford University Press.

Bransford, J., Darling-Hammond, L., & LePage, P. (2005). Introduction. In Darling-Hammond and Bransford (Eds.), *Preparing teachers for a changing world: What teachers should learn and be able to do* (pp. 1–39). San Francisco, CA: Jossey-Bass.

California Commission on Teacher Credentialing. (1997). *California standards for the teaching profession.* Sacramento, CA: California Department of Education.

Charney, R. (1992). *Teaching children to care: Management in the responsive classroom.* Greenfield, MA: Northeast Foundation for Children.

Chorzempa, B., & Lapidus, L. (2009). To find yourself, think for yourself. *Teaching Exceptional Children, 41*(3), 54–59.

Clauss-Ehlers, C. (2006). *Diversity training for classroom teaching: A manual for students and educators.* New York, NY: Springer.

Cochran-Smith, M., & Lytle, S. L. (1993). *Inside/outside: Teacher research and knowledge.* New York, NY: Teachers College Press.

Cochran-Smith, M., & Lytle, S. L. (2009). *Inquiry as stance: Practitioner research for the next generation.* New York, NY: Teachers College Press.

Cole, M. (1996). *Cultural psychology: A once and future discipline.* Cambridge, MA: Belknap Press of Harvard University Press.

Conchas, G. (2006). *The color of success: Race and high-achieving urban youth.* New York, NY: Teachers College Press.

Copeland, M. (2010). *Socratic circles: Fostering critical and creative thinking in middle and high school.* Portland, ME: Stenhouse.

Cummins, J. (1996). *Negotiating identities: Education for empowerment in a diverse society.* Los Angeles, CA: California Association for Bilingual Education.

Cushman, K. (1990). Performance and exhibitions: The demonstration of mastery. *Horace, 6*(3). Retrieved from http://www.essentialschools.org/resources/123.

Darling-Hammond, L. (1997). *The right to learn: A blueprint for creating schools that work.* San Francisco, CA: Jossey-Bass.

Darling-Hammond, L. (2000). Teacher quality and student achievement: A review of state policy evidence. *Education Policy Archives, 8*(1). Retrieved from http://epaa.asu.edu/epaa/v8n1/

Davidson, J. (2009). Exhibitions: Connecting classroom assessment with culminating demonstrations of mastery. *Theory into Practice, 48*(1), 36–43.

Delgado-Bernal, D. (2002). Critical race theory, Latino critical theory, and critical raced-gendered epistemologies: Recognizing students of color as holders and creators of knowledge. *Qualitative Inquiry, 8,* 105–126.

Delpit, L. (2006). *Other people's children: Cultural conflict in the classroom.* New York, NY: The New Press.

Delpit, L. (2012). *Multiplication is for White people: Raising expectations for other people's children.* New York, NY: The New Press.

Dewey, J. (1938). *Experience and education.* New York, NY: Kappa Delta Pi.

Duncan-Andrade, J. (2007). Gangstas, wankstas, and ridas: Defining, developing, and supporting effective teachers in urban schools. *International Journal of Qualitative Studies in Education, 20*(6), 617–638.

Engeström, Y. (2005). *Developmental work research: Expanding activity theory in practice.* Berlin, Germany: Lehmanns Media.

Frank, C. (2009). *Ethnographic interviewing for teacher preparation and staff development.* New York, NY: Teachers College Press.

Freedman, S., & Appleman, D. (2008). "What else would I be doing?": Teacher identity and teacher retention in urban schools. *Teacher Education Quarterly, 35*(3), 109–126.

Freedman, S. W., & Appleman, D. (2009). "In it for the long haul": How teacher education can contribute to teacher retention in high-poverty, urban schools. *Journal of Teacher Education, 60*(3), 323–337.

Freedman, S. W., Delp, V., & Crawford, S. M. (2005). Teaching English in untracked classrooms. *Research in the Teaching of English, 4*(1), 62–126.

Freedman, S. W., Simons, E. R., Kalnin, J. S., & Casareno, A. (1999). *Inside city schools: Investigating literacy in multicultural classrooms.* New York, NY: Teachers College Press.

Freire, P. (1998). *Teachers as cultural workers.* Boulder, CO: Westview Press.

Freire, P. (1993). *Pedagogy of the oppressed* (20th anniv. ed.). New York, NY: Continuum.

Gándara, P. C., & Contreras, F. (2009). *The Latino education crisis: The consequences of failed social policies.* Cambridge, MA: Harvard University Press.

Gandhi, A. (2002). Gandhian Education: The difference between knowledge and wisdom. *Encounter: Education for Meaning and Social Justice, 15*(2), 14–16.

Garcia, O. (2009). Emergent bilinguals and TESOL: What's in a name? *TESOL Quarterly, 43*(2), 322–326.

Garcia, O., & Kleifgen, J. A. (2010). *Educating emergent bilinguals: Policies, programs, and practices for English language learners.* New York, NY: Teachers College Press.

Gay, G. (2010). *Culturally responsive teaching: Theory, research, and practice* (2nd ed.). New York, NY: Teachers College Press.

Genesee, F. (1987). *Learning through two languages: Studies of immersion and bilingual education.* Cambridge, MA: Newbury House.

Giroux, H. (1988). *Schooling and the struggle for public life: Critical pedagogy in the modern age.* Minneapolis: University of Minnesota Press.

Goldenberg, C. (2008). Teaching English language learners: What the research does—and does not—say. *American Educator, 32*(2), 8–23, 42–44.

Gose, M. (2009). When Socratic dialogue is flagging: Questions and strategies for engaging students. *College Teaching, 57*(1), 46.

Gregory, A., & Weinstein, P.S. (2008). The discipline gap and African Americans: Defiance or cooperation in the high school classroom. *Journal of School Psychology, 46*(2), 455–475.

Guthrie, W. K. C. (1968). *The Greek philosophers from Thales to Aristotle.* London, England: Routledge.

Gutierrez, K. D., Baquedano-López, P., & Tejeda, C. (1999). Rethinking diversity: Hybridity and hybrid language practices in the third space. *Mind, Culture, and Activity, 6*(4), 286–303.

Gutiérrez, K. D., Baquedano-López, P., & Turner, M. G. (1997). Putting language back into language arts: When the radical middle meets the third space. *Language Arts,* 368–378.

He, M. F., & Phillion, J. (Eds.). (2008). *Personal-passionate-participatory inquiry into social justice in education.* Charlotte, NC: Information Age.

Heath, S. B. (1983). *Ways with words.* Cambridge, England: Cambridge University Press.

Hopkins, B. (2004). *Just schools: A whole school approach to restorative justice.* London, England: Jessica Kingsley.

hooks, b. (1994). *Teaching to transgress: Education as the practice of freedom.* New York, NY: Routledge.

hooks, b. (2003). *Rock my soul: Black people and self-esteem.* New York, NY: Atria.

Howard, T. C. (2010). *Why race and culture matter in schools: Closing the achievement gap in America's classrooms.* New York, NY: Teachers College Press.

Jensen, E. (2010). *Teaching with poverty in mind.* New York, NY: Association for Supervision and Curriculum Development.

Ladson-Billings, G. (2009). *The dreamkeepers: Successful teachers of African American children* (2nd ed.). San Francisco, CA: Jossey-Bass.

Lantieri, L. (2001). *Schools with spirit: Nurturing the inner lives of children and teachers.* Boston, MA: Beacon Press.

Leontiev, A. N. (1977). Activity and consciousness. In *Philosophy in the USSR: Problems of dialectical materialism* (pp. 180–202, Robert Daglish, Trans.). Moscow, Russia: Progress Publishers.

Lindholm-Leary, K. J. (2001). *Dual language education* (Vol. 28). Tonowanda, NY: Multilingual Matters.

Loreman, T., Deppeler, J., & Harvey, D. (2005). *Inclusive education: A practical guide to supporting diversity in the classroom.* London, England: Routledge-Falmer.

Mahiri, J. (2011). *Digital tools in urban schools: Mediating a remix of learning.* Ann Arbor, MI: University of Michigan Press.

Miller, R. (1997). *What are schools for? Holistic education in American culture.* Jaime, VT: Holistic Education Press.

Milner, H. R. (2010). *Start where you are but don't stay there: Understanding diversity, opportunity gaps, and teaching in today's classrooms.* Cambridge, MA: Harvard Education Press.

Moll, L. C. (2000). The diversity of schooling: A cultural historical approach. In M. Reyes & J. Halcan (Eds.), *The best for our children: Latino researchers on literacy.* New York, NY: Teachers College Press.

National Governors Association Center for Best Practices & Council of Chief State School Officers. (2010). *Common Core State Standards for English language arts and literacy in history/social studies, science, and technical subjects.* Washington, DC: Authors.

Newmann, F. M., & Wehlage, G. G. (1993). Five standards of authentic instruction. *Educational Leadership, 50,* 8–12.

Noffke, S. E. (2009). Revisiting the professional, personal and political dimensions of action research. In S. Noffke & B. Somekh (Eds.), *The Sage handbook of educational action research* (pp. 6–23). London, England: Sage.

Noguera, P. A. (1995). Preventing and producing violence: A critical analysis of responses to school violence. *Harvard Educational Review, 65*(2), 198–212.

Nystrand, M., with Gamoran, A. (1997). *Opening dialogue: Understanding the dynamics of language and learning in the English classroom.* New York, NY: Teachers College Press.

Payne, C. M. (2008). *So much reform, so little change: The persistence of failure in urban schools.* Cambridge, MA: Harvard Education Press.

Pratt, M. L. (1991). Arts of the contact zone. *Profession, 9*(1), 33–40.

Ravitz, J. (2010). Beyond changing culture in small high schools: Reform models and changing instruction with project-based learning. *Peabody Journal of Education, 85*(3), 290–312.

Richards, J. C., & Rodgers, T. S. (2001). *Approaches and methods in language teaching.* Cambridge, England: Cambridge University Press.

Richert, A. E. (2012). *What should I do? Confronting dilemmas of teaching in urban schools.* New York, NY: Teachers College Press.

Saldaña, J. (2009). *The coding manual for qualitative researchers.* Los Angeles, CA: Sage.

Sizer, T. (1986). Rebuilding: First steps by the Coalition of Essential Schools. *The Phi Delta Kappan, 68*(1), 38–42.

Schieffelin, B. B., & Ochs, E. (1986). Language socialization. *Annual Review of Anthropology, 15*(1), 163–191.

Schmidt, R. (1983). Interaction, acculturation, and the acquisition of communicative competence: A case study of an adult. *Sociolinguistics and language acquisition, 137*, 174.

Skiba, R. J., & Peterson, R. L. (2000). School discipline at a crossroads: From zero tolerance to early response. *Exceptional Children, 66*(3), 335–346.

Shank, G., & Takagi, P. (2004). Critique of restorative justice. *Social Justice, 31*(3), 147–163.

Song, A. M. (2003). *Choosing ethnic identity.* Malden, MA: Polity Press.

Valdés, G. (1996). *Con respeto: Bridging the distances between culturally diverse families and schools.* New York, NY: Teachers College Press.

Valdés, G., & Figueroa, R. (1994). *Bilingualism and testing: A special case of bias.* Westport, CT: Ablex.

Valenzuela, A. (1999). Subtractive schooling: US-Mexican youth and the politics of caring. New York: SUNY Press.

Vertovec, S. (2007). Super-diversity and its implications. *Ethnic and Racial Studies, 30*(6), 1024–1054.

Vigil, J. D. (1988). *Barrio gangs: Street life and identity in Southern California.* Austin, TX: University of Texas Press.

Vlastos, G. (1983). The Socratic elenchus. *Oxford Studies in Ancient Philosophy, 1*(3), 27–58.

Wacquant, L. (2008). *Urban outcasts: A comparative sociology of advanced marginality.* Cambridge, MA: Polity Press.

Weiner, L. (2006). *Urban teaching: The essentials.* New York, NY: Teachers College Press.

Wong Fillmore, L. (1991). When learning a second language means losing the first. *Early Childhood Research Quarterly, 6*, 323–346.

Wong Fillmore, L., & Snow, C. (2000). *What teachers need to know about language.* Washington, DC: U. S. Department of Education, Office of Educational Research and Improvement.

Zehr, H. (2002). *The little book of restorative justice.* Intercourse, PA: Good Books.

About the Editors and Contributors

Jabari Mahiri, PhD, is a professor in the Graduate School of Education at the University of California, Berkeley and the William and Mary Jane Brinton Chair of Urban Teaching. He researches learning, literacy, and digital practices of urban youth in and beyond schools. He is faculty director of the Bay Area Writing Project, an elected council member-at-large of the American Educational Researh Association, and a recipient of the Berkeley Chancellor's Award for Advancing Institutional Excellence. He is board chair of REALM Charter Schools and author of *Digital Tools in Urban Schools: Mediating a Re-mix of Learning; Shooting for Excellence: African American and Youth Culture in New Century Schools;* and *Out of Bounds: When Scholarship Atheletes Become Academic Scholars* (with Derek Van Rheenen). He also is editor of *What They Don't Learn in School: Literacy in the Lives of Urban Youth.*

Sarah Warshauer Freedman, PhD, is a professor in the Graduate School of Education at the University of California, Berkeley. She studies the teaching and learning of written language, as well as the ways English is taught in schools. She is a 2013 American Educational Research Association Fellow (honored for exceptional contributions to education research) and has been a fellow at the Center for Advanced Studies in the Behavioral Sciences and the Rockefeller Foundation's Bellagio Center. She is author (with her collaborators) of *Inside City Schools: Investigating Literacy in Multicultural Classrooms*, which won the Multicultural Book Award from the National Association of Multicultural Educators and the Ed Frye Book Award from the National Reading Conference. She also authored *Exchanging Writing, Exchanging Cultures: Lessons in Reform from the United States and Great Britain*, which won the Ed Frye Book Award and the Richard Meade Award from the National Council of Teachers of English. Her study "Teaching English in Untracked Classrooms" won the Alan C. Purves Award for research with important implications for practice.

Paula L. Argentieri is a PhD candidate in the Graduate School of Education at the University of California, Berkeley in the area of social and cultural studies with a designated emphasis in gender and women studies. In addition to teaching for Compton and Berkeley Unified School Districts, she has taught undergraduate classes at UC Berkeley from 2003–2010. In 2009, she received the Chancellors Award for Public Service and Community Engagement. Over the last twenty years, she has worked to facilitate transformational spaces for both social change and personal growth.

Julia R. Daniels is a PhD candidate in multicultural education at the University of Washington. Prior to entering her doctoral program, she taught high school English, literature, and reading classes in the Oakland California Unified School District, and she has worked in literacy education in Ohio and California for nine years. She sees teaching as an extension of activism.

Jennifer DiZio is a PhD candidate and researcher at the Graduate School of Education and the Berkeley Center for New Media at the University of California, Berkeley. In 2012 Jennifer was awarded the National Science Foundation's graduate research fellowship to continue work in online education and STEM literacies. Prior to commencing her studies at Berkeley, Jennifer worked as a producer for film and television in the US and UK.

Katherine K. Frankel, PhD, is an assistant professor of literacy in the School of Education at Boston University. Her doctorate in language, literacy, and culture is from the Graduate School of Education at the University of California, Berkeley. Her research examines teaching and learning in secondary schools with a focus on adolescents' literacies in and out of school. Her most recent work explores the reading and writing opportunities that are available to students in literacy intervention classes and other content-area classes and how these opportunities shape students' identities as readers and writers. She began her career in education as a grammar and composition teacher and reading tutor.

Exequiel "Rex" Ganding is a PhD candidate in the Language, Literacy, and Culture program in the Graduate School of Education at the University of California, Berkeley. His research is focused at the intersection of composition and literacy studies, specifically examining the challenges and potential that digital culture poses for writing pedagogy. He has taught college composition for 5 years at several institutions in the San Francisco Bay Area, instructing courses from below-transfer level to second-year composition.

Nischala Hendricks received her MA in multicultural urban secondary English from the Graduate School of Education at the University of California, Berkeley. She started her career in education working with preschool students with special needs in Santa Cruz, California. In addition to teaching 9th-grade English in the San Francisco Bay Area, she has taught language arts at a Title 1 school in Denver, Colorado.

José R. Lizárraga is a PhD candidate in language, literacy, and culture in the Graduate School of Education at the University of California, Berkeley. His research interests include language and identity, new media literacy, educational technology, art practice, multilingualism, and Latina(o) issues in education. He is currently exploring the out-of-school literacy and language practices of Latina(o) youth as mediated by digital social networks. Previously, he worked as an educator and administrator in schools and after-school literacy programs for over 8 years.

Paul F. Lai is a PhD candidate in language, literacy, and culture in the Graduate School of Education at the University of California, Berkeley, where he also earned his MA in Multicultural Urban Secondary English. His research focuses on immigrant students, language learning, and social and civic engagement. He has taught in San Francisco Bay Area high schools for 8 years.

Danny C. Martinez, PhD, is an assistant professor of adolescent literacy at the University of California, Davis. He received his MA from the Multicultural Urban Secondary English Program at the University of California, Berkeley. His research explores how Black and Latina/o youth use their varied linguistic tools to make meaning despite teaching practices that narrowly define what counts as language and learning. He has taught English as a Second Language and English Language Arts to middle school and high school youth in San Francisco and Los Angeles. His work as a teacher informs his research agenda and the professional development work he does with pre-service and in-service teachers.

Nicola C. Martinez received her MA in multicultural urban secondary English from the University of California, Berkeley. While there she was awarded the Alpha Delta Gamma Excellence In Student Teaching Scholarship and the Stevenson Fellowship for Teachers. She taught English language arts in a San Francisco public school. She served as coordinator of the Discovering the Reality of Our Community Program, an award-winning afterschool drug and alcohol prevention program for high school youth in Richmond, California. Currently, she is assistant program coordinator for the District Attorney's Justice Academy, an academic enrichment and employment program for high school students from urban and suburban high schools in Alameda County, California.

Eva Marie Oliver received her MA in multicultural urban secondary English from the University of California, Berkeley. She began teaching in the Health and Bioscience Department of an Oakland public school. She also has taught 6th- and 9th-grade English, college writing, and digital journalism and is the co-coach of a young women's empowerment group at her high school called

"Real Ambitious Women" (RAW). During the 2011–2012 academic year, RAW co-facilitated the Season of Peace-Building with the young men's group on campus, and she eventually coordinated and edited their writings in an anthology entitled *74 Days Through Our Eyes: Oakland's Voiceless Strive for Peace* that was published in 2013.

Rafael Velázquez Cardenas received his MA in multicultural urban secondary English from the University of California, Berkeley. He teaches in the Hayward California Unified School District. Having taught elementary school, middle school, high school and college students, he believes that education is a powerful driving force for personal development and social justice through which students can become critical thinkers and agents of change.

Sophia Sobko received her MA in multicultural urban secondary English from the University of California, Berkeley. She worked with urban youth for many years throughout Southern California and abroad in Madrid, Spain, prior to graduate school. After teaching 11th and 12th grade English in San Francisco for 2 years, she returned to Southern California to pursue her passion for the arts and explore the field of arts education. She continues to both teach and learn from urban youth through her work at the Museum of Photographic Arts in San Diego, CA.

John M. Scott is a PhD candidate and instructor in the Graduate School of Education and the Berkeley Center for New Media at the University of California, Berkeley. His research explores the use of digital video and multimedia production across a range of educational and social contexts, including those related to youth identity in global contexts, online instruction and pedagogy, civic engagement, and vernacular creativity. He has worked on the development and design of a number of web applications, including most recently PIC Your Future, a college-readiness application that uses digital collage tools to help students picture themselves in college to help develop a college-going identity. Prior to beginning doctoral work, he was an art and English teacher in New York City public schools.

Index